Mastering Classification Algorithms for Machine Learning

Learn how to apply Classification algorithms for effective Machine Learning solutions

Partha Majumdar

www.bpbonline.com

First Edition 2023
REPRINT 2025

ISBN: 978-93-55518-514

LIMITS OF LIABILITY AND DISCLAIMER OF WARRANTY

Distributors:

BPB PUBLICATIONS
20, Ansari Road, Darya Ganj
New Delhi-110002
Ph: 23254990/23254991

DECCAN AGENCIES
4-3-329, Bank Street,
Hyderabad-500195
Ph: 24756967/24756400

MICRO MEDIA
Shop No. 5, Mahendra Chambers,
150 DN Rd. Next to Capital Cinema,
V.T. (C.S.T.) Station, MUMBAI-400 001
Ph: 22078296/22078297

Published by Manish Jain for BPB Publications, 20 Ansari Road, Darya Ganj, New Delhi-110002 and Printed by him at Manipal Technologies, Manipal

www.bpbonline.com

Dedicated to

My beloved wife:

Deepshree

About the Author

Partha Majumdar is not just a programmer. He has been involved in developing more than 10 Enterprise Class products deployed in Customer locations in more than 57 countries. He has worked with key ministries of 8 countries in developing key systems for them. Also, he has been involved in developing key systems for more than 20 enterprises.

Partha has been employed in enterprises including Siemens, Amdocs, NIIT, Mobily, and JP Morgan Chase & Co. Apart from developing company systems, Partha managed highly profitable business units. He has set up three successful companies as of 2021 in India, Dubai, and Saudi Arabia.

Partha has developed OLTP systems for Telcos, Hospitals, Tea Gardens, Factories, Travel Houses, Cricket tournaments, etc. Since 2012, Partha has been developing Data Products and intensively working on Machine Learning and Deep Learning. Partha has a panache for finding patterns in most of what he gets involved in. As a result, Partha has been useful to teams in developing Rapid Development Tools.

Partha has continued to learn new domains and technology throughout his career. After graduating in Mathematics, Partha completed a master's in Telecommunications and a master's in computer security. He has also completed executive MBAs in Information Systems and Business Analytics. He completed a PG Certificate program in AI / ML / DL from Manipal Academy of Higher Education (Dubai), an advanced certificate in Cyber Security from IIT (Kanpur), and a PG-level advanced certificate in Computational Data Sciences from IISc (Bengaluru). He is pursuing a Doctorate in Business Administration from the Swiss School of Business and Management (Geneva).

Partha is an avid traveller. He has had the opportunity to visit twenty-four countries for work and leisure so far. Partha loves experiencing diverse cultures and learns from every interaction.

Partha is married to Deepshree and has two daughters - Riya and Ranoo.

Acknowledgement

I want to express my deepest gratitude to my family for their unwavering support and encouragement throughout this book's writing, especially my wife Deepshree.

I want to express my gratitude which cannot be put into words, for all the professors who have taken the pains to teach all that I know today.

I am also grateful to BPB Publications for their guidance and expertise in bringing this book to fruition. Creating this book was an eventful journey, with valuable participation and collaboration of editors, reviewers, and management.

Finally, I would like to thank all the readers who have taken an interest in my book and for their support in making it a reality. Your encouragement has been invaluable

Preface

Creating models for Machine Learning is a time-consuming process involving hours of work on the machine to tune the models during the training phase. Every model has a mathematical foundation, meaning several hyperparameters must be altered before the final model can arrive. Understanding the mathematics behind every model makes it possible to formulate a scientific mechanism for trying different combinations of the hyperparameters to test. Also, understanding the mathematics behind the models helps understand how the different hyperparameters can be set so that the model converges relatively quickly.

Another aspect is that all models do not suit all types of data. To understand which model can be suitable for building a model for a given dataset, one needs to understand the mathematical formulation of the models.

In summary, to be successful in building machine-learning models, understanding the mathematical formulations is vital. This book provides details of the mathematics of every machine-learning model for solving classification problems. The book starts with simple models and proceeds to state-of-the-art complex models. A detailed algorithm walkthrough is provided with demonstration data for every algorithm discussed in the book.

Last, but not least, every chapter discusses an industry problem solved using machine learning. The book discusses applying classification algorithms to solve Spam Detection, Customer Segmentation, Disease Diagnosis, Malware Detection, Emotion Detection from Speech, and Image Classification.

All the code in this book has been written in Python. Python is by far the most popular programming language for data sciences. However, users of other popular programming languages, including R, Scala, and Octave, can use this book as the mathematics of the models remain the same.

The main library used in this book is Scikit-Learn, which is by far the most popular library for machine learning. While Scikit-Learn is used for Python in this book, Scikit-Learn is also available for R language. I hope you will find this book informative and helpful.

Chapter 1: Introduction to Machine Learning - explains how machines learn. This chapter builds the need to understand that machine-learning models are essentially mathematical formulations. Different types of problems that can be solved using machine learning are discussed. The chapter uses examples to discuss solving Regression, Classification, Clustering, and Dimensionality Reduction problems.

Chapter 2: Naïve Bayes Algorithm - presents a detailed discussion of this simple, yet powerful and popular algorithm. Naïve Bayes algorithm is a probabilistic model and this chapter discusses the involved concepts of probability. As the Naïve Bayes algorithm is a simplification of the Bayes Theory, this chapter discusses the need for simplification and the implications of the simplification. The Naïve Bayes algorithm is applied to solving the problem of Spam Detection. This chapter ends with discussing the different metrics used to evaluate a model.

Chapter 3: K-Nearest Neighbor Algorithm – discusses another simple, yet powerful and popular classification algorithm. The mathematical formulation of this algorithm is discussed in this chapter, along with the possible variations. The problem of Customer Segmentation based on Recency, Frequency, and Monetary Value (RFM) analysis is solved using the KNN algorithm in this chapter.

Chapter 4: Logistic Regression is the foundation of more complex algorithms, including Neural Networks. This chapter uses a simple example to explain the concept of Gradient Descent through a walkthrough. The concepts of the loss and cost functions are discussed in this chapter and will apply to the following chapters. Logistic Regression essentially conducts binary classification. This chapter discusses extending the core algorithm to conduct multi-class classification. This chapter ends with discussing how to classify the outcome of a medical diagnosis.

Chapter 5: Decision Tree Algorithm is used in building many more complex algorithms. So, understanding the Decision Tree algorithm is vital. This chapter walks through the process of building decision trees using the Gini Index. Step-by-step calculations are demonstrated in the process. The chapter rounds off with a discussion of how the Decision Tree algorithm can be applied to detecting malware in JPEG files. Before the Decision Tree algorithm can be applied, we need to be able to extract information from the JPEG files and be able to formulate the data such that it can be used for applying a machine learning algorithm to it. The chapter includes a discussion on how unbalanced datasets can be balanced. Also, the chapter discusses how principal component analysis can be applied to reduce the data dimensions.

Chapter 6: Ensemble Models – discusses how many weak models can be combined to form a strong model. This chapter also discusses how ensemble models can be formulated, including Voting, Bagging, Boosting, and Stacking models. The chapter concludes with a discussion of how Emotions can be detected from Speech. To be able to do this, the chapter discusses how information from audio clips can be extracted and formulated for application to a machine learning model.

Chapter 7: Random Forest Algorithm is a powerful and state-of-the-art algorithm in machine learning. It is a special case of the Bagging Ensemble model. This chapter discusses the formulation of the Random Forest algorithm and what makes the model free from bias and variance that works well on real-life data. The application for detecting malware in ELF files is discussed using the Random Forest algorithm.

Chapter 8: Boosting Algorithm is another state-of-the-art algorithm for solving classification problems. This chapter walks through the AdaBoost algorithm using an example. AdaBoost algorithm primarily uses the Decision Tree algorithm as the core. So, the Decision Tree algorithm is revisited in this chapter. This chapter solves the problem of classifying images using the AdaBoost algorithm. As even a powerful algorithm like AdaBoost does not produce satisfactory results for video classification, the chapter concludes by introducing Neural Networks.

Besides the **eight chapters**, the book has **8 annexures** to supplement the discussions with necessary concepts.

Annexure 1: Jupyter Notebook is the Integrated Development Environment (IDE) used to develop and run all the code discussed in this book. The files containing all the code discussed in this book are provided as supplementary material along with the book. All these codes are in the form of Jupyter Notebooks. This annexure discusses the basics of the Jupyter Notebook.

Annexure 2: Python is the programming language used in this book. This annexure introduces the basics of Python programming.

Annexure 3: Singular Value Decomposition is one of the methods to reduce the data dimensions. This annexure discusses the mathematics behind Singular Value Decomposition (SVD) and shows an application of SVD to Image Compression.

Annexure 4: Preprocessing Textual Data is one of the essential steps before text data can be applied to machine learning. This annexure discusses the essential preprocessing steps for cleaning textual data.

Annexure 5: Stemming and Lamentation are mechanisms applied in preprocessing textual data. This annexure discusses both these techniques with examples.

Annexure 6: Vectorizers are used to convert text data into numbers to be applied to machine learning models. Machine learning models can be built using only numeric data and thus, it is necessary to have a mechanism for converting text data into numbers. This annexure discusses two vectorizers – the Count Vectorizer and the TF-IDF Vectorizer.

Annexure 7: Encoders are used to convert text data into numbers to be applied to machine learning models. Machine learning models can be built using only numeric data and thus, it is necessary to have a mechanism for converting text data into numbers. This annexure discusses various encoders.

Annexure 8: Entropy is used in forming Decision Trees. Chapter 5 discussed how Decision Trees are formed using the Gini Index. This annexure provides an alternative method of forming Decision Trees using Entropy and Information Gain.

Code Bundle and Coloured Images

Please follow the link to download the
Code Bundle and the *Coloured Images* of the book:

https://rebrand.ly/5j8ua05

The code bundle for the book is also hosted on GitHub at **https://github.com/bpbpublications/Mastering-Classification-Algorithms-for-Machine-Learning**. In case there's an update to the code, it will be updated on the existing GitHub repository.

We have code bundles from our rich catalogue of books and videos available at **https://github.com/bpbpublications**. Check them out!

Errata

We take immense pride in our work at BPB Publications and follow best practices to ensure the accuracy of our content to provide with an indulging reading experience to our subscribers. Our readers are our mirrors, and we use their inputs to reflect and improve upon human errors, if any, that may have occurred during the publishing processes involved. To let us maintain the quality and help us reach out to any readers who might be having difficulties due to any unforeseen errors, please write to us at :

errata@bpbonline.com

Your support, suggestions and feedbacks are highly appreciated by the BPB Publications' Family.

Piracy

If you come across any illegal copies of our works in any form on the internet, we would be grateful if you would provide us with the location address or website name. Please contact us at **business@bpbonline.com** with a link to the material.

If you are interested in becoming an author

If there is a topic that you have expertise in, and you are interested in either writing or contributing to a book, please visit **www.bpbonline.com**. We have worked with thousands of developers and tech professionals, just like you, to help them share their insights with the global tech community. You can make a general application, apply for a specific hot topic that we are recruiting an author for, or submit your own idea.

Reviews

Please leave a review. Once you have read and used this book, why not leave a review on the site that you purchased it from? Potential readers can then see and use your unbiased opinion to make purchase decisions. We at BPB can understand what you think about our products, and our authors can see your feedback on their book. Thank you!

For more information about BPB, please visit **www.bpbonline.com**.

Join our book's Discord space

Join the book's Discord Workspace for Latest updates, Offers, Tech happenings around the world, New Release and Sessions with the Authors:

https://discord.bpbonline.com

Table of Contents

CHAPTER 1
Introduction to Machine Learning

Welcome to this book.

In this book, we will explore models for classifying data. We need to classify data for various purposes. For example, from piles of data regarding credit card transactions, we need to find out if there is any fraudulent transaction. So essentially, we are classifying the data into two classes – good transactions and fraudulent transactions. For example, from data regarding pictures of food items, we need to figure out if a food item would suit a diabetic patient.

Human beings are experts in classification in most situations. However, the data to classify is too large in the modern world. So, we need machines to classify as effectively as humans so that it is practical to meet the demand.

This book will discuss various models using which, machines can effectively classify data. Before we discuss these classification models, we start with a discussion on what machine learning is. We will also explore how machines can be made to learn.

Figure 1.1

Structure

In this chapter, we will discuss the following topics:

- Machine learning
    - Traditional programming versus programming for machine learning
    - The learning process of a machine
    - Kinds of data machines can learn from
- Types of machine learning
    - Supervised learning
    - Unsupervised learning

Objectives

After reading this chapter, you can differentiate between traditional programming and programming for machine learning. Also, you will understand what are the different problems that can be solved by machine learning.

Machine learning

Neuroscientist *Warren S. McCulloch* and *Logician Walter H. Pitts* published *A Logical Calculus of the ideas immanent in the Nervous activity* in 1943 in the Bulletin of

Mathematical Biophysics, Vol 5. In this paper, they discussed a mathematical model of neural networks. This is the first attempt to make machines think like the human brain. [1]

"What is being able to think" is a vast subject. We can make a simple abstraction, as shown in *Figure 1.1*. Thinking is a process of collecting data, finding patterns in the data, and making inferences from the patterns.

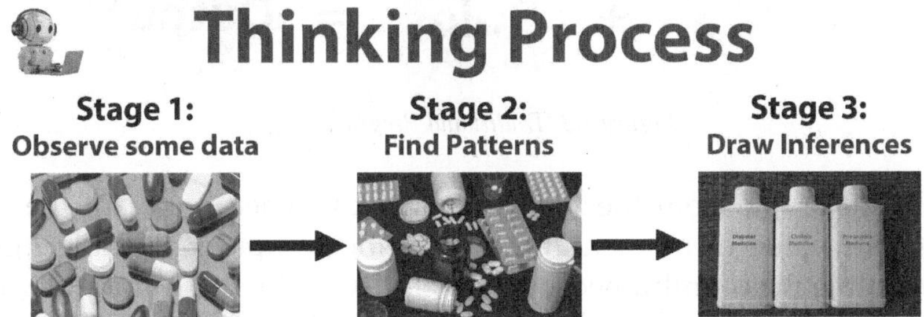

***Figure 1.2**: Abstraction of how thinking is performed*

Let us discuss the process of thinking through an example. Suppose the data provided to us is a massive pile of medicines. On receiving this data, we could find patterns like which medicines are like each other. We may study the composition of the medicines and the manufacturers and many other attributes. We may classify the medicines as which medicine group is for curing what disease based on the patterns we find.

Machine learning is like this. We present data to the machine and sometimes provide information about the data. Based on this information and knowledge, the machine finds patterns and considers the mechanism to see them as its rules. Once the machine has formulated its rules, it makes inferences about a new situation.

Machine learning is a branch of **Artificial Intelligence** (**AI**). In machine learning, using mathematical modeling on data, a machine is made to learn the patterns in the data without any human intervention.

Traditional programming versus programming for machine learning

Programming for machine learning is different from traditional programming.

1 **https://www.cse.chalmers.se/~coquand/AUTOMATA/mcp.pdf.**

In traditional programming, we have data and rules. We apply the rules to the data to get the Output. Refer to *Figure 1.3*:

***Figure 1.3**: Traditional Programming*

Consider this example from the world of Physics. When we want the computer to calculate the value of momentum, we tell the computer that the formula for momentum is the mass multiplied by the velocity and tell the computer the value of mass and velocity. Here, the value of mass and velocity is the **Data**. On this data, the computer applies the **Rule**, that is, the formula for momentum, to find the momentum value for us. The value of momentum calculated by the computer is the **Output**.

$$Momentum = Mass * Velocity$$

Generally written as,

$$Momentum = mv$$

In contrast to traditional programming, in machine learning, we supply the computer with Data and Output, and we expect the computer to generate the Rules as shown in *figure 1.4*:

Programming for Machine Learning

***Figure 1.4**: Programming for Machine Learning*

Suppose we had a mechanism to get values of momentum from some experiment. And we knew the values of mass and velocity in each of the experiments. Now, if we want the computer to determine the formula for momentum, that would be a machine learning situation. So, we would input the values of mass, velocity, and momentum and tell the machine to determine the formula for calculating momentum.

The learning process of a machine

Let us discuss a simplistic way the machines learn. As you would imagine, the actual process is much more complex.

Consider that we have the following data, (Refer to *Figure 1.5*) from an experiment. We ask the machine to provide a relationship between momentum mass and velocity.

Mass (KG)	Velocity (KM/h)	Momentum (KG*KM/h)
m	v	M
2	20	42
4	100	403
5	50	245
8	60	477
3	30	94

***Figure 1.5**: Input to a computer to create a Machine Learning Model*

For the machine to build a model, the data scientist must tell the machine what model to make. Generally, the data scientist tries to understand the data. This step is called **Exploratory Data Analysis**. In the preceding situation, we have two independent variables, m, and v, and one dependent variable, M. We can plot this data on a 2-dimensional chart as shown in *Figure 1.6*:

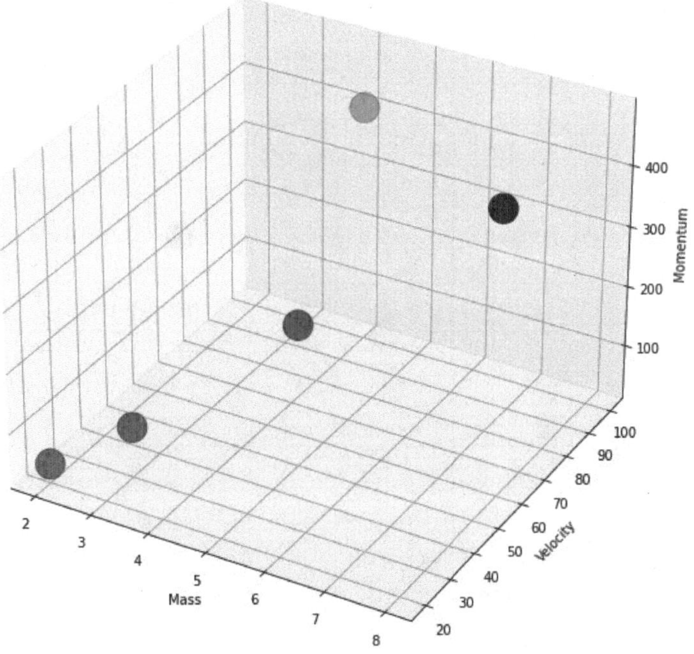

***Figure 1.6**: Scatter Plot based on data in Figure 1.4*

Let us say that data scientist decides to create a linear model of the form $M = \beta_0 + \beta_1 * m + \beta_2 * v$. The machine needs to estimate the values of β_0, β_1, and β_2.

The Data Scientist provides a starting value of β_0, β_1, and β_2. Let us say that these values are $\beta_0 = 5$, $\beta_1 = 5$, and $\beta_2 = 5$. Using these values, the machine calculates the values for M, as shown in *Figure 1.7*. We call the value calculated by the machine Mhat.

Mass (KG)	Velocity (KM/h)	Momentum (KG*KM/h)	For β0 = 5, β1 = 5, β2 = 5
m	v	M	Mhat
2	20	42	115
4	100	403	525
5	50	245	280
8	60	477	345
3	30	94	170

β0	5
β1	5
β2	5

***Figure 1.7**: Initial estimates of Momentum (M) made by the machine*

If we plot this data, we get the chart shown in *Figure 1.8*, where the dots are the actual values of M as provided to the machine. The stars are the values of M estimated by the machine:

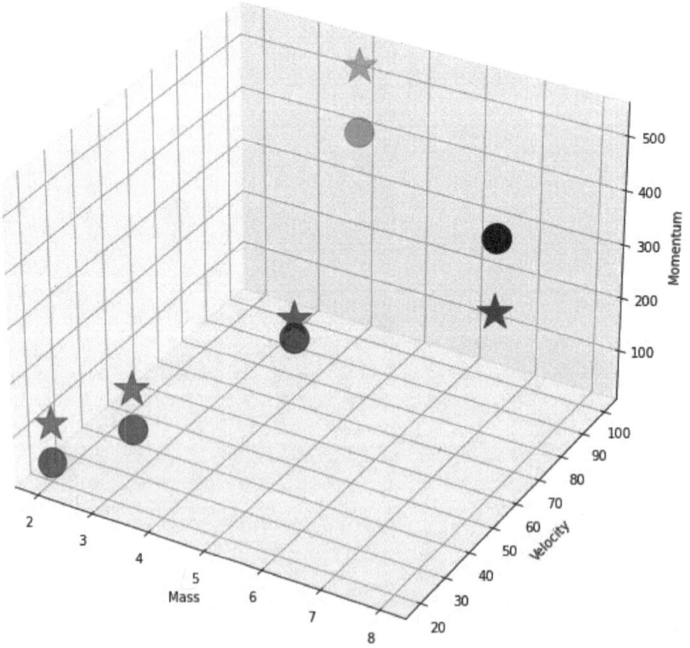

***Figure 1.8**: Plot of the machine's initial Momentum (M) estimates*

We can see that the machine did not do so well. However, the machine continues. The machine calculates its error in making the estimates, as shown in *Figure 1.9*. We see that the machine can overestimate or underestimate. So, the error can be negative or positive. Instead of considering the value of the error, we consider the value of the square of the error. Further, we calculate the **mean of the squared error (MSE)** across all the data points by averaging the squares of error.

Mass (KG)	Velocity (KM/h)	Momentum (KG*KM/h)	For β0 = 5, β1 = 5, β2 = 5	ERROR	E^2
m	v	M	Mhat	E = M - Mhat	
2	20	42	115	-73	5329
4	100	403	525	-122	14884
5	50	245	280	-35	1225
8	60	477	345	132	17424
3	30	94	170	-76	5776

β0 5
β1 5
β2 5

Mean Square Error = 8927.6

***Figure 1.9**: Computation of error in estimates made by the machine*

Now, the machine considers other values of β_0, β_1 and β_2 so that the value of the MSE is minimized. After some rounds of calculations, the machine gets the following values of β_0, β_1 and β_2 as shown in *Figure 1.10*:

Mass (KG)	Velocity (KM/h)	Momentum (KG*KM/h)	For β0 = 0, β1 = 32.7423630419487, β2 = 2.50428859372717	ERROR	E^2
m	v	M	Mhat	E = M - Mhat	
2	20	42	115.570498	-73.57049796	5412.61817
4	100	403	381.3983115	21.60168846	466.632944
5	50	245	288.9262449	-43.9262449	1929.51499
8	60	477	412.19622	64.80378004	4199.52991
3	30	94	173.3557469	-79.35574694	6297.33457

β0 0
β1 32.74236304
β2 2.504288594

Mean Square Error = 3661.12612

***Figure 1.10**: Estimate of Momentum after minimizing MSE*

The estimates, though better, could be more reasonable. So, the data scientist considers another strategy. This time the data scientist asks the computer to try and find a relationship between m*v and M. They want the machine to create an equation of the form $M = \beta_0 + \beta_1 * m * v$. As in the earlier case, the data scientist gives initial values for β_0 and β_1 as $\beta_0 = 5$ and $\beta_1 = 5$.

The setup is shown in *Figure 1.11*:

Mass (KG)	Velocity (KM/h)	Feature	Momentum (KG*KM/h)	For β0 = 5, β1 = 5	ERROR	E^2
m	v	m * v	M	Mhat	E = M - Mhat	
2	20	40	42	205	-163	26569
4	100	400	403	2005	-1602	2566404
5	50	250	245	1255	-1010	1020100
8	60	480	477	2405	-1928	3717184
3	30	90	94	455	-361	130321

β0 5
β1 5

Mean Square Error = 1492115.6

***Figure 1.11**: New setup*

The machine tries to minimize the MSE for this setup and calculate the values of β_0 and β_1, as shown in *Figure 1.12*:

Mass (KG)	Velocity (KM/h)	Feature	Momentum (KG*KM/h)	For β0 = 2.46214616625777, β1 = 0.991020053873143	ERROR	E^2
m	v	m * v	M	Mhat	E = M - Mhat	
2	20	40	42	42.10294832	-0.102948321	0.01059836
4	100	400	403	398.8701677	4.129832284	17.0555147
5	50	250	245	250.2171596	-5.217159635	27.2187547
8	60	480	477	478.151772	-1.151772025	1.3265788
3	30	90	94	91.65395101	2.346048985	5.50394584

β0 2.462146166
β1 0.991020054

Mean Square Error = 10.2230785

***Figure 1.12**: Estimate of Momentum after minimizing MSE for the new model devised in Figure 1.11*

The machine has done much better. Let us plot this data and check (Refer to *Figure 1.13*):

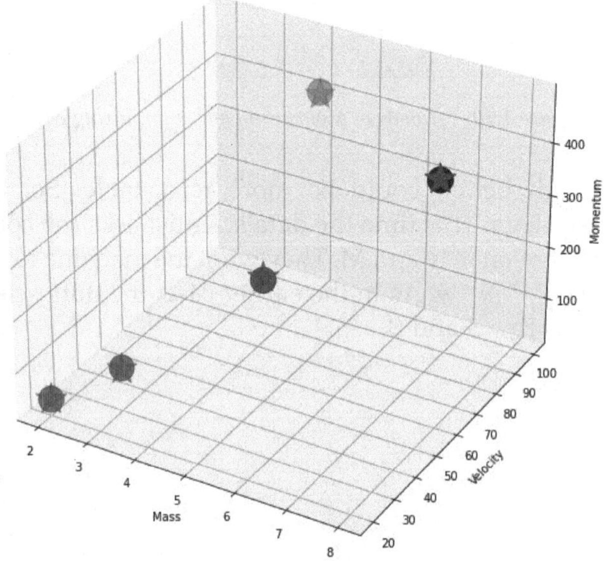

***Figure 1.13**: Plot of new estimates made by the machine. The RED crosses are the estimates*

So, the machine has given us a formula for calculating momentum based on the data provided to the machine. According to the machine:

$$Momentum = 2.46214616625777 + 0.991020053873143 * Mass * Velocity$$

Now, for any new value of Mass and Velocity, say *Mass = 7 kg* and *Velocity = 8 km/h*, the machine would say that:

$$Momentum = 2.46214616625777 + 0.991020053873143 * 7\ kg * 8\ km/h = 57.95926918\ kg * km/h$$

This is pretty good as, according to the formula from physics, the value of momentum for *Mass = 7 kg* and *Velocity = 8 km/h* should be *56 kg * km/h*.

Kinds of data the machines can learn from

From nature, human beings can gather data through the five sense organs. We can see, hear, smell, taste, and feel. Out of these five types of data, human beings have been able to digitize what they see and hear. Likewise, machines can also understand data from images and sounds.

Human beings have created a lot of digital data from various activities we perform. This data is either structured or unstructured.

- Structured data is organized in tabular form and follow definite semantics. It is by far the data most processed by machines. As of 2022, about 80% of the data machines learn from are structured data. Machines are extremely good with structured data. Also, machines are very useful in working on structured data as humans fail to cope with the volumes of structured data. Examples of structured data can be found in any system where some transactions are conducted. For example, the data regarding credit card system transactions is structured. In a credit card system, millions of transactions are performed daily. Tasks like detecting fraudulent transactions are extremely difficult for human beings. So, here machines are best suited for the job.
- Unstructured data is a more recent phenomenon. This has mainly exploded due to social media. Unstructured data has no definite semantics, so, such data must be expressed with some semantics before the machines can work on them. Over the years, many representations of unstructured data have emerged; thus, machines can work efficiently on such data. Examples of unstructured data include tweets and newspaper articles. Images and audio/video clips are also unstructured data.
- We can also categorize data as semi-structured, containing portions of structured and unstructured data. For example, data from emails have a structure in that it contains structured information regarding the date the email was sent, who sent it, whom it was sent to, what the subject is, does

it have attachments, and so on. However, the body of the emails contains unstructured data. As machines work well with structured and unstructured data, machines work well with semi-structured data too.

No matter the type of data, it must be understood that machines can only work on numbers. So, any data the machines need to understand must be presented to the machine in numbers. In this book, we will discuss various techniques for converting non-numeric data to numbers without any loss of context and allowing machines to learn from them. These discussions will be spread across all the remaining chapters as we will discuss different problems to be solved by the machines.

Types of machine learning

Machine learning can be classified into two main types. They are **Supervised learning** and **Unsupervised learning**.

- In Supervised learning, we can perform two tasks: **regression** and **classification**.
- In Unsupervised learning, we can do two tasks: **clustering** and **dimensionality reduction**.
    - o There is a special case of Clustering tasks called **Anomaly Detection**.

Figure 1.14 summarizes all types of machine learning and the tasks that can be performed:

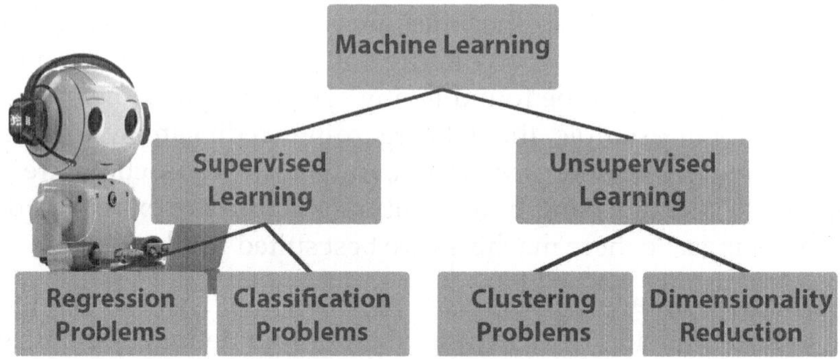

***Figure 1.14**: Types of machine learning*

Some people also consider **Reinforcement learning** as one type of Machine Learning. At the same time, some people argue that Reinforcement learning is approximate dynamic programming.

Let us discuss each type of machine learning in more detail. However, this book focuses on the classification task, a type of supervised learning.

Supervised learning

In Supervised learning, the machine is provided data along with labels. The machine learns based on the data and the associated labels and then makes inferences. So, we are providing the machine with prior knowledge, and then after the machine learns from this knowledge, it can make decisions within the boundaries of this provided knowledge.

Labels are the analysis of the data as determined by humans. For example, if we want the machine to learn to differentiate between images of dogs and cats, we need to provide data regarding dogs and cats to the machines. Along with this data, we need to provide labels stating which are the images of dogs and which are the images of cats. Suppose we want the machine to predict the marks in an exam. In that case, we need to provide historical data along with labels stating how many marks were obtained under the circumstances provided in the data.

The bottom line in Supervised learning is that we provide existing knowledge to the machine and expect the machine to find patterns in the provided knowledge and make rules that the machine can use to answer future questions asked on the same subject.

Let us understand this with an example. Consider that we want the machine to be able to detect spam emails. So, we gather the data as shown in *Table 1.1*:

Contains spelling mistakes	Contains the word "Urgent"	Contains the word "ASAP"	Contains a link to click	Label
NO	NO	NO	YES	Benign
NO	NO	NO	NO	Benign
YES	NO	YES	NO	Spam
NO	YES	YES	YES	Spam
YES	NO	NO	YES	Benign
YES	YES	YES	YES	Spam

Table 1.1*: Example dataset of emails for spam detection*

In this example, the dataset in *Table 1.1* contains only 6 data points. In real situations, the datasets have thousands and millions of data points. Nevertheless, the dataset contains data in 4 variables: Contains spelling mistakes, Contains the word "Urgent", Contains the word "ASAP", and Contains a link to click. In machine language parlance, these variables are called **Independent Variables**. For these four variables, there is data in each data point. In normal circumstances, experts would have studied real emails and gathered these four characteristics for each email. Apart from collecting data regarding the characteristics of the emails, experts would also assign a label as to whether the email is benign or spam. The variable we refer to as the label is also called the **dependent variable** in machine learning parlance.

In Supervised learning, the machine would form patterns from the independent variables considering the associated dependent variable. From the pattern would emerge a rule that the machine will use when given new values for the independent variables.

The preceding example is a **Classification problem** where the machine needs to decide whether an email is benign or spam. This type of Classification problem is called a **Binary classification problem**, as the machine must decide between two options or classes.

There are classification problems where the machine needs to choose between more than two classes. Such classification problems are called **Multi-class classification problems**.

Implementation of classification on the example data provided in *Table 1.1* is as follows:

```
import pandas as pd

df = pd.DataFrame([['NO', 'NO', 'NO', 'YES', 'Benign'],
                   ['NO', 'NO', 'NO', 'NO', 'Benign'],
                   ['YES', 'NO', 'YES', 'NO', 'Spam'],
                   ['NO', 'YES', 'YES', 'YES', 'Spam'],
                   ['YES', 'NO', 'NO', 'YES', 'Benign'],
                   ['YES', 'YES', 'YES', 'YES', 'Spam']
                  ],
                  columns = ['ContainsSpellingMistakes',
'ContainsUrgent', 'ContainsASAP',  'ContainsLink', 'Label']
                 )

df
```

```
  ContainsSpellingMistakes ContainsUrgent ContainsASAP ContainsLink 
Label
0                  NO             NO            NO          YES    Benign
1                  NO             NO            NO          NO     Benign
2                  YES            NO            YES         NO     Spam
3                  NO             YES           YES         YES    Spam
4                  YES            NO            NO          YES    Benign
5                  YES            YES           YES         YES    Spam
```

```
X = df.drop('Label', axis = 1, inplace = False)
y = df['Label']

print(X, '\n\n', y)
  ContainsSpellingMistakes ContainsUrgent ContainsASAP ContainsLink
0                       NO             NO           NO          YES
1                       NO             NO           NO           NO
2                      YES             NO          YES           NO
3                       NO            YES          YES          YES
4                      YES             NO           NO          YES
5                      YES            YES          YES          YES

0    Benign
1    Benign
2      Spam
3      Spam
4    Benign
5      Spam
Name: Label, dtype: object
from sklearn.preprocessing import LabelEncoder

# Convert all data to numbers
leX = LabelEncoder()
XL = X.apply(leX.fit_transform)

leY = LabelEncoder()
yL = leY.fit_transform(y)

print(XL, '\n\n', yL)
   ContainsSpellingMistakes  ContainsUrgent  ContainsASAP  ContainsLink
0                         0               0             0             1
1                         0               0             0             0
2                         1               0             1             0
3                         0               1             1             1
4                         1               0             0             1
5                         1               1             1             1
```

```
[0 0 1 1 0 1]
from sklearn.linear_model import LogisticRegression

# Build Model
lr = LogisticRegression()
lr.fit(XL, yL)

# Prepare Test Data
testData = ['NO', 'YES', 'NO', 'YES']
Xtest = leX.transform(testData)

prediction = lr.predict(Xtest.reshape(1, -1))
print('Prediction =', leY.inverse_transform(prediction))
Prediction = ['Benign']
```

Take another example. Suppose we have the temperatures of a city, say Bengaluru, every day for many years. We have three attributes, that is, the date, whether it was cloudy on that date, and the temperature on that date, as shown in *Table 1.2*:

Date	Cloudy	Temperature (in Celsius)
01-Jan-2001	YES	14.3
02-Jan-2001	NO	13.7
03-Jan-2001	NO	13.6
04-Jan-2001	YES	14.2
05-Jan-2001	NO	12.8
...	...	...

***Table 1.2**: Example dataset of temperatures in a city*

Suppose we have this data from 01-Jan-2001 till 31-Dec-2015. Also, we want to know what the temperature would be on 25-Oct-2022. We should be able to predict the same using a Machine learning system with a Regression model. We need historical data for all the independent and associated dependent variables in Regression problems. In the example in *t*able 1.2, the date and whether cloudy or not are the independent variables or features. From some independent variables, we can derive many more independent variables. For example, from our data in *Table 1.2*, from the feature date, we can derive other independent variables like month, day of the year, etc. So, instead of using the date as the independent variable, we could use the month of the date and the day of the year as our features. Generating independent variable(s) or feature(s) from the existing independent variable(s) is called Feature Engineering (Refer to *Table 1.3*).

Date	Month	Day of the Year	CLOUDY	Temperature (in Celsius)
01-Jan-2001	1	1	YES	14.3
02-Jan-2001	1	2	NO	13.7
03-Jan-2001	1	3	NO	13.6
04-Jan-2001	1	4	YES	14.2
05-Jan-2001	1	5	NO	12.8
...	...	...	...	...

***Table 1.3**: Feature Engineered dataset of temperatures in a city*

The temperature is the dependent variable or target variable. Given this data, we want the machine to learn the patterns and create a rule. Then, given any date in the future and whether it is cloudy, the machine should predict the temperature on that day. So, this is also Supervised Learning.

A regression implementation on the example data provided in *Table 1.2* is as follows:

```
import pandas as pd

df = pd.DataFrame([['01-01-2001', 'YES', 14.3],
                   ['01-02-2001', 'NO', 13.7],
                   ['01-03-2001', 'NO', 13.6],
                   ['01-04-2001', 'YES', 14.3],
                   ['01-05-2001', 'NO', 14.2],
                   ['01-06-2001', 'YES', 12.8],
                   ['01-07-2001', 'NO', 14.7],
                   ['01-08-2001', 'NO', 11.3],
                   ['01-09-2001', 'NO', 11.7],
                   ['01-10-2001', 'NO', 12.1],
                  ],
                  columns = ['Date', 'Cloudy', 'Temperature']
                 )

df

        Date Cloudy  Temperature
0 01-01-2001    YES         14.3
1 01-02-2001     NO         13.7
```

```
2  01-03-2001     NO         13.6
3  01-04-2001    YES         14.3
4  01-05-2001     NO         14.2
5  01-06-2001    YES         12.8
6  01-07-2001     NO         14.7
7  01-08-2001     NO         11.3
8  01-09-2001     NO         11.7
9  01-10-2001     NO         12.1
import datetime
import numpy as np
from sklearn.preprocessing import LabelEncoder

# Feature Engineering
# Get Month and Day of the Year
df['Month'] = pd.to_datetime(df['Date']).dt.month
referenceDate = np.array([datetime.datetime(2001, 1, 1)] * len(df))
df['DayOfYear'] = (pd.to_datetime(df['Date']) - referenceDate).dt.days

# Convert Cloudy to numbers
leC = LabelEncoder()
df['Cloudy'] = leC.fit_transform(df['Cloudy'])

df
         Date  Cloudy  Temperature  Month  DayOfYear
0  01-01-2001       1         14.3      1          0
1  01-02-2001       0         13.7      1          1
2  01-03-2001       0         13.6      1          2
3  01-04-2001       1         14.3      1          3
4  01-05-2001       0         14.2      1          4
5  01-06-2001       1         12.8      1          5
6  01-07-2001       0         14.7      1          6
7  01-08-2001       0         11.3      1          7
8  01-09-2001       0         11.7      1          8
9  01-10-2001       0         12.1      1          9
X = df[['Month', 'DayOfYear', 'Cloudy']]
y = df['Temperature']

from sklearn.ensemble import RandomForestRegressor
from dateutil import parser
```

```
import numpy as np

# Build Model
rfr = RandomForestRegressor()
rfr.fit(X, y)

# Prepare Test Data
testData = ['01-22-2001', 'NO']

Xtest = [0, 0, 0]
Xtest[0] = parser.parse(testData[0]).month
Xtest[1] = (parser.parse(testData[0]) - referenceDate[0]).days
Xtest[2] = leC.transform([testData[1]])[0]
print('Transformed test data:', Xtest)

# Make the prediction
prediction = rfr.predict(np.array(Xtest).reshape(1, -1))
print('\nPredicted temperature on %s = %f' % (testData[0], prediction))
Transformed test data: [1, 21, 0]

Predicted temperature on 01-22-2001 = 12.012000
```

You may have realized that Regression models can be developed when the dependent variable is continuous. In contrast, Classification models can be created when the dependent variable is discrete. A **discrete variable** is a variable that takes a finitely infinite number of values (for example, a set of whole numbers). A **continuous variable** is a variable that takes an infinitely infinite number of values (for example, a set of rational numbers).

Unsupervised learning

Unlike Supervised learning, in Unsupervised learning, we provide data to the machine without labels. Under these circumstances, the machine can perform two kinds of tasks – **Clustering** and **Dimensionality Reduction**.

In Clustering, the machine can separate similar objects into separate clusters. Suppose we provide a vast volume of Customer information to the machine along with information regarding the customers on various attributes. By analyzing the attributes, the machine can form similar customer clusters. There are several uses for such applications. For example, in clustering customers, we can study the clustered customers and plan specific marketing drives for each cluster. Or when we have the clusters created by the machine, we can use that information to tell the machine to determine the cluster for future customers that engage with the business. So, we can use the results from the clustering exercise for classification.

Let us understand clustering through an example. Suppose we have data regarding sales, as shown in *Table 1.4*. We want to find similar customers.

Customer ID	Last Invoice Date	Invoice Amount (in Rs.)
1	03-Jan-2022	300.00
2	03-Jan-2022	2000.00
2	04-Jan-2022	500.00
6	06-Feb-2022	200.00
5	17-Feb-2022	1200.00
3	25-Feb-2022	3000.00
1	20-Mar-2022	250.00
3	22-Mar-2022	300.00
2	26-Mar-2022	1750.00
4	28-Mar-2022	600.00

***Table 1.4**: Example dataset of retail sales*

```
import pandas as pd

df = pd.DataFrame([[1, '01-03-2022', 300],
                   [2, '01-03-2022', 2000],
                   [2, '01-04-2022', 500],
                   [6, '02-06-2022', 200],
                   [5, '02-17-2022', 1200],
                   [3, '02-25-2022', 3000],
                   [1, '03-20-2022', 250],
                   [3, '03-22-2022', 300],
                   [2, '03-26-2022', 1750],
                   [4, '03-28-2022', 600]
                  ],
                  columns = ['CustomerID', 'InvoiceDate', 'InvoiceAmount']
                 )
df

   CustomerID InvoiceDate  InvoiceAmount
```

```
0            1  01-03-2022            300
1            2  01-03-2022           2000
2            2  01-04-2022            500
3            6  02-06-2022            200
4            5  02-17-2022           1200
5            3  02-25-2022           3000
6            1  03-20-2022            250
7            3  03-22-2022            300
8            2  03-26-2022           1750
9            4  03-28-2022            600
# Feature Engineering
df['InvoiceDate'] = pd.to_datetime(df['InvoiceDate'])
gb = df.groupby('CustomerID')
counts = gb.size().to_frame(name = 'Frequency')
dfRFM = \
(counts
    .join(gb.agg({'InvoiceDate': 'max'}).rename(columns={'InvoiceDate':
'MostRecentPurchase'}))
    .join(gb.agg({'InvoiceAmount': 'sum'}).
rename(columns={'InvoiceAmount': 'MonetaryValue'}))
    .reset_index()
)

#from datetime import datetime, date
dfRFM['MostRecentPurchaseDate'] = pd.to_
datetime(dfRFM['MostRecentPurchase']).dt.date
dfRFM['Recency'] = (df.InvoiceDate.max().date() -
dfRFM['MostRecentPurchaseDate']).dt.days
dfRFM.drop(['MostRecentPurchaseDate', 'MostRecentPurchase'], axis = 1,
inplace = True)
print('Shape of Customer Data:', dfRFM.shape)
print('\n')
print(dfRFM.head())
Shape of Customer Data: (6, 4)
```

```
   CustomerID  Frequency  MonetaryValue  Recency
0           1          2            550        8
1           2          3           4250        2
2           3          2           3300        6
3           4          1            600        0
4           5          1           1200       39
# Scale Data
X = dfRFM.drop('CustomerID', axis = 1, inplace = False)
y = dfRFM['CustomerID']

from sklearn.preprocessing import StandardScaler
sc = StandardScaler()
X = sc.fit_transform(X.to_numpy())
X = pd.DataFrame(X, columns=['Frequency', 'MonetaryValue', 'Recency'])
X.head()
   Frequency  MonetaryValue   Recency
0   0.447214      -0.739480 -0.486540
1   1.788854       1.674705 -0.793829
2   0.447214       1.054846 -0.588970
3  -0.894427      -0.706856 -0.896258
4  -0.894427      -0.315366  1.101117
# Visualise the Data
import matplotlib.pyplot as plt
%matplotlib inline
import numpy as np

np.random.seed(19680801)

fig = plt.figure(figsize = (15, 10))
ax = fig.add_subplot(projection = '3d')

xs = X.Recency
ys = X.Frequency
zs = X.MonetaryValue
```

```
ax.scatter(xs, ys, zs, marker = 'o', s = 500)

ax.set_xlabel('Recency')
ax.set_ylabel('Frequency')
ax.set_zlabel('Monetary Value')

plt.show()
```

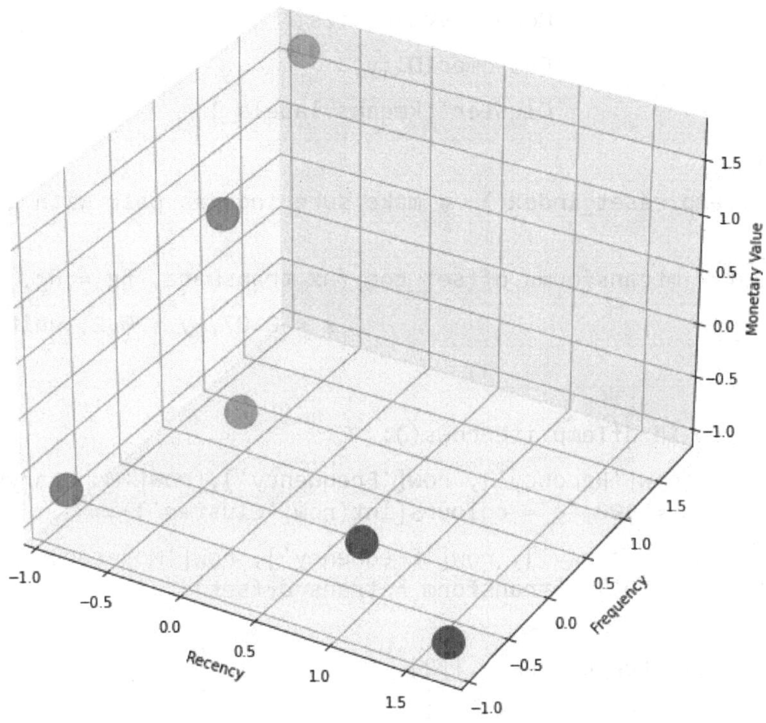

Figure 1.15: *Visualization of the Customer data*

```
# Create Clusters
from sklearn.cluster import KMeans
import matplotlib.transforms as mtransforms

kmeans = KMeans(n_clusters = 3, random_state = 42)
kmeans.fit(X, y)

# Visualise
np.random.seed(19680801)
```

```
fig = plt.figure(figsize = (15, 10))
ax = fig.add_subplot(projection = '3d')

colours = ['r', 'b', 'g']
dfTemp = pd.DataFrame({'Recency':xs,
                       'Frequency':ys,
                       'MonetaryValue':zs,
                       'CustomerID':y,
                       'Cluster':kmeans.labels_}
                       )
dfTemp = dfTemp.reset_index()  # make sure indexes pair with number of
rows
trans_offset = mtransforms.offset_copy(ax.transData, fig = fig,
                                        x = 0.07, y = 0.2, units =
'inches')

for index, row in dfTemp.iterrows():
    ax.scatter(row['Recency'], row['Frequency'], row['MonetaryValue'],
marker = 'o', s = 500, c = colours[int(row['Cluster'])])
    ax.text(row['Recency'], row['Frequency'], row['MonetaryValue'],
int(row['CustomerID']), transform = trans_offset)

xs1 = kmeans.cluster_centers_.T[2]
ys1 = kmeans.cluster_centers_.T[1]
zs1 = kmeans.cluster_centers_.T[0]
ax.scatter(xs1, ys1, zs1, marker = 'x', s = 800, c = 'r')

ax.set_xlabel('Recency')
ax.set_ylabel('Frequency')
ax.set_zlabel('Monetary Value')

plt.show()
```

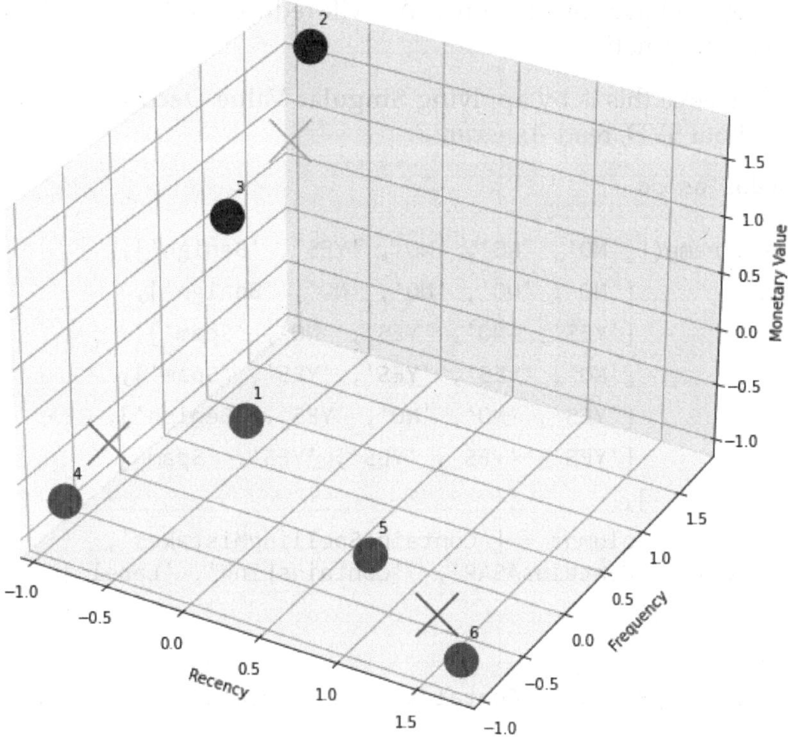

***Figure 1.16**: Customers grouped in 3 clusters*

Unsupervised learning is also used for **Dimensionality reduction**. Dimensionality reduction is the process of reducing the features while building a model so that only the essential features are utilized for building the model. Reducing the number of features reduces the complexity of the models, and thus the models become more robust.

Let us understand Dimensionality Reduction through an example. Let us consider the data in *table 1.5*:

Contains spelling mistakes	Contains the word "Urgent"	Contains the word "ASAP"	Contains link to click	Label
NO	NO	NO	YES	Benign
NO	NO	NO	NO	Benign
YES	NO	YES	NO	Spam
NO	YES	YES	YES	Spam
YES	NO	NO	YES	Benign
YES	YES	YES	YES	Spam

***Table 1.5**: Example dataset of emails for spam detection*

In this dataset, we have four features. We will reduce the number of features to 2 without losing information.

One way to achieve this is by applying **Singular Value Decomposition (SVD)**. To know more about SVD, read *Annexure 3*.

```
import pandas as pd

df = pd.DataFrame([['NO', 'NO', 'NO', 'YES', 'Benign'],
                   ['NO', 'NO', 'NO', 'NO', 'Benign'],
                   ['YES', 'NO', 'YES', 'NO', 'Spam'],
                   ['NO', 'YES', 'YES', 'YES', 'Spam'],
                   ['YES', 'NO', 'NO', 'YES', 'Benign'],
                   ['YES', 'YES', 'YES', 'YES', 'Spam']
                  ],
                  columns = ['ContainsSpellingMistakes',
'ContainsUrgent', 'ContainsASAP',  'ContainsLink', 'Label']
                 )
df
  ContainsSpellingMistakes ContainsUrgent ContainsASAP ContainsLink
Label
0                NO             NO            NO            YES  Benign
1                NO             NO            NO             NO  Benign
2                YES            NO            YES            NO    Spam
3                NO             YES           YES           YES    Spam
4                YES            NO            NO            YES  Benign
5                YES            YES           YES           YES    Spam
X = df.drop('Label', axis = 1, inplace = False)
y = df['Label']

print(X, '\n\n', y)
  ContainsSpellingMistakes ContainsUrgent ContainsASAP ContainsLink
0                       NO             NO           NO          YES
1                       NO             NO           NO           NO
2                      YES             NO          YES           NO
3                       NO            YES          YES          YES
4                      YES             NO           NO          YES
5                      YES            YES          YES          YES
```

```
 0    Benign
1    Benign
2      Spam
3      Spam
4    Benign
5      Spam
Name: Label, dtype: object
from sklearn.preprocessing import LabelEncoder

# Convert all data to numbers
leX = LabelEncoder()
XL = X.apply(leX.fit_transform)

leY = LabelEncoder()
yL = leY.fit_transform(y)


print(XL, '\n\n', yL)
   ContainsSpellingMistakes  ContainsUrgent  ContainsASAP  ContainsLink
0                         0               0             0             1
1                         0               0             0             0
2                         1               0             1             0
3                         0               1             1             1
4                         1               0             0             1
5                         1               1             1             1

 [0 0 1 1 0 1]
from sklearn import decomposition

pca = decomposition.PCA(n_components = 2)
pca.fit(XL)
X = pca.transform(XL)
X = pd.DataFrame(X, columns = ['Feature1', 'Feature2'])
X
   Feature1  Feature2
0 -0.569933 -0.580462
1 -0.882814 -0.010497
2  0.042248  0.973800
3  0.715967 -0.614335
```

```
4 -0.295684  0.132684
5  0.990216  0.098810
import matplotlib.pyplot as plt
%matplotlib inline

fig = plt.figure(figsize = (10, 6))
ax = fig.add_subplot(1, 1, 1)

plt.scatter(X.Feature1, X.Feature2, marker = 'o', s = 500, c = yL)

ax.set_xlabel('Feature 1')
ax.set_ylabel('Feature 2')

plt.show()
```

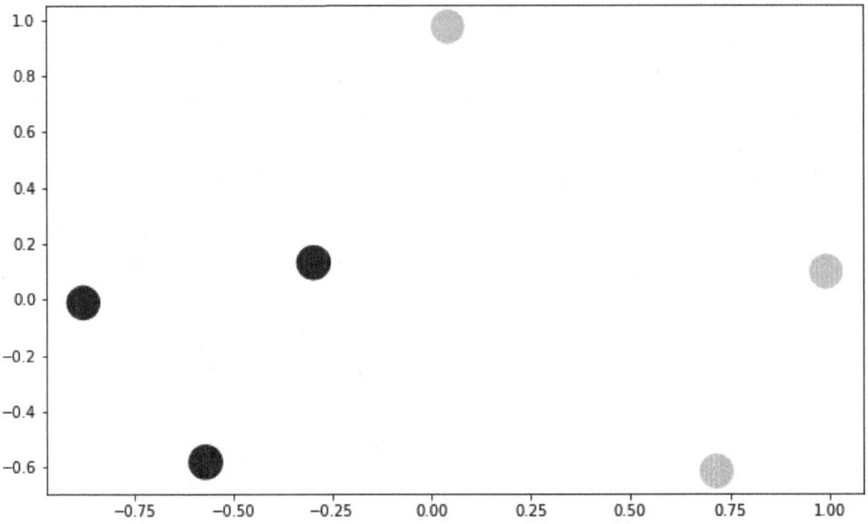

***Figure 1.17**: Visualization of the spam dataset after reducing to 2 dimensions*

Conclusion

The effort to make machines learn has been in action for more than 70 years. However, these efforts have accelerated only in the last 15-20 years. This is mainly because the amount of data available has exploded in the last 15-20 years mainly because of the development of many digital devices and the advent of social media. To date, machines can be relied on for many prediction and prescription activities like Fraud detection, Weather forecasting, election forecasting, medical diagnostics, and so on. However, many more developments are required before machines can become reliable in performing tasks on their own.

Machines learn through mathematical models. We got the essence of that in this chapter. The remaining chapters will discuss the mathematical models used to create classification algorithms.

In the next chapter, we will start this series by discussing the Naïve Bayes algorithm.

Points to remember

- Machines can only understand numbers.
- Data can be available as numbers and non-numbers. All data available as non-numbers should be converted to numbers. There are many methods for achieving this.
- Machines can learn from tabular data, text, images, videos, and sound clips.
- Machines learn through mathematical models.
- Machine learning can be divided into two main types: supervised and unsupervised.
- In Supervised learning, we can do two tasks – Regression and classification.
- In Unsupervised learning, we can do two tasks – Clustering and dimensionality reduction.
- Anomaly detection is a special case of Unsupervised learning for clustering.

Chapter 2
Naïve Bayes Algorithm

In *Chapter 1, Introduction to Machine Learning,* we discussed the types of activities a machine can perform. We underlined the fact that machines essentially learn based on mathematical models. This chapter discusses one such mathematical model, that is, the Naïve Bayes Algorithm. Using Naïve Bayes Algorithm, we will develop a machine-learning model for Spam detection.

The Naïve Bayes algorithm simplifies the Bayes theorem by making some assumptions. So, first, we will discuss the Bayes Theorem before moving to Naïve Bayes Algorithm.

As Bayes theorem is based on probability, we will start this chapter with a discussion on probability.

Figure 2.1

Structure

In this chapter, we will discuss the following topics:

- Basics of probability
    - Conditional probability
    - Multiplication rule of probability
    - Independent events
- Total probability theorem
- Bayes theorem
- Detecting spam using Bayes theorem
- Detecting spam using Naïve Bayes theorem
- Variations of Naïve Bayes algorithm
- Applying Naïve Bayes algorithm to detect spam SMS
    - Creating training and test sets
    - Pre-processing the data
        - Function to detect whether one or more URLs are present in the text
        - Function to remove non-essential elements from the text
        - Forming TF-IDF (Converting text to numbers)
    - Building the model
    - Confusion matrix
        - Accuracy score
        - Precision score
        - Recall score
        - F1 score
    - Checking the model's training accuracy
    - Validating the model
    - Making predictions using the model

Objectives

After reading this chapter, you will understand the mathematics behind the Naïve Bayes algorithm. Also, you will understand the nuances of a basic spam detection model.

Basics of probability

Many definitions of probability exist in mathematics textbooks. For the context of this book, **Probability could be defined as the chance of occurrence of an event under an experiment**.

Let us understand this through an example. Suppose the experiment is to toss a coin with a head on one side and a tail on the other ten times. The event of interest is the number of heads we obtain. We are interested in determining the probability of getting a head in this experimental setup.

Suppose the outcomes of each of the ten tosses are as given in *Table 2.1:*

Toss Number	1	2	3	4	5	6	7	8	9	10
Outcome	H	T	T	H	H	T	T	T	T	H

Table 2.1: *Outcomes of the experiment of tossing a coin ten times*

We see that we got Heads 4 times out of 10 tosses. So, the probability of getting a head per this experiment is 4/10.

We would write this as:

$$P(\text{Head}) = 4/10 = 0.4$$

Let us simulate the process of tossing the coin n number of times using the following program:

```
import numpy as np
import scipy.stats as stats
from scipy.stats import norm, beta
import matplotlib.pyplot as plt
import warnings
warnings.filterwarnings("ignore")

def probabilityOfHead(numberOfTrials):
    plt.figure(figsize=(8, 5))

    data = stats.bernoulli.rvs(0.5, size = numberOfTrials)
    x = np.linspace(0, 1, 100)

    heads = data[:numberOfTrials].sum()
```

```
    a = 1
    b = 1
    s = heads
    f = numberOfTrials - s
    y = beta.pdf(x, a + s, b + f)
   plt.plot(x, y, label = 'observe %d tosses,\n %d heads' % (numberOfTrials,
heads))
    plt.fill_between(x, 0, y, color='#348ABD', alpha = 0.4)
    plt.vlines(0.5, 0, max(y), color = "k", linestyles = "--", lw = 1)

    leg = plt.legend()
    leg.get_frame().set_alpha(0.4)
    plt.autoscale(tight=True)

     plt.title('Probability of getting Heads, P(Head) = %f' % (heads /
numberOfTrials))

    plt.show()
```

Let us run the above function for 20 tosses. The result obtained is shown in *Figure 2.1*. The result you get upon running the same command may be different.

```
probabilityOfHead(20)
```

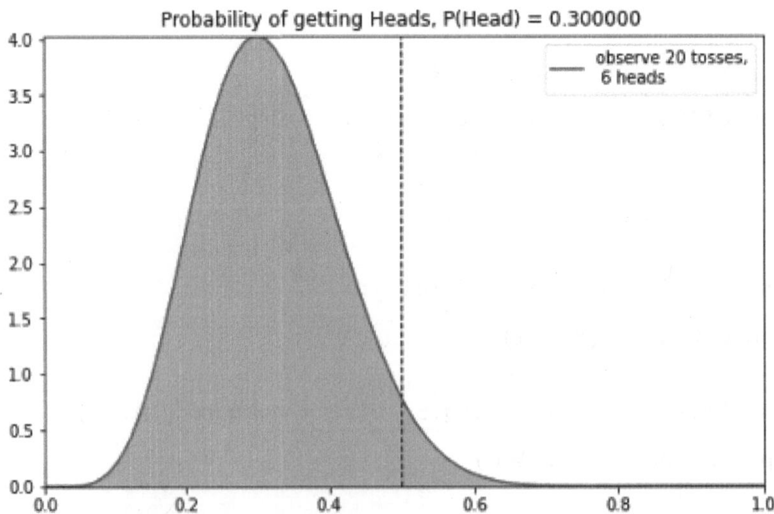

***Figure 2.2**: Probability of getting a head on tossing a coin 20 times*

Let us run the function for 50, 100, 500, and 1000 tosses. The result obtained is shown as follows:

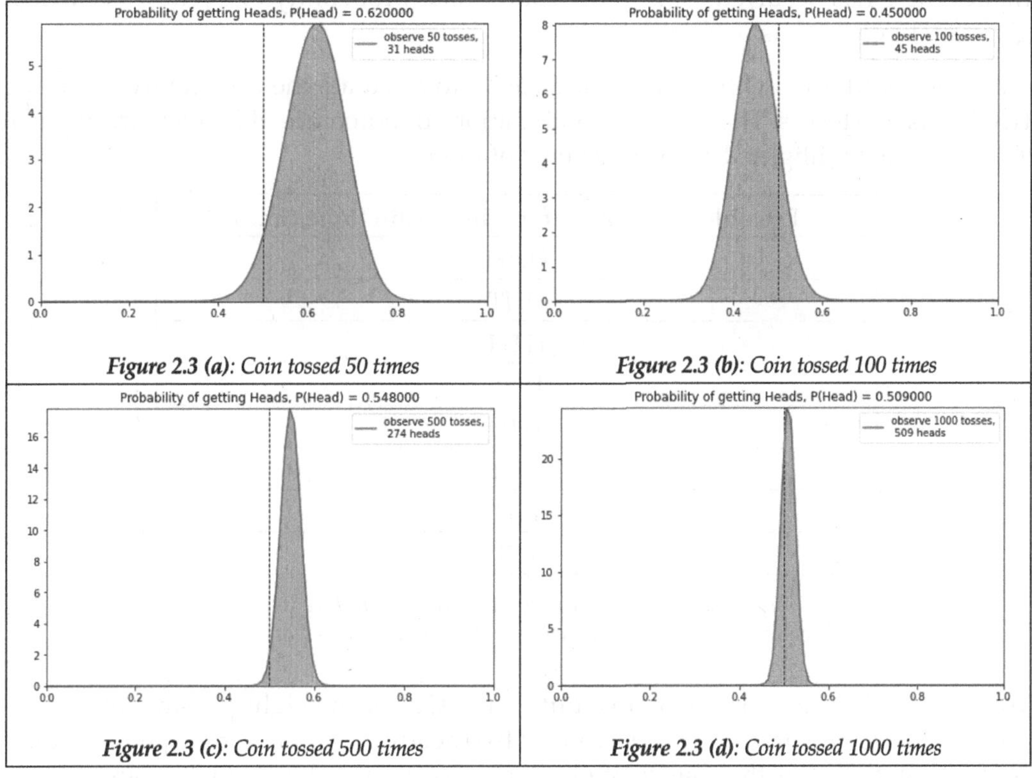

***Figure 2.3 (a)**: Coin tossed 50 times*

***Figure 2.3 (b)**: Coin tossed 100 times*

***Figure 2.3 (c)**: Coin tossed 500 times*

***Figure 2.3 (d)**: Coin tossed 1000 times*

***Figure 2.3**: Distributions of getting heads in different numbers of tosses of a fair coin*

We can see that as we toss the coin a greater number of times, the probability of getting a head tends toward 0.5 or 1/2.

We would denote the event by a variable. So, let us say that the variable X represents our event. We want to find the probability that X = head. Then, we would write P(X = head).

Under the assumption that all the outcomes of tossing a coin are equally likely, we can state that P(X = Head) = 1/2.

Conditional probability

Continuing with the example of tossing a coin and obtaining a head, let us say that we want to find the probability of getting two heads in 3 tosses, given that we have obtained a head in the first toss. So, here we have two events. Let us denote the two events as X and Y. Y is the event where we have obtained a head in the first toss. Then, X will be the event of getting one head for the successive two tosses.

We would write this as P(X = 1 head in toss 2 to 3 | Y = head in toss 1). In regular work, we would write this as P(X | Y). This is read as the probability of event X, given that event Y has occurred. This is the conditional probability of event X occurring, given that event Y has occurred.

Now, we could use the illustration in *Table 2.2* to calculate the probability of getting two heads in 3 tosses. The possible combinations of outcomes of 3 tosses are given in *Table 2.2*. The highlighted rows are events of interest:

Possible Outcomes of tossing a coin three times
HHH
HHT
HTH
HTT
THH
TTH
THT
TTT

***Table 2.2**: Possible outcomes on tossing a coin three times. Highlighted rows are the outcomes of two heads obtained in 3 tosses*

We see that there are eight possible outcomes. Out of the eight possible outcomes, there are three outcomes where we can get two heads in 3 tosses (Some people would prefer to state this as the chance of obtaining exactly two heads in 3 tosses). So, the probability of getting two heads in 3 tosses is 3/8.

We could have calculated the above as follows as well. There are $^3C_2$ ways to get 2 heads of 3 tosses. And the probability of getting a head in each toss is 1/2. So, the likelihood of getting two heads in 3 tosses is $^3C_2$ (= 3/8.

Now, it is given that we have obtained a head in the first toss. Therefore, the possible outcomes of the three tosses in this circumstance are shown in *Table 2.3*:

Possible Outcomes on tossing a coin three times, given that the outcome of the first toss is a head
HHH
HHT
HTH
HTT

***Table 2.3**: Possible outcomes on tossing a coin three times where a head has been obtained in the first toss. Highlighted rows are the outcomes where two heads are in 3 tosses*

So, in this example, the probability of getting two heads in 3 tosses, given that the outcome of the first toss is a head, is 2/4 = 1/2.

So, $P(X \mid Y) = 1/2$.

We could have calculated this as $P(X \mid Y) = {}^{2}C_{1} (1/2^{2} = 1/2$ (one head in 2 tosses as we already have a head from the first toss).

We can understand this through another example. Let us say that event Y is an event of a person purchasing an iPhone 14. X is the event that a person might consider purchasing a screen guard for iPhone 14. So, we have the following:

X = Event of a person buying an iPhone 14 screen guard

Y = Event of a person purchasing an iPhone 14

So, for $P(X \mid Y)$, we want to find the conditional probability of event X, given that event Y has occurred.

Remember that $P(X \mid Y) \neq P(Y \mid X)$

Multiplication rule of probability

Suppose X and Y are two events, as shown in *Figure 2.4*. We see that events X and Y have some common items. The common items between events X and Y are called the **Intersection** of events X and Y.

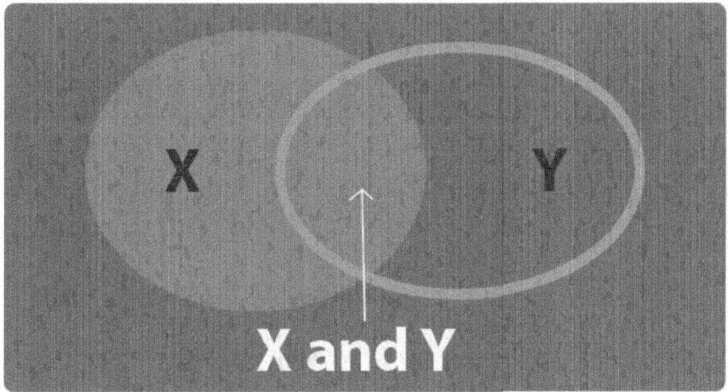

***Figure 2.4**: Intersection between 2 events*

The probability of the intersection of the events X and Y is called the Joint probability of the events X and Y and is denoted as P(X, Y).

Now, the multiplication rule of probability states that

$$P(X \text{ and } Y) = P(X \cap Y) = P(X,Y) = P(Y \mid X) * P(X)$$

Let us understand this through an example. Suppose X is the event that a student is a Female and Y is the event that the student is a Graduate. Then, the event (X and Y) is that the student is a Female graduate.

Consider the data in *Table 2.4*:

	Graduate	Non-Graduate	TOTAL
Male	126	55	181
Female	133	32	165
TOTAL	259	87	346

Table 2.4: *Illustration Data*

From *Table 2.4*, we get the following:

$$P(X = Female) = 165/346$$

$$P(Y = Graduate) = 259/346$$

$$P(Y \mid X) = 133/165$$

$$P(X \mid Y) = 133/259$$

Then, by multiplication rule of probability, we get:

$$P(X,Y) = 165/346 * 133/165 = 133 / 346$$

$$P(Y,X) = 259/346 * 133/259 = 133 / 346$$

Note that $P(X, Y) = P(Y, X)$.

From the multiplication rule of probability, we get a formula for conditional probability as follows:

$$P(Y \mid X) = (P(X,Y))/(P(X))$$

Or

$$P(X \mid Y) = (P(X,Y))/(P(Y))$$

Independent events [1]

Two events, A and B, are said to be independent if $P(A \mid B) = P(A)$, that is, if the probability of event A given that event B has occurred is the same as the probability of event A, then events A and B are independent.

Consider that we have two events, X and Y, such that Y is the event of getting a three on tossing a dice, and X is the event of getting a head on tossing a coin. Suppose we perform event Y first, and the outcome is three being obtained. Then, $P(X \mid Y)$ is the probability of getting a head on tossing a coin when we have obtained a three on throwing a dice.

Now, $P(X) = 1/2$ because the head is one of the two possible outcomes: head and tail.

Also, $P(X \mid Y) = 1/2$.

As $P(X \mid Y) = P(X)$, we say X and Y are independent events.

Total probability theorem

Suppose we have two disjoint sets, B_1 and B_2, in a sample space, as shown in *Figure 2.5*:

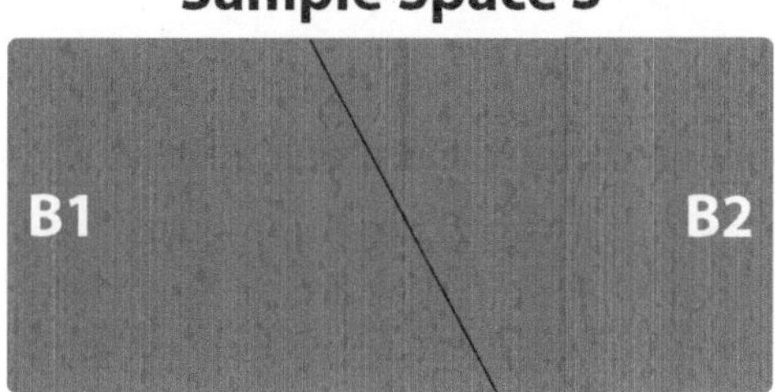

***Figure 2.5**: A sample space S with two disjoint sets B1 and B2*

Now, we have a set A, as shown in the green ellipse in *Figure 2.6*:

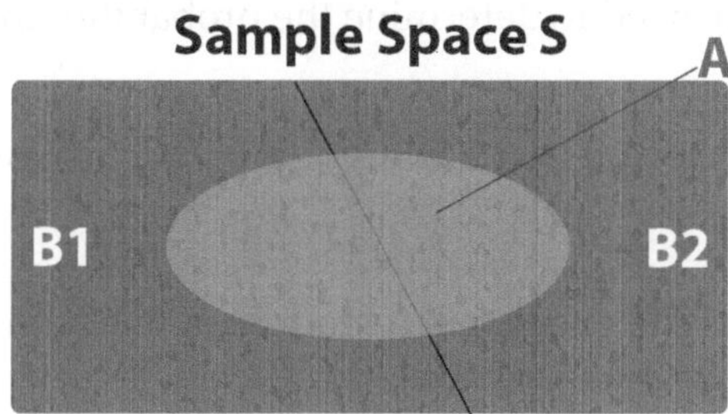

***Figure 2.6**: Set A in green ellipse added to the sample space S*

Let us represent set A as two sets, A_1 and A_2, as shown in *Figure 2.7*:

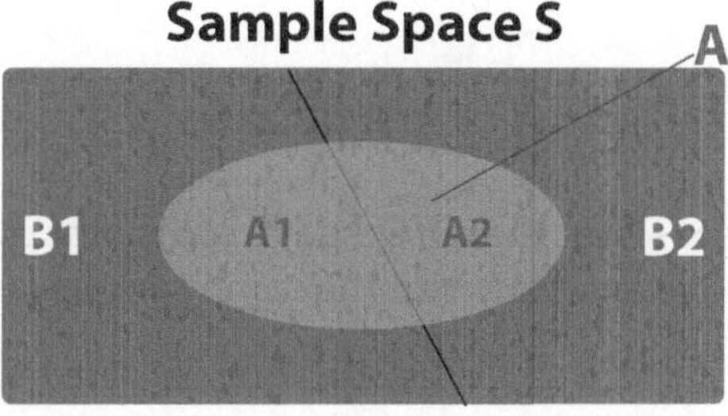

***Figure 2.7**: Set A represented as two sets, A1 and A2*

So, we see that $A = A1 \cup A2$, or the union of A1 and A2 or (A1 or A2).

Now, $A1 = B1 \cap A$ and $A2 = B2 \cap A$ (There are intersections).

So, $A = (B1 \cap A) \cup (B2 \cap A)$.

Now, let

A = Probability of the event $Y = P(Y)$,

B1 = Probability of the event $X1 = P(X1)$ and,

B2 = Probability of the event $X2 = P(X2)$.

Then, we can state that:

$$P(Y) = P(X1 \cap Y) + P(X2 \cap Y) = P(X1, Y) + P(X2, Y)$$

Now, from our discussion on conditional probability, we know

$$P(A, B) = P(B \mid A) * P(A)$$

So, we get:

$$P(Y) = P(X1,Y) + P(X2,Y) = P(Y \mid X1) * P(X1) + P(Y \mid X2) * P(X2)$$

Let us consider an example. Suppose that in a class, 20% of the Males are 6′ (read, 6 feet) tall and 1% of the Females are 6′ tall. Furthermore, we know that 40% of the students are females. We need to determine the probability that a student in the class is 6′ tall.

We consider that Y is the event that a student is 6′ tall. So, we need to determine.

$$P(6') = P(Y)$$

Also, consider that X1 is the event that a student is male, and X2 is the event that a student is a female. We know that:

$P(Female) = P(X2) = 40\%$ and $P(Male) = P(X1) = 1 - P(Female) = 1 - P(X2) = 60\%$

$P(6' \mid Male) = P(Y \mid X1) = 20\%$ and $P(6' \mid Female) = P(Y \mid X2) = 1\%$

So, we get:

$P(Y) = P(Y \mid X1) * P(X1) + P(Y \mid X2) * P(X2) = 20\% * 60\% + 1\% * 40\% = 12\% * 0.4\% = 4.8\%$

Total Probability theorem states that if we have n disjoint events X1, X2, …, Xn in a sample space and we have an event Y in the same sample space, then:

$P(Y) = P(Y \mid X1) * P(X1) + P(Y \mid X2) * P(X2) + \ldots + P(Y \mid Xn) * P(Xn)$

$$P(Y) = \sum_{i=1}^{n} P(Y|X_i) * P(X_i)$$

Bayes theorem [2]

Suppose X and Y are two events. Then, Bayes theorem states that:

$$P(X \mid Y) = \frac{P(Y|X) * P(X)}{P(Y)}$$

We will focus on the aspect of the Bayes theorem that we need to work with the Naïve Bayes algorithm.

Notice that we inverted the probability we need to find in the Bayes theorem. To find P(X | Y), we will determine P(Y | X) along with P(X) and P(Y). This is useful in many circumstances. Let us understand this through an example.

We consider the same example we used to understand the Total Probability theorem. So, we have 40% females in a class. The probability that a male student is 6′ tall is 20%, and the likelihood that a female student is 6′ tall is 1%. Now, suppose that we observed a 6′ tall student. We want to determine the probability that this 6′ tall student is a female.

We consider that Y is the event that a student is 6′ tall. So, *P(6′) = P(Y).*

Also, consider that X_1 is the event that a student is a Male, that is, $P(Male) = P(X_1)$ and X_2 is the event that a student is a Female, that is, $P(Female) = P(X_2)$. So, we know that:

$$P(Female) = P(X_2) = 40\% \text{ and } P(Male) = P(X_1) = 1 - P(Female) = 1 - P(X_2) = 60\%$$

$$P(6' \mid Male) = P(Y \mid X_1) = 20\% \text{ and } P(6' \mid Female) = P(Y \mid X_2) = 1\%$$

We need to find the probability that a student is a female, given that the student is 6′ tall. or we want to find $P(Female \mid 6') = P(X_2 \mid Y)$.

Using Bayes theorem, we know that:

$$P(X2 \mid Y) = (P(Y \mid X_2) * P(X_2) \not{)} P(Y)$$

From the Total probability theorem, we know that:

$$P(Y) = P(Y \mid X_1) * P(X_1) + P(Y \mid X_2) * P(X_2)$$

So, we get:

$$P(X_2 \mid Y) = \frac{P(Y|X_2)*P(X_2)}{P(Y|X_1)*P(X_1)+P(Y|X_2)*P(X_2)}$$

The important thing to notice is that we do not have the value for $P(X_2 \mid Y)$. So, we could compute its value by inverting the requirement.

So, we get $P(X_2 \mid Y) = \frac{1\% * 40\%}{20\% * 60\% + 1\% * 40\%} = 3.226\%$.

Notice another aspect. Our base knowledge was that 1% of the 6′ tall students are females. When we know that a student is 6′ tall, our knowledge that the student could be a female has increased to 3.226%. The initial knowledge is called **Prior knowledge**. The knowledge we obtain after having some data is called **Posterior knowledge**. So, we also write the Bayes theorem, as shown in *Figure 2.8*:

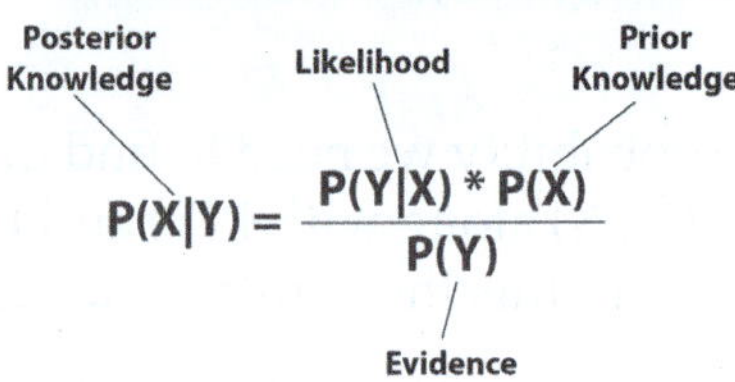

***Figure 2.8**: Bayes theorem*

Many scientists believe that the human brain works in the Bayesian way. They call it Bayesian thinking. In our daily lives, we apply Bayesian thinking in most of our decisions. Let us take one example from an incident.

One person works as an Infrastructure **Subject Matter Expert (SME)**. They faced an issue with a server that had McAfee Antivirus installed on it for one of their customers. After the **Root Cause Analysis (RCA)**, it was concluded that the presence of the McAfee software was causing the problem, and they uninstalled the McAfee software from all the servers.

I asked her, "How many servers were there?" Answer: 30

"How many had McAfee software installed on it?" Answer: 10

"How many of the servers with McAfee installed on them had a problem?" Answer: 1

"How many servers with no McAfee software installed had a problem?" Answer: 1

So, I got the following:

$$P(McAfee) = 10/30 = 1/3$$

$$P(NoMcAfee) = 20/30 = 2/3$$

$$P(Problem \mid McAfee) = 1/10$$

$$P(Problem \mid NoMcAfee) = 1/20$$

So, by the total probability theorem,

$P(Problem) = P(Problem \mid McAfee) * P(McAfee) + P(Problem \mid NoMcAfee) * P(noMcAfee) = 1/10 * 1/3 + 1/20 * 2/3 = 1/30 + 1/30 = 2/30$

So, by Bayes theorem, the probability of the presence of the McAfee software is the cause of the problem = $P(McAfee \mid Problem) = \frac{P(Problem|McAfee) * P(McAfee)}{P(Problem)} = \frac{1/10 * 1/3}{2/30} = 1/2 = 50\%$

This Bayes theorem analysis shows that the decision to uninstall the McAfee software from all the servers may not have been the best. Instead, they could have isolated that server and analyzed it further.

Detecting spam using Bayes theorem

Now that we have discussed the Bayes theorem let us apply it for one application, that is, spam detection. This is a Supervised learning model; thus, we will need labeled data to start. Let us say that our labeled data is shown in *Table 2.5*:

Message Text	Label
Please wake me up at 6 AM	Benign
Click this link asap	Spam
Call 9111122222 asap	Spam
Please review my document	Benign
Can we meet today	Benign

***Table 2.5**: Sample dataset to use for Spam Detection*

Let us pre-process the data in *Table 2.5* and remove **me, up, at, 6 AM, this, 9111122222, my, can** and **we**. The words we remove will not impact the spam detection algorithm. We have the data as shown in *Table 2.6*:

Pre-processed Message Text	Label
Please wake	Benign
Click link asap	Spam
Call asap	Spam
Please review document	Benign
Meet today	Benign

***Table 2.6**: Pre-processed dataset to be used for spam detection*

From *Table 2.6*, we can see that we have a total of 12 words in all the messages. Now, let us make a list of unique words in the data in *Table 2.6* and note the frequency of occurrence of each word across all the message texts. From the frequency of the occurrence of the words, we can calculate the probability of the occurrence of each word. It is shown in *Table 2.7*:

Word	Frequency	P(Word)	Word	Frequency	P(Word)
please	2	2/12	wake	1	1/12
click	1	1/12	link	1	1/12
asap	2	2/12	call	1	1/12
review	1	1/12	document	1	1/12
meet	1	1/12	today	1	1/12

***Table 2.7**: Frequency of each unique word and thus their probability in our dataset*

So, the probability of the word "please" occurring in our dataset is *P(please) = 2/12*.

Look at the column "label" in *Table 2.5* (or *Table 2.6*). We see that there are two unique labels – benign and spam. So, our data has two classes, and we can use this data to build a model for determining whether a message is benign or spam. We also notice that we have a total of 5 data points. So, the probability of a message being benign as per our dataset is , as we have 3 out of 5 messages in the dataset, which are labeled as benign. Similarly, the probability of a message being spam, as per our dataset, is .

So,

$$P(Benign) = 3/5$$

$$P(Spam) = 2/5$$

We see that the total number of words in the benign message is seven and the total number of words in the spam messages is 5 (refer to *Table 2.6* and count the number of words in the messages labeled benign and count the number of words in the messages labeled Spam).

Next, for each unique word in the messages, let us find out the probability of the word appearing in a benign and spam message. It is shown in *Table 2.8*:

Word	Occurrences in Benign messages	P(Word | Benign)	Occurrences in Spam messages	P(Word | Spam)
please	2	2/7	0	0
click	0	0	1	1/5
asap	0	0	2	2/5

review	1	1/7	0	0
meet	1	1/7	0	0
wake	1	1/7	0	0
link	0	0	1	1/5
call	0	0	1	1/5
document	1	1/7	0	0
today	1	1/7	0	0

***Table 2.8**: Probabilities of occurrences of each word in benign and spam messages*

So, we have the following information:

- Probability of a message being benign.
- Probability of a message being spam.
- Probabilities of occurrence of a word in the messages.
- Probabilities of occurrences of a word given that the message is benign.
- Probabilities of occurrences of a word given that the message is spam.

Now, we want to find the probability of a message being spam, given that a particular word appears in it. We want to find the probability of a message being Spam, given that the word "please" appears in it. So, we want to find P(Spam | please).

Now, by Bayes Theorem, we know that:

$$P(Spam \mid please) = \frac{P(please|Spam) * P(Spam)}{P(please)}$$

We have the values of P(please | Spam), P(Spam), and P(please). So, we get:

$$P(Spam \mid please) = \frac{0*(^2/_5)}{^2/_{12}} = 0.$$

Similarly, we can find the probability of a message being Spam for another word like "asap". We get:

$$P(Spam \mid asap) = \frac{P(asap|Spam) * P(Spam)}{P(asap)} = \frac{(^2/_5)*(^2/_5)}{^2/_{12}} = {}^2/_{300} = {}^1/_{150}.$$

Let us try one last example. Let us determine the probability of a message being Benign given that the word "please" appears in the message:

$$P(Benign \mid please) = \frac{P(please|Benign) * P(Benign)}{P(please)} = \frac{(^2/_7)*(^3/_5)}{^2/_{12}} = {}^3/_{420} = {}^1/_{140}.$$

Now, see that P(Benign | please) > P(Spam | please). So, if a message contains the word "please", there is more chance that the message is Benign.

We have devised a mechanism to determine whether a message is Benign or Spam based on a particular word appearing in the message. However, a message will contain more than one word, and the presence of each word and the combinations of words in the message can lead to a message being Benign or Spam. So, we need to further our model.

We have determined P(Spam | asap) in the above example. Suppose the message also contains "call" apart from "asap." So, we need to find P(Spam | (call AND asap)), which is written as P(Spam | (call, asap)).

By Bayes Theorem, we get:

$$P(Spam \mid (call, asap)) = \frac{P((call,asap)|Spam) * P(Spam)}{P(call,asap)} \quad \text{--- } eqA$$

Here, P(call, asap) is P(call AND asap) or P(call asap). Using the multiplication rule of probability, we know that:

$$P(call, asap) = P(call \mid asap) * P(asap)$$

We know P(asap). However, to calculate P(call | asap), we will have to scan all the messages where "asap" exists and then see if "call" also exists. This may be possible for a small number of words. However, our datasets typically contain tens of thousands of words or a combination of words. So, performing these operations would be very expensive on any computer. We simplify our solution by assuming that the events of each word appearing in the messages are independent of the appearance of any other word. This is rarely a reality. Nevertheless, this assumption can lead us to a reasonable solution called the **Naïve Bayes theorem**.

Detecting Spam using Naïve Bayes theorem

Continuing with our example, we were stuck in the phase for calculating P((call | asap) and P((call, asap) | Spam). Now, if we consider that the event of the word "call" appearing in the message is independent of the event of the word "asap" appearing in the message, then we know that:

$$P(call \mid asap) = P(call)$$

Also, by the multiplication rule of probability and from the assumption that the event of the word "call" appearing in the message is independent of the event of the word "asap" appearing in the message, we get:

$$P((call, asap) \mid Spam) = \frac{P((call,asap),Spam)}{P(Spam)} = \frac{P(call,Spam)*P(asap,Spam)}{P(Spam)}$$

$$= \frac{[P(call|Spam) *P(Spam)][P(asap|Spam)* P(Spam)]}{P(Spam)}$$

$$= P(call \mid Spam) * P(asap \mid Spam) * P(Spam)$$

Making this substitution in equation eqA, we get:

$$P(Spam \mid (call, asap)) = \frac{P(call|Spam) * P(asap|Spam) * P(Spam)}{P(call,asap)} \quad \text{--- } eqB$$

In the Naïve Bayes algorithm, we remove the denominator in the equation eqB to get:

$$P(Spam \mid (call, asap)) = P(call \mid Spam) * P(asap \mid Spam) * P(Spam) \quad \text{--- } eqC$$

Let us generalize the equation eqC. Let the event of the message being Spam be event X. The occurrences of the words in the message are the events $A_1, A_2, \ldots, A_n$ (Here, we consider that we have n words in the message). So, eqC can be written as:

$$\mathbf{P(X \mid (A_1, A_2, \ldots, A_n)) = P(A_1 \mid X) * P(A_2 \mid X) * \ldots * P(A_n \mid X) * P(X)} \quad \text{--- } eqD$$

Equation eqD is the Naïve Bayes theorem.

Using Naïve Bayes theorem, let us calculate P(Spam | (call, asap)).

From *Table 2.8*, we get

$$P(call \mid Spam) = 1/5, P(asap \mid Spam) = 2/5.$$

We know that P(Spam) = 2 / 5.

So,

$$P(Spam \mid (call, asap)) = (1/5) * (2/5) * 2/5() = 4/125$$

If we also calculate *P(Benign | (call, asap))*, then we could compare *P(Benign | (call, asap))* and *P(Spam | (call, asap))*. Whichever of these two would be greater, the chances of the message being in that class, given that these two words are present in the message, would be greater. Generalization of this idea to any number of events $A_1, A_2, \ldots, A_n$ for another event X in the same sample space is the **Naïve Bayes Algorithm**.

Variations of Naïve Bayes algorithm

Naïve Bayes algorithm can be used for binary classification (that is, classifying into two classes) or multi-class type. These variations of the Naïve Bayes algorithm implementation are available in the Scikit-Learn library. Let us discuss these implementations.

Note: Discrete variables can assume a finitely finite number of values or a finitely infinite number of values. For example, if a variable can assume the values [0, 1], it is discrete as the number of values in the set is finitely finite. Suppose a variable can assume any natural number; it is also discrete as the number of values is finitely infinite. Discrete variables are also categorical variables.

Continuous variables are variables that assume an infinitely infinite number of values. For example, if a variable can assume any rational number, it is a continuous variable, as the set of rational numbers is infinitely infinite.

We can perform classification only if the target variable (or the dependent variable) is discrete. If the target variable is continuous, we can only perform regression.

Bernoulli Naïve Bayes

Bernoulli Naïve Bayes implementation performs binary classification, that is, only two classes are in the dependent variable. For example, in the spam detection example, if the need is only to classify whether a message is a spam, Bernoulli Naïve Bayes implementation could be used. However, if there is a need to also classify the nature of the spam-like Virus, Botnet, DDOS, etc., then there are more than two classes, and thus Bernoulli Naïve Bayes implementation cannot be used.

Multinomial Naïve Bayes

Multinomial Naïve Bayes implementation allows for classifying two or more classes. Multinomial Naïve Bayes implementation works well if the independent variables are categorical or continuous. This variation works significantly better than the other variations in text data if vectorizers like TF-IDF Vectorizers and Count Vectorizers are used to create independent variables. Refer to *Annexure 6* for details on *Vectorizers.*

Complement Naïve Bayes

Complement Naïve Bayes implementation is a variation of the Multinomial Naïve Bayes implementation. Complement Naïve Bayes works well when the dataset is imbalanced.

Note: A dataset is considered imbalanced if the number of data points in each class varies hugely. For example, suppose we have a dataset of spam emails containing 1000 data points in 2 classes – spam and not spam. We would consider the dataset balanced if we have about 50-50% or 60-40% or 40-60% between data points for spam emails and not spam emails in the dataset. Otherwise, the dataset could be regarded as imbalanced.

Any fraud dataset, like spam email, spam SMS, Credit Card fraud, etc., is heavily imbalanced. Fraud could happen once in a thousand or even a million transactions.

Categorical Naïve Bayes

Categorical Naïve Bayes is used when all the independent variables are categorical. It can be used for classifying two or more than two classes.

Gaussian Naïve Bayes

In Gaussian Naïve Bayes implementation, the likelihood function is:

$$P(X_i \mid Y) = \frac{1}{\sqrt{2\pi\sigma_y^2}} e^{-\frac{(x_i-\mu_y)^2}{2\sigma_y^2}}$$

where μ_y and σ_y are the mean and standard deviations of the target class.

Gaussian Naïve Bayes implementation is used when all the independent variables are continuous, and all the independent variables are distributed normally.

Note: A distribution is said to be normal if it is evenly distributed around the mean and forms a bell-shaped curve. The distributions in Figures 2.1, 2.2, 2.3, 2.4, and 2.5 are normally distributed.

Applying Naïve Bayes algorithm to detect spam SMS

Short Messaging Service (SMS) is a service provided by Mobile service providers using which Mobile users can send messages to other Mobile users. Using SMS, mobile users can send a message which can, at the most, contain 160 characters. The messages can contain any character and can include hyperlinks.

We will feed data containing spam SMS and good SMS along with labels into the machine. The labels contain information regarding which SMS is a spam which is a good. We make the machine learn to detect spam SMS and good SMS. Once the model is ready, if we feed any SMS to the model, the model should respond by stating whether the input SMS is spam or good.

The first step in building a supervised learning model is to load the data based on which the model will be prepared. The data for building this model is available on the github link mentioned in the beginning of the book. We will use the pandas **read_csv()** function to read the data into a pandas data frame.

```
# Import the pandas library
import pandas as pd
# Read the data into a data frame and display the data frame
df = pd.read_csv('spamSMSDataset.csv', encoding = 'latin-1')
df
```

```
        v1                                                v2 Unnamed: 2  \
0      ham  Go until jurong point, crazy.. Available only ...        NaN
1      ham                      Ok lar... Joking wif u oni...        NaN
2     spam  Free entry in 2 a wkly comp to win FA Cup fina...       NaN
3      ham  U dun say so early hor... U c already then say...        NaN
4      ham  Nah I don't think he goes to usf, he lives aro...        NaN
...    ...                                               ...        ...
5567  spam  This is the 2nd time we have tried 2 contact u...        NaN
5568   ham               Will Ì_ b going to esplanade fr home?        NaN
5569   ham  Pity, * was in mood for that. So...any other s...        NaN
5570   ham  The guy did some bitching but I acted like i'd...        NaN
5571   ham                         Rofl. Its true to its name       NaN

     Unnamed: 3 Unnamed: 4
0           NaN        NaN
1           NaN        NaN
2           NaN        NaN
3           NaN        NaN
4           NaN        NaN
...         ...        ...
5567        NaN        NaN
```

```
5568        NaN        NaN
5569        NaN        NaN
5570        NaN        NaN
5571        NaN        NaN

[5572 rows x 5 columns]
```

If the data frame is uploaded correctly, you will notice that the data frame has 5 columns and 5572 rows. The columns should be named v1, v2, Unnamed: 2, Unnamed: 3, and Unnamed: 4. The column v2 contains the SMS text, and column v1 has the label when the associated SMS text in column v2 is a Spam SMS or a Good SMS. We only need columns v1 and v2. So, we will first retain only columns v1 and v2.

```
df = df[['v1', 'v2']]
df.head()
     v1                                                 v2
0   ham  Go until jurong point, crazy.. Available only ...
1   ham                      Ok lar... Joking wif u oni...
2  spam  Free entry in 2 a wkly comp to win FA Cup fina...
3   ham  U dun say so early hor... U c already then say...
4   ham  Nah I don't think he goes to usf, he lives aro...
```

Column v2 is our independent variable, and column v1 is the dependent variable.

Let us see the unique values in this column v1:

```
# Checking the unique values in the column v1 in the data frame df
df.v1.unique()
array(['ham', 'spam'], dtype=object)
```

Notice that column v1 has ham and spam values. Here, **`ham`** indicates that the corresponding SMS is good, and **`spam`** suggests that the corresponding SMS is spam.

Let us check how many SMS of the two types we have in the dataset.

```
df.v1.value_counts()
ham     4825
spam     747
Name: v1, dtype: int64
```

We see that the dataset needs to be balanced, as the number of good SMS examples is nearly seven times that of the number of spam SMS.

Column v1 (our dependent variable) contains the text 'ham' or 'spam'. However, we know that the computer cannot make anything out of the text available in column v1. So, we need to convert the contents of column v1 to numbers. We will use the **Label Encoder** to encode the values in column v1 to numbers. Label Encoders pick up the unique values in a column and assign a value starting with 0 till (n - 1), where n is the number of unique values in the column. To know more about Encoders, refer to *Annexure 7*.

```
from sklearn.preprocessing import LabelEncoder

le = LabelEncoder()
df['label'] = le.fit_transform(df['v1'])
print(df.head())
print('\nUnique values of the column "label"', df.label.unique())
```

```
     v1                                                 v2  label
0   ham  Go until jurong point, crazy.. Available only ...      0
1   ham                      Ok lar... Joking wif u oni...      0
2  spam  Free entry in 2 a wkly comp to win FA Cup fina...      1
3   ham  U dun say so early hor... U c already then say...      0
4   ham  Nah I don't think he goes to usf, he lives aro...      0

Unique values of the column "label" [0 1]
```

Let us take the contents of column v2 to a variable X.

X will be our independent variable.

Let us take the contents of the column label to a variable Y.

Y will be our dependent variable.

```
X = df['v2']
y = df['label']
```

Creating training and test sets

We will split the data at random so that we have two sets. We will use one set to train our model and the other set to validate the model's goodness. We will split the data such that 90% of the data will be used for training, and the rest 10% will be used for validation.

We will split the data into training and test sets using the function **`train_test_split()`** from the Scikit-Learn library:

```
from sklearn.model_selection import train_test_split

X_train, X_test, y_train, y_test = train_test_split(X, y, test_size = 0.10, random_state = 42)

print("Number of data points in the training set = %d" % (X_train.shape[0]))

print("Number of data points in the test set = %d" % (X_test.shape[0]))

Number of data points in the training set = 5014

Number of data points in the test set = 558
```

`train_test_split()` returns four datasets. We have captured these datasets in the variables **`X_train`**, **`X_test`**, **`y_train`**, and **`y_test`**. **`X_train`** contains 90% (in our case) of the rows from the original dataset (that is, X) chosen randomly and only contains the columns related to the independent variables. **`y_train`** has the corresponding values of the dependent variable in relation to the dataset **`X_train`**. **`X_test`** contains the rest of the 10% of the rows from the original dataset (that is, X) and contains only the columns corresponding to the independent variables. **`y_test`** contains the corresponding values of the dependent variable corresponding to the dataset **`X_test`**.

We will train the model using **`X_train`** and **`y_train`**.

We will test the model by making predictions using **`X_test`**.

We will measure the model's goodness by comparing the predictions made on **`X_test`** to the actual values in **`y_test`**.

Pre-processing the data

As stated before, we must find a way to represent the text data as numbers. One way to do this is by preparing **Term Frequency - Inverse Document Frequency (TF-IDF)** for every data point. We refer to such data as a vector of TF-IDFs. To learn more about TF-IDF, refer to *Annexure 6*.

However, before we create the vector of TF-IDFs, we can remove non-essential words/elements from our data.

Among the non-essential words/elements are the following:

- Commonly used words like a, an, the, and so on. These are referred to as Stop words.
- Punctuations and special characters
- URLs
- Numbers
- Extra white spaces

Among the above categories, URL is a special category. Generally, spam SMS contains some URLs. As we cannot let the computer infer from the URL, we will make a column in our X data frame with a value of 1 if an URL is present in X and 0 if there is no URL in X. Let us do this first.

Function to detect whether one or more URLs are present in the text

Let us write a function to detect whether one or more URL is present in a provided text. The function returns a 1 if one or more URL is present in the text and removes the URL from the text. The function should return a 0 if the text contains no SMS.

```
import re


def identifyAndRemoveURLs(text):
        present = re.search(r'\w+:\/{2}[\d\w-]+(\.[\d\w-]+)*(?:(?:\/
[^\s/]*))*', text)
    if present:
      return re.sub(r'\w+:\/{2}[\d\w-]+(\.[\d\w-]+)*(?:(?:\/[^\s/]*))*',
'', text), 1
    else:
        return text, 0
```

Let us test this function.

```
print('Example 1:', identifyAndRemoveURLs("Click this link to register -
https://www.fake.com OR this link for information - http://info.org or
download this file - file://test.txt"))

print('Example 2:', identifyAndRemoveURLs('This contains no URLs'))

Example 1: ('Click this link to register -  OR this link for information
-  or download this file - ', 1)

Example 2: ('This contains no URLs', 0)
```

Let us apply this function to the training dataset and remove all the URLs from the text. Also, let us make a new Series called URLPresent, which will contain a 1 or 0 to indicate whether the corresponding text in **X_train** has a URL or not respectively.

Once we have converted **X_train** to TF-IDF, we will add URLPresent to the TF-IDF to form the data for training the model.

```
URLPresent = pd.Series([identifyAndRemoveURLs(text)[1] for text in X_
train])

X_train = pd.Series([identifyAndRemoveURLs(text)[0] for text in X_train])


print('New Text:\n', X_train.head())

print('\nURL Present Indicator:\n', URLPresent.head())

New Text:

 0    LookAtMe!: Thanks for your purchase of a video...

1          Aight, I'll hit you up when I get some cash

2                                Don no da:)whats you plan?

3                             Going to take your babe out ?

4    No need lar. Jus testing e phone card. Dunno n...

dtype: object


URL Present Indicator:

 0    0

1    0

2    0

3    0

4    0

dtype: int64
```

Functions to remove non-essential elements from the data.

We will now write a function to remove the non-essential elements from the data. We will then apply this function to the text in our dataset. To learn more about Pre-processing Textual Data, refer to *Annexure 4*.

```
import nltk
from  nltk.corpus import stopwords
from  nltk.tokenize import word_tokenize

# Gather the list of Stop Words
stopWordList = nltk.corpus.stopwords.words('english')

# Function to remove Stop Words
def removeStopWords(text):
    # splitting strings into tokens (list of words)
    tokens = word_tokenize(text)
    tokens = [token.strip() for token in tokens]
    # filtering out the stop words
   filtered_tokens = [token for token in tokens if token not in stopWordList]
    filtered_text = ' '.join(filtered_tokens)

    return filtered_text
def removeSpecialCharacters(text):
    pattern = r'[^a-zA-z0-9\s]'
    return re.sub(pattern, '', text)
def removeNumbers(text):
    return re.sub('([0-9]+)', '', text)
def removeExtraWhiteSpaces(text):
    return " ".join(text.split())
def cleanData(text):
    text = removeSpecialCharacters(text)
    text = removeStopWords(text)
    text = removeNumbers(text)
    text = removeExtraWhiteSpaces(text)

    return text
```

Now that our function is ready, we will apply this function to our input data. We will treat only the text in the **X_train** dataset for the moment, as this is what we will use for training our model.

Before applying the function, we convert all the data to lowercase. This is so that all the similar words appear the same. For example, the word "Same" may be used in the text as "Same", "SAME", "same" or in any other way. If we do not convert all the text to lower or upper case, all the different representations of the same word will appear as distinct entities. Having the same word as different entities does not add value to the spam detector. Suppose we consider that the word "free" is used in Spam. So, we need to determine how frequently "free" is used in SMS texts. If we treat the other representations of "free" differently, our model will weaken.

```
X_train = X_train.str.lower()
X_train = X_train.apply(cleanData)
X_train.head()
0    lookatme thanks purchase video clip lookatme y...
1                                 aight ill hit get cash
2                                           dawhats plan
3                                       going take babe
4    need lar jus testing e phone card dunno networ...
dtype: object
```

Forming TF-IDF (Converting text to numbers)

Now that we have a clean data set, we need to convert this text data to numbers so the computer can use it to model it. There are several ways to convert text data to numbers. We will see two such methods.

We will now create **TF-IDF Vectors**. To make the TF-IDF Vectors, we will use the **TfidfVectorizer** from the Scikit-Learn library as follows:

```
from  sklearn.feature_extraction.text import TfidfVectorizer

tfidf = TfidfVectorizer(min_df = 0, use_idf = True, ngram_range = (1, 4))
tfidfText = tfidf.fit_transform(X_train)
print('Shape of original Training Data:', X_train.shape)
print('Shape of transformed Training Data:', tfidfText.shape)
Shape of original Training Data: (5014,)
Shape of transformed Training Data: (5014, 87653)
```

We see that we originally had one column containing all the text. After transforming using **TfidfVectorizer**, we now have 87653 columns.

Let us see what this transformed data looks like.

```
tfidfText.todense()
matrix([[0., 0., 0., ..., 0., 0., 0.],
        [0., 0., 0., ..., 0., 0., 0.],
        [0., 0., 0., ..., 0., 0., 0.],
        ...,
        [0., 0., 0., ..., 0., 0., 0.],
        [0., 0., 0., ..., 0., 0., 0.],
        [0., 0., 0., ..., 0., 0., 0.]])
```

We convert TF-IDF vectors to a data frame:

```
dfTrain = pd.DataFrame(tfidfText.todense(), columns=tfidf.get_feature_
names())
dfTrain
```

```
      ____  ____ joys  ____ joys father  ____ joys father ans  _ll  \
0      0.0        0.0               0.0                   0.0  0.0
1      0.0        0.0               0.0                   0.0  0.0
2      0.0        0.0               0.0                   0.0  0.0
3      0.0        0.0               0.0                   0.0  0.0
4      0.0        0.0               0.0                   0.0  0.0
...    ...        ...               ...                   ...  ...
5009   0.0        0.0               0.0                   0.0  0.0
5010   0.0        0.0               0.0                   0.0  0.0
5011   0.0        0.0               0.0                   0.0  0.0
5012   0.0        0.0               0.0                   0.0  0.0
5013   0.0        0.0               0.0                   0.0  0.0

      _ll finish  _ll finish buying  _ll submitting  _ll submitting da  \
0            0.0                0.0             0.0                0.0
1            0.0                0.0             0.0                0.0
2            0.0                0.0             0.0                0.0
3            0.0                0.0             0.0                0.0
```

```
4            0.0            0.0            0.0            0.0
...          ...            ...            ...            ...
5009         0.0            0.0            0.0            0.0
5010         0.0            0.0            0.0            0.0
5011         0.0            0.0            0.0            0.0
5012         0.0            0.0            0.0            0.0
5013         0.0            0.0            0.0            0.0

     _ll submitting da project  ...  zoom cine zoom cine actually  \
0                          0.0  ...        0.0                0.0
1                          0.0  ...        0.0                0.0
2                          0.0  ...        0.0                0.0
3                          0.0  ...        0.0                0.0
4                          0.0  ...        0.0                0.0
...                        ...  ...        ...                ...
5009                       0.0  ...        0.0                0.0
5010                       0.0  ...        0.0                0.0
5011                       0.0  ...        0.0                0.0
5012                       0.0  ...        0.0                0.0
5013                       0.0  ...        0.0                0.0

      zoom cine actually tonight  zouk  zouk nichols  zouk nichols
parisfree  \
0                          0.0   0.0           0.0           0.0
1                          0.0   0.0           0.0           0.0
2                          0.0   0.0           0.0           0.0
3                          0.0   0.0           0.0           0.0
4                          0.0   0.0           0.0           0.0
...                        ...   ...           ...           ...
5009                       0.0   0.0           0.0           0.0
5010                       0.0   0.0           0.0           0.0
5011                       0.0   0.0           0.0           0.0
5012                       0.0   0.0           0.0           0.0
5013                       0.0   0.0           0.0           0.0
```

```
      zouk nichols parisfree roses   zs  zs subscription  zs subscription
pw
0                                0.0  0.0             0.0              0.0
1                                0.0  0.0             0.0              0.0
2                                0.0  0.0             0.0              0.0
3                                0.0  0.0             0.0              0.0
4                                0.0  0.0             0.0              0.0
...                              ...  ...             ...              ...
5009                             0.0  0.0             0.0              0.0
5010                             0.0  0.0             0.0              0.0
5011                             0.0  0.0             0.0              0.0
5012                             0.0  0.0             0.0              0.0
5013                             0.0  0.0             0.0              0.0

[5014 rows x 87653 columns]
```

To the above data frame, we will add the series **URLPresent**, indicating whether the text contains a URL:

```
dfTrain['URLPresent'] = URLPresent
dfTrain.head()
```

```
   ____  ____ joys  ____ joys father  ____ joys father ans  _ll  _ll finish
\
0   0.0         0.0               0.0                  0.0  0.0         0.0
1   0.0         0.0               0.0                  0.0  0.0         0.0
2   0.0         0.0               0.0                  0.0  0.0         0.0
3   0.0         0.0               0.0                  0.0  0.0         0.0
4   0.0         0.0               0.0                  0.0  0.0         0.0

   _ll finish buying  _ll submitting  _ll submitting da  \
0                0.0             0.0                0.0
1                0.0             0.0                0.0
2                0.0             0.0                0.0
3                0.0             0.0                0.0
4                0.0             0.0                0.0
```

```
   _ll submitting da project  ...  zoom cine actually  \
0                        0.0  ...                 0.0
1                        0.0  ...                 0.0
2                        0.0  ...                 0.0
3                        0.0  ...                 0.0
4                        0.0  ...                 0.0

   zoom cine actually tonight  zouk  zouk nichols  zouk nichols parisfree  
\
0                         0.0   0.0           0.0                     0.0
1                         0.0   0.0           0.0                     0.0
2                         0.0   0.0           0.0                     0.0
3                         0.0   0.0           0.0                     0.0
4                         0.0   0.0           0.0                     0.0

   zouk nichols parisfree roses   zs  zs subscription  zs subscription 
pw  \
0                           0.0  0.0              0.0              0.0
1                           0.0  0.0              0.0              0.0
2                           0.0  0.0              0.0              0.0
3                           0.0  0.0              0.0              0.0
4                           0.0  0.0              0.0              0.0

   URLPresent
0           0
1           0
2           0
3           0
4           0

[5 rows x 87654 columns]
```

Building the model

Our target variable has two classes, so we could use Bernoulli Naïve Bayes implementation to build our model. However, as we have prepared our data using

TF-IDF Vectorizer, we will use Multinomial Naïve Bayes implementation as this implementation works better with vectorized data.

Tip: In the code provided in this section, you could replace the Multinomial Naïve Bayes implementation with the Bernoulli Naïve Bayes implementation and check the difference.

We need the training data and associated labels to build the model. We built and stored the TF-IDF vectors for the training data set in dfTrain. We have the corresponding labels in **`y_train`**. Using this, we can make our model.

```
from sklearn.naive_bayes import MultinomialNB

model = MultinomialNB()
model.fit(dfTrain.values, y_train)
MultinomialNB()
```

Confusion Matrix

Now, we have built the model. The next step is to test the model. Let us pause here and discuss how we will test the model.

The intuition for testing the model is that we will make predictions using the model and then compare the predictions with the results we already have. Either the machine makes the same prediction as the original data or makes an error. We can represent the result in a **Confusion Matrix**.

Let us understand the confusion matrix with the simplest case possible. As in our example, we have two classes – Spam and Not Spam. So, there are two possibilities in the data we have. These are the **Actual values**. The machine will use its algorithm and predict two values as well. These are the **Predicted values**. If we put the actual and predicted values in a matrix, we will get the Confusion Matrix, as shown in *Figure 2.9*:

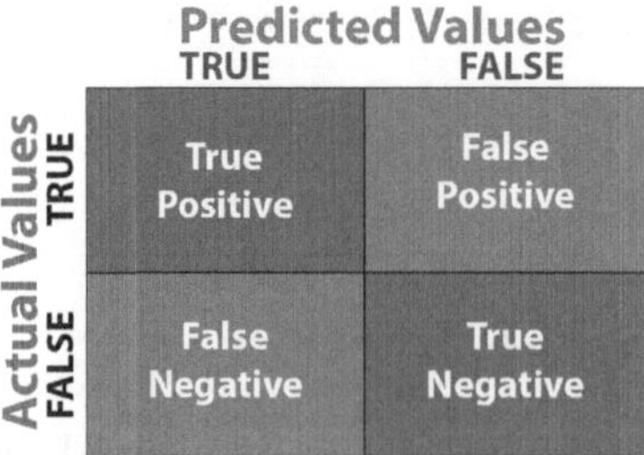

***Figure 2.9**: Generic Confusion Matrix*

In *Figure 2.9*, we have four quadrants. When the Actual and Predicted values are True, we say these cases are the **True Positives (TP)**. These cases were predicted correctly when the actual value was True.

When the Actual Value is False and the Predicted Value is False, we say these cases are the **True Negatives (TN)**. These cases were predicted correctly when the actual value was False. So, True Positives and True Negatives are the cases that were predicted correctly.

When the Actual Value is True and the Predicted Value is False, we say these are **False Positives (FP)**. Lastly, when the Actual Value is False and the Predicted Value is True, we say these are the **False Negatives (FN)**. False Positives and False Negatives are the values that were incorrectly predicted.

Now, we discuss the metrics used to measure the goodness of a classification model.

Accuracy

Accuracy states how many predictions were made correctly out of the total predictions.

$$Accuracy = \frac{Total\ number\ of\ correct\ predictions}{Total\ number\ of\ datapoints} = \frac{TP+TN}{TP+TN+FP+FN}$$

Precision

Precision indicates how consistently the model behaves when the same input is provided to the model.

$$Precision\ (\ P\ ) = \frac{TP}{TP+FP}$$

Recall

Recall indicates the ability of the model to identify the relevant cases in the dataset.

$$Recall\ (\ R\ ) = \frac{TP}{TP+FN}$$

F1 Score

F1 Score combines Precision and Recall into a single number. F1 Score is the harmonic mean of Precision and Recall.

$$F1\ Score = \frac{2\ (Precision * Recall)}{Precision + Recall} = \frac{2\ (P * R)}{P + R}$$

Checking the model's training accuracy

We have built our model. First, we need to find out how well the model is working on the Training data. Remember that the model used the Training data to create its rules. Before we can generate the metrics for the model, we need to make predictions from the model. Let us first make the predictions on the Training set.

```
yTrainPred = model.predict(dfTrain.values)
```

Let us generate the Confusion Matrix. We can calculate the accuracy, precision, recall, and F1 score from the confusion matrix. Let us calculate the accuracy.

```
print("Training Accuracy = %5.5f" % (metrics.accuracy_score(y_train, yTrainPred)))

Training Accuracy = 0.97527
```

So, our model is predicting at an accuracy of 97.527%. This indicates that the machine is doing reasonably well.

Validating the model

Training Data is what the machine has used to create the model. However, the machine has not seen the Test Data yet. So, we use the Test Data to validate the model. If the model performs well on the Test Data, then we can be confident that the model is good.

To validate the model, we need to feed the test dataset to the model and ask the model to make predictions. However, before presenting the test data to the model, we need to preprocess the test data the same way we preprocessed the training data:

```
URLPresentTest = pd.Series([identifyAndRemoveURLs(text)[1] for text in X_test])

X_test = pd.Series([identifyAndRemoveURLs(text)[0] for text in X_test])

X_test = X_test.str.lower()

X_test = X_test.apply(cleanData)

X_test.head()

0    funny fact nobody teaches volcanoes erupt tsun...

1    sent scores sophas secondary application schoo...

2     know someone know fancies call find pobox lshb p

3    promise getting soon youll text morning let kn...

4    congratulations ur awarded either cd gift vouc...
```

```
dtype: object
tfidfTestText = tfidf.transform(X_test)
dfTest = pd.DataFrame(tfidfTestText.todense(), columns=tfidf.get_feature_
names())
dfTest['URLPresent'] = URLPresentTest
print('Shape of original Test Data:', X_test.shape)
print('Shape of transformed Test Data:', dfTest.shape)
Shape of original Test Data: (558,)
Shape of transformed Test Data: (558, 87654)
```

The important aspect is that we applied the same instance of TF-IDF Vectorizer that we used for the training dataset. This is because we fit the TF-IDF Vectorizer on the training dataset and **only transformed the test data using the fit we generated from the training dataset**.

Now that we have transformed the test dataset, we can use it to make predictions using the model we developed:

```
yTestPred = model.predict(dfTest.values)
```

Let us generate the Confusion Matrix for the predictions made on the test dataset and check the model's goodness:

```
confusionMatrix = metrics.confusion_matrix(y_test, yTestPred)
cmDisplay = metrics.ConfusionMatrixDisplay(confusion_matrix =
confusionMatrix, display_labels = [False, True])
cmDisplay.plot()
plt.show()
```

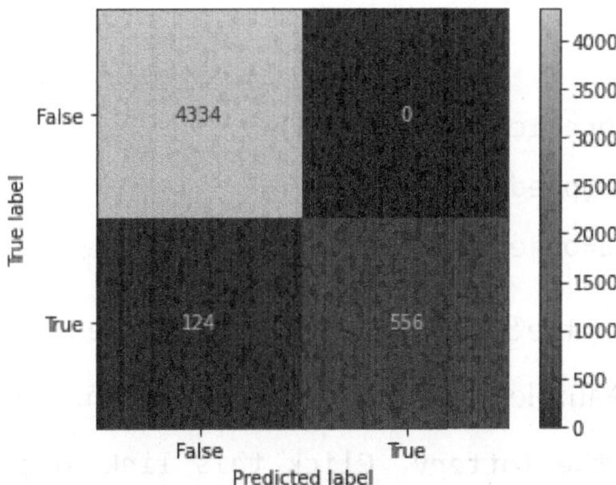

***Figure 2.10**: Confusion Matrix for predictions made on the Test Set*

Let us check the test accuracy of our model:

```
print("Test Accuracy = %5.5f" % (metrics.accuracy_score(y_test,
yTestPred)))
```

```
Test Accuracy = 0.97491
```

So, the model has a test accuracy of 97.491%.

Making predictions using our model

We can feed a new SMS into our model and get the predictions from the model. I will use a simple sentence in the English language. Notice the mechanics. The same mechanics can be used by applying them to real data.

```
testSMS = "This is a test SMS to be checked for spam"
URLPresentInSMS = identifyAndRemoveURLs(testSMS)[1]
testSMS = identifyAndRemoveURLs(testSMS)[0]
testSMS = testSMS.lower()
testSMS = cleanData(testSMS)
testSMS
'test sms checked spam'
import numpy as np


tfidfTestSMS = tfidf.transform([testSMS])
arrTestSMS = tfidfTestSMS.toarray()
arrTestSMS = np.append(arrTestSMS, URLPresentInSMS).reshape(1, -1)
arrTestSMS.shape
(1, 87654)
prediction = model.predict(arrTestSMS)
le.inverse_transform(prediction)
array(['ham'], dtype=object)
```

Our model predicts that the SMS may not be spam if the text is as we have given.

We will test one last example to conclude this discussion.

```
testSMS = "You won the lottery. Click this link http://fake.com as soon
as possible"
```

```
URLPresentInSMS = identifyAndRemoveURLs(testSMS)[1]
testSMS = identifyAndRemoveURLs(testSMS)[0]
testSMS = testSMS.lower()
testSMS = cleanData(testSMS)
tfidfTestSMS = tfidf.transform([testSMS])
arrTestSMS = tfidfTestSMS.toarray()
arrTestSMS = np.append(arrTestSMS, URLPresentInSMS).reshape(1, -1)

prediction = model.predict(arrTestSMS)
le.inverse_transform(prediction)
array(['spam'], dtype=object)
```

Our model predicts that this SMS could be spam.

Conclusion

In this chapter, we have discussed the first mathematical model that can be used to train a computer. The Naïve Bayes Algorithm is a simple algorithm to implement. However, its utility is limited because it assumes that the events are independent, which is rarely practical. However, Naïve Bayes Algorithm can be applied to the data as the first model for classification to understand the data.

In the next chapter, we discuss another simple mathematical model, i.e., the K-Nearest Neighbor algorithm.

Points to remember

- The probability of an event is the ratio of the number of favorable outcomes and the total number of outcomes.
- The Conditional Probability of event A, when event B has already occurred, is written as P(A | B).
- The Multiplication Rule of Probability states that if A and B are two events, $P(A, B) = P(B \mid A) * P(A)$.
- Two events, A and B, are independent if $P(A \mid B) = P(A)$.
- Total Probability Theorem states that if $X_1, X_2, \ldots, X_n$ and Y are events in the same sample space and if $X_1, X_2, \ldots, X_n$ are disjoint events, then $P(Y) = \sum_{i=1}^{n} P(Y|X_i) * P(X_i)$.

- Bayes Theorem states that if A and B are 2 events, then $P(A \mid B) = \frac{P(B|A)*P(A)}{P(B)}$.
- To find $P(Y \mid (A_1,A_2,\ldots,A_n)$, the Naïve Bayes Theorem assumes that events A_1, A_2, …, A_n are independent.
- Naïve Bayes Theorem states that $P(Y \mid (A_1,A_2,\ldots,A_n) = P(A_1 \mid Y) * P(A_2 \mid Y) * \ldots * P(A_n \mid Y) * P(Y)$.

Join our book's Discord space

Join the book's Discord Workspace for Latest updates, Offers, Tech happenings around the world, New Release and Sessions with the Authors:

https://discord.bpbonline.com

CHAPTER 3
K-Nearest Neighbor Algorithm

In the previous chapter, we discussed a simple but powerful classification algorithm. This chapter discusses another simple but powerful classification algorithm called the **K-Nearest Neighbor** (**KNN**) algorithm. The KNN algorithm is used for solving both classification and regression problems. While discussing how the K-Nearest Neighbor algorithm is used for classification, we will touch upon how the algorithm can be altered to solve regression problems.

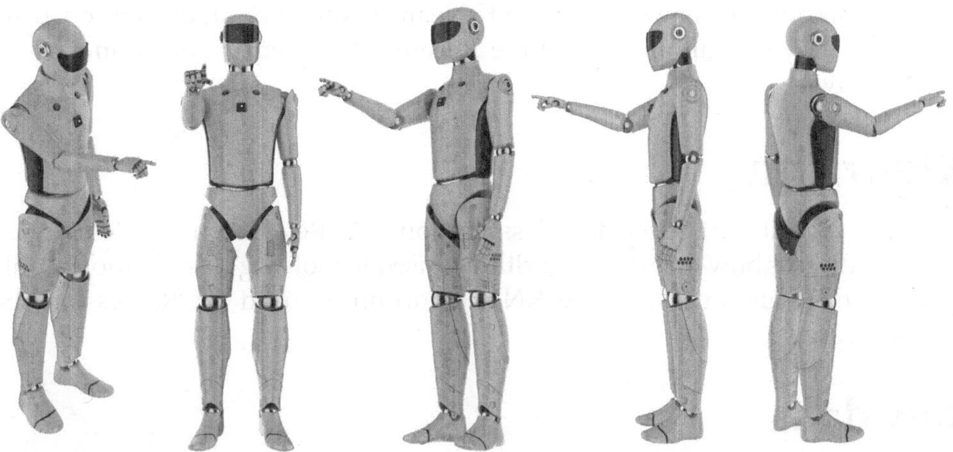

Figure 3.1

Structure

In this chapter, we will discuss the following topics:

- Algorithm
  - Raw data
  - Preparing the data for modelling
  - Finding the distance between the data points
  - Standardizing the data
  - Applying the KNN algorithm for classification
- Mechanisms to measure the distance
  - Manhattan distance
  - Hamming distance
- Classifying customers based on RFM analysis
  - Using the model to predict Customer Segments on live data
    - Preprocessing the data
    - Transforming the data
    - Applying the Model to Segment Customers

Objectives

After reading the chapter, you will understand the mathematics behind the K-Nearest Neighbor algorithm. As we apply the K-Nearest Neighbor algorithm to Customer Classification, you will understand the **Recency, Frequency, and Monetary Value** (**RFM**) analysis.

Algorithm

The KNN algorithm is used for classification and Regression problems. We will primarily discuss how the KNN algorithm is used for solving classification problems. From these discussions, how the KNN algorithm is used for Regression should become clear.

Raw data

As with any classification problem, we would start with the data with associated labels. Consider that we have the Customer Data and the associated labels, as shown in *Table 3.1* for the class of the Customers. The labels associated with each customer are some forms of classification assigned by the experts of the Retail Store (from which the data has been taken). Almost all companies try to categorize their customers into different classes for various analyses like planning appropriate promotions for the different classes of customers, planning new pricing strategies for the different classes of customers, planning new products/brands for the different classes of customers, etc.

Customer ID	Last Invoice Date	Total Amount (Rs.)	Customer Class
A1	29-Aug-2022	1,500	A
A2	29-Sep-2022	1,000	A
A3	31-Aug-2022	6,000	B
A4	12-Sep-2022	1,100	A
A5	02-Oct-2022	1,250	A
A6	20-Aug-2022	2,000	A
A7	20-Sep-2022	5,500	B
A8	20-Sep-2022	1,000	A
A9	22-Sep-2022	2,000	A
A10	09-Sep-2022	5,000	B

***Table 3.1**: Invoice data from a retail store*

Let us understand the data in *Table 3.1*. Each record represents a customer of some retail store for whom the detail of the last invoice date and the total values of all purchases for a period is recorded. So, we know how recently the customer made a purchase. Also, we know the total amount the customer has spent in the retail store for a period (let us assume that the period is the period of interest for the analysis). So, based on this information, the retail store has classified these ten customers into two classes: A and B.

The retail store would want to classify any other customer based on the same data points (that is, last invoice date and total amount) into classes A and B. For doing this classification, we can use the KNN algorithm.

Preparing the data for modelling

Before we can use the data in *Table 3.1* for modeling, we must make it suitable. For the data to be suitable for modeling, all data elements must be numbers. However, we have one data element (that is, the last invoice date): a date. We convert this date to a number by calculating how many days it has been since the customer's last purchase. In marketing parlance, we call this **recency**.

To calculate the recency, we need to consider a reference date. Let us say that our reference date is 09-Oct-2022. We will calculate the recency for each customer as the difference between the reference date and the last invoice date. The results are shown in *Table 3.2*:

Customer ID	Last Invoice Date	Recency	Total Amount (Rs.)	Customer Class
A1	29-Aug-2022	41	1,500	A
A2	29-Sep-2022	10	1,000	A
A3	31-Aug-2022	39	6,000	B
A4	12-Sep-2022	27	1,100	A
A5	02-Oct-2022	7	1,250	A
A6	20-Aug-2022	50	2,000	A
A7	20-Sep-2022	19	5,500	B
A8	20-Sep-2022	19	1,000	A
A9	22-Sep-2022	17	2,000	A
A10	09-Sep-2022	30	5,000	B

***Table 3.2**: Recency calculated with reference date as 09-Oct-2022*

We can use the data in *Table 3.2* to apply the KNN algorithm. For every customer, we will use the data points for "Recency" and "Total amount" to determine the "Customer class". For the ten customers in *Table 3.2*, we already know the "Customer class" as this has been provided to us by some human experts. Using this data provided by the experts, we will make predictions for any new customer.

Finding the distance between the data points

Now, let us say that we have a new customer to analyze, and we know the *Last Invoice Date* and the *Total Amount* for this customer. Let us say that this customer has an ID of C1, the last invoice date is 25-Sep-2022, and the total amount purchased by this customer is Rs. 7,000.

From the above data, we can calculate the "Recency" for this customer. So, recency for customer *C1 = (09-Oct-2022 – 25-Sep-2022) = 14 days*. So, what we have is shown in *Table 3.3*:

Customer ID	Last Invoice Date	Recency	Total Amount (Rs.)	Customer Class
C1	25-Sep-2022	14	7,000	???

***Table 3.3**: Data for the new Customer C1*

To determine the "Customer Class" for C1, we will find the distance of the data points of C1 from all the other data points available to us in *Table 3.2*. To find the distance, we can use the Euclidean distance.

We know that for 2-dimensional data, the Euclidean distance between 2 points (x_1, y_1) and (x_2, y_2) is defined as:

$$\sqrt{(x_1 - x_2)^2 + (y_1 - y_2)^2}$$

Using this formula, we can find the distance between each customer considering "Recency" as x and "Total Amount" as y.

So, the Euclidean distance between customer C1 and A1 can be calculated as:

$$\sqrt{(14 - 41)^2 + (7000 - 1500)^2} = \sqrt{(-27)^2 + (5500)^2} = \sqrt{729 + 30250000} = \sqrt{30250729} =$$

5500.06627

So, we have a mechanism. However, we note that the calculation for the Euclidean distance is heavily biased towards the "Total Amount" value. This is because the "Total Amount" value is much larger than the value of "Recency". To overcome this problem, we need to **standardize** our data.

Standardizing the data

To standardize the data, we can find the z-value of each data point. The z-value can be found using the formula:

$$z = \frac{x-\mu}{\sigma}$$

Here, x is the data point, μ, and σ is the mean and the standard deviation of the attribute for which x is the data point:

Let us understand this practically. Let us take the attribute "Recency". For all the data points, we can find the mean as:

$$\mu_{Recency} = \frac{\sum_{i=1}^{n} x_i}{n} = \frac{41+10+39+27+7+50+19+19+17+30}{10} = \frac{259}{10} = 25.9$$

Now, we can find the Standard Deviation for the data points of "Recency" as:

$$\sigma_{Recency} = \sqrt{\frac{\sum_{i=1}^{n}(x_i-\mu)^2}{n}} = \sqrt{\frac{(41-25.9)^2+(10-25.9)^2+\cdots+(30-25.9)^2}{10}} = 13.35$$

Now, we can calculate the standardized values of "Recency" as shown in *Table 3.4*:

Customer ID	Recency	Standardized Recency	Total Amount (Rs.)	Customer Class
A1	41	$\frac{(41 - 25.9)}{13.35} = 1.13$	1,500	A
A2	10	$\frac{(10 - 25.9)}{13.35} = -1.19$	1,000	A
A3	39	0.98	6,000	B
A4	27	0.08	1,100	A
A5	7	-1.42	1,250	A
A6	50	1.80	2,000	A
A7	19	-0.52	5,500	B
A8	19	-0.52	1,000	A
A9	17	-0.67	2,000	A
A10	30	0.31	5,000	B

***Table 3.4**: Calculation of Standardized Recency*

Notice that all "Standardized Recency" values range from -2 to +2. Generally, for any observation, we should get most of the standardized values in the range of -3 to +3. This is because if the data distribution is normal or near normal, ~99% should be within three standard deviations.

Next, let us standardize the value of "Total Amount". We can find the values of μ and σ for "Total Amount" just like in "Recency". We leave it to you to conduct the calculations. We will get $\mu_{TotalAmount} = 2{,}635$ *and* $\sigma_{TotalAmount} = 1{,}919.38$. So, we can calculate the standardized "Total Amount" values as shown in *Table 3.5*:

Customer ID	Recency	Standardized Recency	Total Amount (Rs.)	Standardized Total Amount	Customer Class
A1	41	1.13	1,500	$\frac{(1500 - 2635)}{1919.38} = -0.59$	A
A2	10	-1.19	1,000	$\frac{(1000 - 2635)}{1919.38} = -0.85$	A
A3	39	0.98	6,000	1.75	B
A4	27	0.08	1,100	-0.80	A
A5	7	-1.42	1,250	-0.72	A
A6	50	1.80	2,000	-0.33	A
A7	19	-0.52	5,500	1.49	B

A8	19	-0.52	1,000	-0.85	A
A9	17	-0.67	2,000	-0.33	A
A10	30	0.31	5,000	1.23	B

***Table 3.5**: Calculation of Standardized Total Amount*

Now that we have the standardized values of "Recency" and "Total Amount", we can use these values to find the distance between new data for customer C1 and all our customer data. Before doing that, we need to standardize the values of "Recency" and "Total Amount" for customer C1. Now, note that we will standardize the values of customer C1 with respect to the means and standard deviations we found for our dataset as shown in the following table:

Customer ID	Last Invoice Date	Recency	Total Amount (Rs.)	Customer Class
C1	25-Sep-2022	14	7,000	???
Standardized Recency		$\frac{(14 - 25.9)}{13.35} = -0.89$		
Standardized Total Amount			$\frac{(7000 - 2635)}{1919.38} = 2.27$	

***Table 3.6**: Standardized Data for the new Customer C1*

Using the standardized values, we can find the Euclidean distance between C1 and the customers in our dataset. Let us calculate the Euclidean distance between C1 and A1.

$$\sqrt{(-0.89 - 1.13)^2 + (2.27 - (-0.59))^2} = \sqrt{(-2.02)^2 + (2.86)^2} = \sqrt{4.0804 + 8.1796} = \sqrt{12.26} = 3.51$$

Let us find the Euclidean distance between customer C1 and all the customers in our dataset, as shown in *Table 3.7*:

Customer ID	Recency	Standardized Recency	Total Amount (Rs.)	Standardized Total Amount	Distance from C1	Customer Class
A1	41	1.13	1,500	-0.59	3.51	A
A2	10	-1.19	1,000	-0.85	3.14	A
A3	39	0.98	6,000	1.75	1.94	B
A4	27	0.08	1,100	-0.80	3.22	A
A5	7	-1.42	1,250	-0.72	3.04	A
A6	50	1.80	2,000	-0.33	3.75	A

Customer ID	Recency	Standardized Recency	Total Amount (Rs.)	Standardized Total Amount	Distance from C1	Customer Class
A7	19	-0.52	5,500	1.49	0.87	B
A8	19	-0.52	1,000	-0.85	3.15	A
A9	17	-0.67	2,000	-0.33	2.61	A
A10	30	0.31	5,000	1.23	1.59	B

Table 3.7: *Finding the distance between new data to classify with the existing data points*

Note: Many Statisticians consider the formula for Standard Deviation as:

$$\sigma = \sqrt{\frac{\sum_{i=1}^{n}(x_i-\mu)^2}{n-1}}$$

In Machine learning, we will deal with massive datasets with thousands, if not millions, of data points. Now, dividing a number by 10,000 and 9,999 does not produce much difference. Thus, we can safely use the formula for Standard Deviation with "n" as the denominator.

In Microsoft Excel, the formula STDEV() to find Standard Deviation considers "n – 1" as the denominator. The formula STDEV.P() to find Standard Deviation in Microsoft Excel considers "n" as the denominator.

Applying the KNN algorithm for classification

In *Table 3.7*, we found the distance between the new data point to classify with all the data points in our dataset. To apply the Algorithm, the first thing to do is to decide a value for K. K is the number of nearest neighbors of the data point to classify that we will analyze.

For our example, let us consider *K* = 3. This implies we must find the three nearest neighbors of our data point to classify. *Table 3.8* shows that the three nearest neighbors for customer C1 are customers A7, A10, and A3 in that order. This is because the Euclidean distance from C1 to the customers A7, A10, and A3 are the lowest.

Customer ID	Recency	Standardized Recency	Total Amount (Rs.)	Standard-ized Total Amount	Distance from C1	Customer Class
A1	41	1.13	1,500	-0.59	3.51	A
A2	10	-1.19	1,000	-0.85	3.14	A
A3	**39**	**0.98**	**6,000**	**1.75**	**1.94**	**B**
A4	27	0.08	1,100	-0.80	3.22	A

A5	7	-1.42	1,250	-0.72	3.04	A
A6	50	1.80	2,000	-0.33	3.75	A
A7	**19**	**-0.52**	**5,500**	**1.49**	**0.87**	**B**
A8	19	-0.52	1,000	-0.85	3.15	A
A9	17	-0.67	2,000	-0.33	2.61	A
A10	**30**	**0.31**	**5,000**	**1.23**	**1.59**	**B**

***Table 3.8**: 3 Nearest Neighbors to the Customer C1 marked in BOLD*

Having determined the nearest neighbors, we study the Customer Class of the nearest neighbors. *Table 3.8* shows that the Customer class of customers A7, A10, and A3 is B.

So, we decide that the Customer class for customer C1 would be B.

Just for the experiment, let us now consider K = 5. So, we need to find the five nearest neighbors for customer C1. See *Table 3.9,* where the five nearest neighbors of customer C1 are marked in **BOLD**:

Customer ID	Recency	Standardized Recency	Total Amount (Rs.)	Standard-ized Total Amount	Distance from C1	Customer Class
A1	41	1.13	1,500	-0.59	3.51	A
A2	10	-1.19	1,000	-0.85	3.14	A
A3	**39**	**0.98**	**6,000**	**1.75**	**1.94**	**B**
A4	27	0.08	1,100	-0.80	3.22	A
A5	**7**	**-1.42**	**1,250**	**-0.72**	**3.04**	**A**
A6	50	1.80	2,000	-0.33	3.75	A
A7	**19**	**-0.52**	**5,500**	**1.49**	**0.87**	**B**
A8	19	-0.52	1,000	-0.85	3.15	A
A9	**17**	**-0.67**	**2,000**	**-0.33**	**2.61**	**A**
A10	**30**	**0.31**	**5,000**	**1.23**	**1.59**	**B**

***Table 3.8**: 5 Nearest Neighbors to the Customer C1 marked in BOLD*

Now, we see that the nearest neighbors, A7, A10, and A3, belong to Customer Class B, whereas the nearest neighbors, A9 and A5, belong to Customer Class A. Here again, we will classify customer C1 as belonging to Customer Class B as the majority of the neighbors of customer C1 belong to Customer Class B.

Note: As you would have realized, we need to choose K such that we do not have a tie between the number of classes to classify. For example, if we have 2 classes to classify, then we must choose K to be an odd number.

Also, we must choose the value of K proportionate to the total number of data points in the dataset. Otherwise, we may make the wrong classification.

Mechanisms to measure the distance

So far, we have used the Euclidean distance to find the similarity between data points for evaluating neighbors for use in the KNN algorithm. Euclidean distance is also called the **L2 Norm**. We have calculated the Euclidean distance between 2 points in the 2-dimensional space. We could generalize this for n-dimensional space as follows. Suppose that we have 2 points as $(x_1, x_2, \ldots, x_n)$ and $(y_1, y_2, \ldots, y_n)$. Then,

$$Euclidean\ Distance = \sqrt{(x_1 - y_1)^2 + (x_2 - y_2)^2 + \cdots + (x_n - y_n)^2}$$

$$= \sqrt{\sum_{i=1}^{n}(x_i - y_i)^2}$$

We will discuss the other measures of distance that we could use to find the distance between 2 points.

Manhattan distance

Manhattan distance is the absolute value of the difference between 2 vectors. Let us say that the 2 points are $(x_1, x_2, \ldots, x_n)$ and $(y_1, y_2, \ldots, y_n)$. Then,

$$Manhattan\ Distance = |x_1 - y_1| + |x_2 - y_2| + \cdots + |x_n - y_n|$$

$$= \sum_{i=1}^{n} |x_i - y_i|$$

Manhattan Distance is also called the **L1 Norm**.

Hamming distance

Hamming distance is used to find the distance between 2 points if the data elements are categorical. Recall that categorical variables can only assume discrete values. Let us say that the 2 points are $(x_1, x_2, \ldots, x_n)$ and $(y_1, y_2, \ldots, y_n)$. Then,

$$Hamming\ Distance = \frac{1}{n}\sum_{i=1}^{n} \delta_i$$

Where $\delta_i = 1$ *if* $x_i = y_i$, *else 0*

Classifying customers based on RFM analysis

In Marketing management, one popular analysis is classifying customers based on **Recency, Frequency, and Monetary** (**RFM**) value, hence, this analysis is called RFM analysis. Here:

- Recency refers to how recently a customer has made a purchase.
- Frequency refers to how frequently the customer makes a purchase, or, in other words, how many times a customer has made a purchase in a period.
- Lastly, Monetary value refers to what value was spent by the customer in a period.

Marketing departments conduct the RFM Analysis to group together similar customers so that they can plan targeted campaigns for each group, plan specific products for each group, or make other similar plans.

From a retail store, the following data was gathered. Here, the RFM values of different customers were captured, and experts grouped the customers into 12 groups numbered 0 to 11. Let us look at the data first. The data link can be found in the GitHub link mentioned in the beginning of the book.

The first step is to load the data file:

```
import pandas as pd

df = pd.read_csv("./CustomerData.csv")
print("Shape of the data", df.shape)
print("\n", df.head())
Shape of the data (4333, 5)

    CustomerID  Frequency  MonetaryValue  Recency  Segment
0      12346.0          1       77183.60      325        8
1      12347.0        171        4091.80        2        5
2      12348.0         26        1395.48       75        7
3      12349.0         67        1345.01       18        0
4      12350.0         16         294.40      310       10
```

In the given data, "Segment" is the dependent variable. And "Recency", "Frequency", and "MonetaryValue" are the independent variables. We need the field "CustomerID" as, finally, we need to identify which customer belongs to which segment. However, the field "CustomerID" is unnecessary for building the model.

Next, we check data regarding how many segments are available and how many samples we have for each segment:

```
df.Segment.value_counts()

0     1701
7      907
1      587
5      506
10     494
9      100
8       21
2        6
3        5
4        3
6        2
11       1
Name: Segment, dtype: int64
```

We notice that the data is imbalanced. Also, this data is unsuitable for applying the KNN algorithm as there are only 1, 2, 3, or a minimal number of samples for some segments. There are many datasets where we find such issues. For example, if we are developing a system for fraud detection, we will have a few data points for the fraud (which may be <1% of the complete data). *We will tackle this situation by balancing the data subsequently.*

Let us now separate the dependent variables and the independent variables:

```
X = df.drop(['CustomerID', 'Segment'], axis = 1)
y = df['Segment']
print(X.head())

   Frequency  MonetaryValue  Recency
0          1       77183.60      325
1        171        4091.80        2
2         26        1395.48       75
3         67        1345.01       18
4         16         294.40      310
```

So, the variable x contains all the independent variables, and the variable y contains the dependent variable.

From the data, we notice that the values for Recency and Frequency are much smaller than those for Monetary Value. This will result in the calculation of distances heavily influenced by the values of Monetary Value. So, we will scale the data so that the values for all the independent variables are in a similar range. For scaling the data, we use the **`StandardScaler()`** class available in Scikit-Learn. Notice that the package where **`StandardScaler()`** is available is present in **`sklearn.preprocessing`**.

When we use the **`StandardScaler()`**, we must first fit the model with the existing data. In the case of **`StandardScaler()`**, when we invoke the **`fit()`** method, the mean and standard deviation values for the data are calculated. Once the data's mean and standard deviation are available, we can call the **`transform()`** method to calculate the z-values for each data item. An alternate method (the one used here) is to call the method **`fit_transform()`**. The **`fit_transform()`** method first performs the **`fit()`** operation and then executes the **`transform()`** method.

```
from sklearn.preprocessing import StandardScaler

sc = StandardScaler()
XS = sc.fit_transform(X.to_numpy())
XS = pd.DataFrame(XS, columns=['Frequency', 'MonetaryValue', 'Recency'])
XS.head()
```

	Frequency	MonetaryValue	Recency
0	-0.397111	8.785658	2.324680
1	0.398556	0.253157	-0.900354
2	-0.280101	-0.061603	-0.171476
3	-0.088205	-0.067495	-0.740600
4	-0.326905	-0.190139	2.174911

Notice that after scaling all the values of the independent variables, their values are in a similar range.

At this stage, we will separate the data to be used for training the model and the data to be used for testing the model. We will keep 80% of the data for training and 20% for testing. To create the training and test sets, we can use the **`train_test_split()`** method available in Scikit-Learn. The method **`train_test_split()`** is available in **`sklearn.model_selection`**. To **`train_test_split()`**, we need to pass all the values of the independent variable(s) (in our case, these are available in **`XS`**) and the dependent variable (in our case, these are stored in y). The parameter **`test_size`** determines the number of samples to choose at random to include in the test set.

The remaining data points are assigned to the training set. We set a value for the parameter **random_state** so that the results are the same every time we run this script.

```
from sklearn.model_selection import train_test_split

X_train, X_test, y_train, y_test = train_test_split(XS, y, test_size =
0.2, random_state = 42)
print("Shape of X_train = ", X_train.shape)
print("Shape of X_test = ", X_test.shape)
print("\nDistribution of labels in X_train\n", y_train.value_counts())
Shape of X_train =  (3466, 3)
Shape of X_test =  (867, 3)

Distribution of labels in X_train
 0      1358
7      737
1      470
5      419
10     376
9       79
8       13
2        5
3        5
6        2
4        1
11       1
Name: Segment, dtype: int64
```

After having created the training and the testing set, we noticed that the data points in the training set need to be balanced to have a similar number of samples for all the segments. One way to balance the dataset is to **Over Sample** the data. By over-sampling the data, we create extra data points randomly for the labels where the number of data points is less. There are many algorithms for Over Sampling. We will use the RandomOverSampler algorithm to create the additional data points.

However, before we can use the RandomOverSampler library, we need to upload the library where this functionality is available. RandomOverSampler is available in the package **imblearn** (or imbalanced learn). Usually, you would need to install this package in your environment:

```
!pip install imblearn
```

Once the **imblearn** package is successfully installed, we can use RandomOverSampler.

We need to pass all the values of the independent variable(s) (available in X_train in our case) and the dependent variable (available in y_train in our case). RandomOverSampler has the method **fit()** to fit the data, the method **resample()** to create random samples for the data, and the method **fit_resample()** to fit the data and create the samples. The method **fit_resample()** is used here. The resultant dataset after over-sampling is stored in the variables XO and yO:

```
from imblearn.over_sampling import RandomOverSampler


oversample = RandomOverSampler(random_state = 42)
XO, yO = oversample.fit_resample(X_train, y_train)
print("Number of samples for each label after oversampling\n", yO.value_counts())
print("\nShape of X after oversampling = ", XO.shape)
Number of samples for each label after oversampling
 7     1358
0     1358
1     1358
10    1358
5     1358
9     1358
8     1358
6     1358
2     1358
3     1358
4     1358
11    1358
Name: Segment, dtype: int64

Shape of X after oversampling =  (16296, 3)
```

After over-sampling, we see we have the same number of samples for each segment.

Now that the training data is ready, we can build the KNN model and check its goodness during the training phase. For classification, there is **KNeighborsClassifier** class from Scikit-Learn. Notice that KNeighborClassifier class is available from **`sklearn.neighbors`** package:

```
from sklearn.neighbors import KNeighborsClassifier


model = KNeighborsClassifier()
model.fit(XO, yO)
```

Notice that we fit the model using the datasets stored in XO and yO, that is, the data we obtained after over-sampling.

Now that the model is ready, we can make predictions from the model and check the metrics. We got an accuracy of 99.74227% for the training dataset. This can be considered an excellent training accuracy score.

Next, we make the predictions on the test dataset and check the accuracy:

```
import matplotlib.pyplot as plt
from sklearn.metrics import ConfusionMatrixDisplay
from sklearn.metrics import accuracy_score


y_testPred = model.predict(X_test)
availableClasses = list(set(y_testPred) & set(y_test))


disp = ConfusionMatrixDisplay.from_predictions(y_test,
                                               y_testPred,
                                               display_labels =
availableClasses)
fig = disp.ax_.get_figure()
fig.set_figheight(10)
fig.set_figwidth(15)
plt.show()
print("\nTest Accuracy = %5.5f%s" % (accuracy_score(y_test, y_testPred)
* 100, "%"))
```

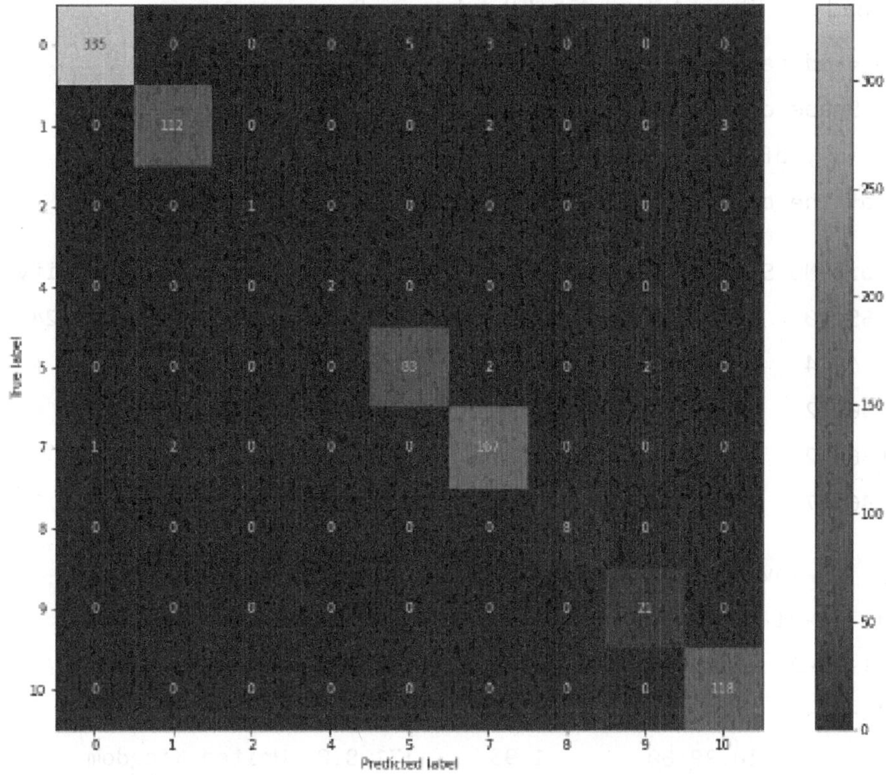

Figure 3.2: Confusion Matrix for Customer Segmentation using KNN Algorithm on the Test Dataset

```
Test Accuracy = 97.69319%
```

Notice that the test accuracy is 97.69319%.

Using the model to predict customer segments on live data

Once the model is ready, it is used on live data to make predictions. In this case, the model will be used to segment customers. However, in most cases, we will never receive readymade data that can be applied to get predictions from the model. The live data needs to be preprocessed before it can be applied to the model to get predictions for the business. We will discuss this aspect.

There are business rules associated with this data. We will not discuss these business rules. However, as we preprocess the data, we will see why the preprocessing step is being taken, and this should make some of the business rules associated with the data known.

Let us load this file and check what the data contains:

```
dfLive = pd.read_csv("./Online_Retail_Test.csv")
print("Shape of the data:", dfLive.shape)
print("\n", dfLive.head())
Shape of the data: (27096, 8)

  InvoiceNo StockCode                          Description  Quantity  \
0    555200     71459    HANGING JAM JAR T-LIGHT HOLDER         24
1    554974     21128                 GOLD FISHING GNOME          4
2    550972     21086         SET/6 RED SPOTTY PAPER CUPS          4
3    576652     22812  PACK 3 BOXES CHRISTMAS PANETTONE          3
4    546157     22180                      RETROSPOT LAMP          2

           InvoiceDate  UnitPrice  CustomerID         Country
0  2011-06-01 12:05:00       0.85     17315.0  United Kingdom
1  2011-05-27 17:14:00       6.95     14031.0  United Kingdom
2  2011-04-21 17:05:00       0.65     14031.0  United Kingdom
3  2011-11-16 10:39:00       1.95     17198.0  United Kingdom
4  2011-03-10 08:40:00       9.95     13502.0  United Kingdom
```

This data has been taken from an Online Retailer in the United Kingdom. The data is the data of sales made by the Online Retailer. The data contains eight columns – Invoice Date, Stock Code (The code for the item sold), Description (The description of the item sold), Quantity, Invoice Date, Unit Price, Customer ID (unique Customer Code), and Country (Country where the customer belongs to). We need to formulate the Recency, Frequency, and Monetary Value from this data to apply our model for segmenting the customers.

Preprocessing the data

The first step is to preprocess the data to remove any unnecessary element or aspect of the data.

We first remove all the duplicate data:

```
print("Before Dropping Duplicates:", dfLive.shape)
dfLive.drop_duplicates(keep= 'first', inplace = True)
print("After Dropping Duplicates:", dfLive.shape)
```

```
Before Dropping Duplicates: (27096, 8)
After Dropping Duplicates: (27082, 8)
```

We see that 14 records were duplicates.

The data contains records of all the invoices. The invoices are raised by the Online Retailer when a sale is made or when an order is canceled, or when an adjustment is passed on a previous sale. Invoice numbers for the canceled orders start with "C" and the invoice numbers for adjustments start with "A". The invoice numbers for the routine sales only contain digits. We do not require the data for the canceled and adjusted invoices (in our present context). So, we will remove all the records about the canceled and adjusted invoices.

```
print("Before Dropping Invalid Invoice Types:", dfLive.shape)

# Classify the Invoices as Normal, Cancelled, and Adjusted
# Delete all the rows except for the Normal Invoices
dfLive['InvoiceType1'] = dfLive['InvoiceNo'].astype(str).str[0]
dfTemp = dfLive.copy()
dfLive['InvoiceType'] = [invoiceType if invoiceType in ['C', 'A'] else
'N' for invoiceType in dfTemp.InvoiceType1]
dfLive = dfLive[dfLive.InvoiceType == 'N']
dfLive.drop(['InvoiceType', 'InvoiceType1'], axis = 1, inplace = True)

print("After Dropping Invalid Invoice Types:", dfLive.shape)
Before Dropping Invalid Invoice Types: (27082, 8)
After Dropping Invalid Invoice Types: (26591, 8)
```

Next, we drop the records where the quantity is negative. An invoice can have a negative quantity if it is for returning some items or simply because of a data entry error. In the present context, we do not need such data. So, we will remove these records:

```
print("Before Dropping Invoice with Negative Quantity:", dfLive.shape)

# Delete the rows where Quantity is less than or equal to 0
dfLive = dfLive[dfLive.Quantity > 0]

print("After Dropping Invoice with Negative Quantity:", dfLive.shape)
Before Dropping Invoice with Negative Quantity: (26591, 8)
After Dropping Invoice with Negative Quantity: (26542, 8)
```

Next, we treat the Stock Codes. They are unique identifiers for the items that the Online Retailer sells. However, they have also included Stock codes for Bank charges, postage, etc. We do not need this data as these do not pertain to the customers. So, we will remove these records from our data.

```
# Classify the Invoices based on the Stock Code
# Remove the rows with invalid Stock Codes
dfTemp = dfLive.copy()
dfLive['StockCodeType'] = ['Remove' if stockCode in ['POST', 'PADS', 'M',
'DOT', 'C2', 'BANK CHARGES'] else 'Keep'
                           for stockCode in dfTemp.StockCode ]
dfLive = dfLive[dfLive.StockCodeType == 'Keep']
dfLive.drop('StockCodeType', axis = 1, inplace = True)

print("After Dropping Invalid Stock Codes:", dfLive.shape)
Before Dropping Invalid Stock Codes: (26542, 8)
After Dropping Invalid Stock Codes: (26423, 8)
```

Lastly, we will create a new column to store the value of the invoice. The value of the invoice is the Quantity of the item sold multiplied by the Unit Price applied to the item for this invoice. We store the value of the invoice in a new column titled "TotalAmount".

```
# Create a column to store the Invoice Amount
dfLive['TotalAmount'] = dfLive.Quantity * dfLive.UnitPrice
```

Transforming the data

Now the data has been preprocessed. However, we cannot use this data against our model as its structure differs from what the model expects. So, we need to transform the data to the structure that the model expects.

To transform the data, we need to establish the Recency, Frequency, and Monetary Value for each Customer. The current data is against the invoices. So, we need to transform this data so that it represents the characteristic of every customer and not the characteristic of the invoices.

The first action we can take is to group the data by Customers and count the number of records for each Customer. This count would give us the value of the Frequency for each Customer.

```
gb = dfLive.groupby('CustomerID')
```

```
counts = gb.size().to_frame(name = 'Frequency')
print(counts)
            Frequency
CustomerID
12347.0            11
12348.0             1
12349.0             5
12353.0             2
12354.0             3
...               ...
18272.0            10
18276.0             1
18282.0             1
18283.0            46
18287.0             2

[3307 rows x 1 columns]
```

So, we have the data for 3307 unique customers and the number of times each customer has purchased from the online retailer.

Now that the original data has been grouped by the Customer, we can find the total Monetary Value of each Customer by summing up all the invoice values of each Customer. Similarly, we can find the last Invoice Date of each Customer.

```
dfCustomerDF = \
(counts
    .join(gb.agg({'TotalAmount':  'sum'}).rename(columns={'TotalAmount':
'MonetaryValue'}))
    .join(gb.agg({'InvoiceDate':  'max'}).rename(columns={'InvoiceDate':
'MostRecentPurchase'}))
  .reset_index()
)
dfCustomerDF.head()
   CustomerID  Frequency  MonetaryValue   MostRecentPurchase
0     12347.0         11         218.20  2011-12-07 15:52:00
1     12348.0          1          41.76  2011-01-25 10:42:00
```

```
2      12349.0          5           112.54  2011-11-21 09:51:00
3      12353.0          2            59.70  2011-05-19 17:47:00
4      12354.0          3            41.35  2011-04-21 13:11:00
```

We have the sum of the invoices for each Customer in the column "MonetaryValue". And we have the last invoice date for each Customer in the column "MostRecentPurchase".

So, we have the values for Frequency and the Monetary Value. We only need to establish the values of Recency for each Customer. For calculating Recency, we would normally consider a Reference Date. However, as this data is comparatively very old (we are in 2022, and this data is from 2011), we will take the maximum invoice date across all the Customers as the reference date:

```
from datetime import datetime, date

dfCustomerDF['MostRecentPurchaseDate'] = pd.to_
datetime(dfCustomerDF['MostRecentPurchase']).dt.date
dfCustomerDF['Recency'] = (datetime.strptime(dfCustomerDF.
MostRecentPurchase.max(), "%Y-%m-%d %H:%M:%S").date() -
                         dfCustomerDF['MostRecentPurchaseDate']).
dt.days
dfCustomerDF.drop(['MostRecentPurchaseDate', 'MostRecentPurchase'], axis
= 1, inplace = True)
dfCustomerDF.head()
```

	CustomerID	Frequency	MonetaryValue	Recency
0	12347.0	11	218.20	2
1	12348.0	1	41.76	318
2	12349.0	5	112.54	18
3	12353.0	2	59.70	204
4	12354.0	3	41.35	232

Now the data is in the format we can use against the model we developed for segmenting customers.

Applying the model to segment customers

The first step before we can apply the model is to Standardize the data. Before we can apply Standardization, let us remove the column "CustomerID" from the data.

```
XLive = dfCustomerDF.drop('CustomerID', axis = 1, inplace = False)

XLive.head()

   Frequency  MonetaryValue  Recency
0         11         218.20        2
1          1          41.76      318
2          5         112.54       18
3          2          59.70      204
4          3          41.35      232
```

We can apply the Standardizer to the Recency, Frequency, and Monetary Value values. Remember that to Standardize the live data, we must apply the Standardizer we fit on the Training data.

```
XTest = sc.transform(XLive.to_numpy())

XTest = pd.DataFrame(XTest, columns=['Frequency', 'MonetaryValue',
'Recency'])

XTest.head()

   Frequency  MonetaryValue   Recency
0  -0.350307      -0.199035 -0.900354
1  -0.397111      -0.219632  2.254788
2  -0.378389      -0.211369 -0.740600
3  -0.392430      -0.217538  1.116541
4  -0.387750      -0.219680  1.396110
```

Now the data is ready for us to make predictions using the Model we have developed:

```
yPredLiveData = model.predict(XTest)

pd.DataFrame(yPredLiveData).value_counts()

0     1539
7      827
1      519
10     417
5        5
dtype: int64
```

We see that the live data has got classified into 5 Customer Segments.

The segments can be assigned to the Customer as has been assigned by the Model:

```
dfCustomerDF['Segment'] = yPredLiveData
dfCustomerDF.head()
```

```
   CustomerID  Frequency  MonetaryValue  Recency  Segment
0     12347.0         11         218.20        2        0
1     12348.0          1          41.76      318       10
2     12349.0          5         112.54       18        0
3     12353.0          2          59.70      204        1
4     12354.0          3          41.35      232        1
```

Lastly, we can visualize the Customer Segments of the live data:

```
import numpy as np

# Fixing random state for reproducibility
np.random.seed(19680801)

fig = plt.figure(figsize=(15, 10))
ax = fig.add_subplot(projection = '3d')

xs = dfCustomerDF.Recency
ys = dfCustomerDF.Frequency
zs = dfCustomerDF.MonetaryValue
ax.scatter(xs, ys, zs, marker = 'o', c = dfCustomerDF.Segment)

ax.set_xlabel('Recency')
ax.set_ylabel('Frequency')
ax.set_zlabel('Monetary Value')

plt.show()
```

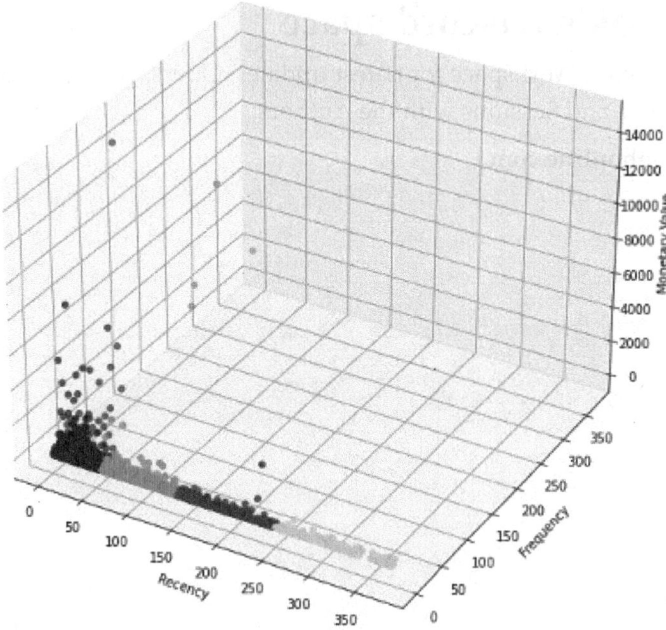

Figure 3.3*: Customer Segments of the Live Data*

Conclusion

As you would have noticed in the discussion on the K-Nearest Neighbor algorithm, this algorithm does not require the machine to be trained. Instead, the machine takes the data and applies the algorithm to perform classification (or regression). So, the K-Nearest Neighbor algorithm is also called a **Lazy Algorithm**. However, the algorithm solves classification (and regression) problems in many circumstances.

In the next chapter, we will discuss the Logistic Regression Algorithm, where we will delve into Gradient Descent for the first time.

Points to remember

- KNN stands for K-Nearest Neighbor.
- KNN Algorithm can be used for Classification and Regression.
- In KNN Algorithm, we find the distance between the data points and assign a class based on the class of the nearest neighbors.
- We can use Euclidean distance, Manhattan distance, or Hamming distance to find the distance between the data points.
- KNeighborClassifier is the class in **`sklearn.neighbors`** package which implements the KNN Algorithm for classification.

Join our book's Discord space

Join the book's Discord Workspace for Latest updates, Offers, Tech happenings around the world, New Release and Sessions with the Authors:

https://discord.bpbonline.com

CHAPTER 4
Logistic Regression

The Logistic Regression algorithm is one of the earliest algorithms for solving classification problems. The word "Regression" in the algorithm's name may be confusing, as this indicates an algorithm for solving Regression problems. *Chapter 1, Introduction to Machine Learning* discusses that the machine learning model is built for solving Regression problems when the output variable is continuous. The machine learning model is built for solving classification problems when the output variable is categorical. In Logistic Regression, taking the formulation of the Linear Regression algorithm, we estimate the probability of the occurrence of a class. As the probabilities are a number between 0 and 1, the Logistic Regression algorithm outputs a number between 0 and 1. Setting a threshold, like 0.5, we can say that if the output of the Logistic Regression algorithm is less than or equal to the threshold, it belongs to one class, and if the output is greater than the threshold, then it belongs to the other class.

In this chapter, we will discuss the formulation of the Logistic Regression algorithm and then apply this algorithm to classify whether a patient has hepatitis.

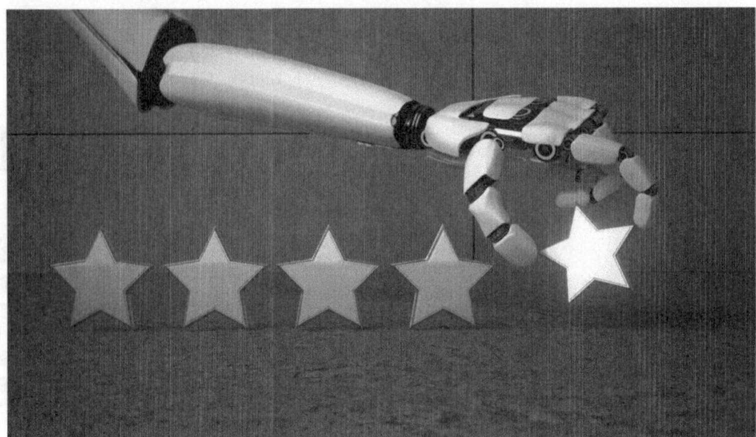

Figure 4.1

Structure

In this chapter, we will discuss the following topics:

- Formulating the Logistic Regression algorithm
    - o Understanding the Linear Regression algorithm
    - o Transitioning to the Logistic Regression algorithm
- Applying the Logistic Regression algorithm
    - o Decision boundary
- Multi-Class classification
- Hepatitis diagnosis prediction classifier
    - o Loading the data
    - o Imputing the missing values
    - o Building and testing the model

Objectives

After reading this chapter, you will understand the nuances of the Gradient Descent. Gradient Descent is the core of the Logistic Regression algorithm and for Neural Networks. You will understand the Sigmoid Function and its applications. You will understand the need for the Loss function and Cost function. As we apply the Logistic Regression algorithm to Disease classification, you will understand how machine learning is applied to the medical field.

Formulating the Logistic Regression algorithm

Before we discuss the Logistic Regression algorithm, we need to discuss the Linear Regression algorithm.

Linear Regression algorithm is an algorithm for solving Regression problems. In Regression problems, we need to predict a continuous variable, and in the classification problem, we need to predict a categorical variable.

Understanding the Linear Regression algorithm

Consider that we set up an experiment to determine the length of the hypotenuse of right-angled triangles. This experiment can be conducted by drawing right-angled triangles on a piece of paper and measuring the length of the sides using a scale. Let us say that the data obtained from our experiment is shown in *Figure 4.2*. We will give this data to the machine to learn how to determine the length of the Hypotenuse.

Features		***Target***
A	B	C
4	2	4.45
6	6	8.5
3	9	9.5
7	5	8.6
2	12	12.2
3	9	9.4
4	7	8

***Figure 4.2**: Results from the Experiment to be used as input data by the machine.*

To analyze the data in *Figure 4.2*, the Data Scientist creates a visualization, as shown in *Figure 4.3*:

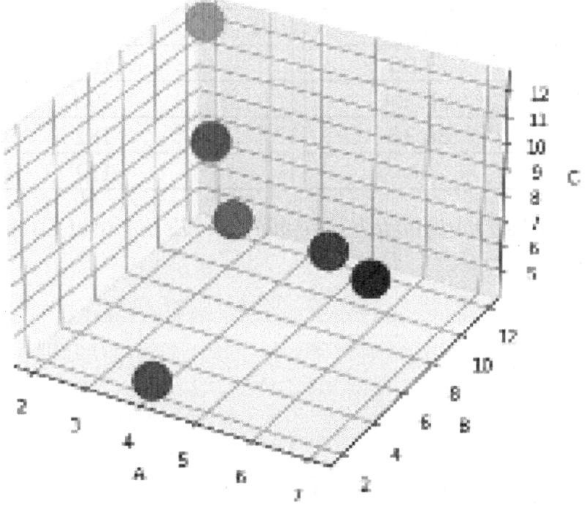

***Figure 4.3**: Vsualization of Data in Figure 4.2*

Suppose the Data scientist has a hunch that there might be a linear relationship between A, B, and C squares, that is, between , and . We will denote as , as and as y. So, and are our features, and y is the target variable.

Features		Target	Engineered Features		Engineered Target
A	B	C	x1 = A^2	x2 = B^2	y = C^2
4	2	4.45	16	4	19.8025
6	6	8.5	36	36	72.25
3	9	9.5	9	81	90.25
7	5	8.6	49	25	73.96
2	12	12.2	4	144	148.84
3	9	9.4	9	81	88.36
4	7	8	16	49	64

***Figure 4.4**: The Engineered problem as shown on the right*

So, the Data scientist instructs the machine to try and create a linear model based on the problem, as shown in *Figure 4.4*. The machines attempts to create an equation as follows:

$$y = \beta_0 + \beta_1 x_1 + \beta_2 x_2$$

To calculate the value of y, the machine has the values of and as the machine has the values of A and B. So, the machine needs to calculate the values of $\beta_0 + \beta_1$ and β_2 to estimate the value of y and compare how reasonable the estimates were by comparing them with the actual values of y. The Data scientist provides the initial values of β_0, β_1 and β_2 as 2, 2, and 2, respectively. So, the machine estimates the value of C, as shown in *Figure 4.5*:

Engineered Features		Engineered Target	Estimate at β0 = 2, β1 = 2, β2 = 2	Estimate of C
x1 = A^2	x2 = B^2	y = C^2	yhat = β0 + β1 * x1 + β2 * x2	Chat = sqrt(yhat)
16	4	19.8025	42	6.480740698
36	36	72.25	146	12.08304597
9	81	90.25	182	13.49073756
49	25	73.96	150	12.24744871
4	144	148.84	298	17.2626765
9	81	88.36	182	13.49073756
16	49	64	132	11.48912529

***Figure 4.5**: First Estimate made by the machine. Estimate of C represented as Chat*

We plot the machine's estimates as shown in *Figure 4.6*:

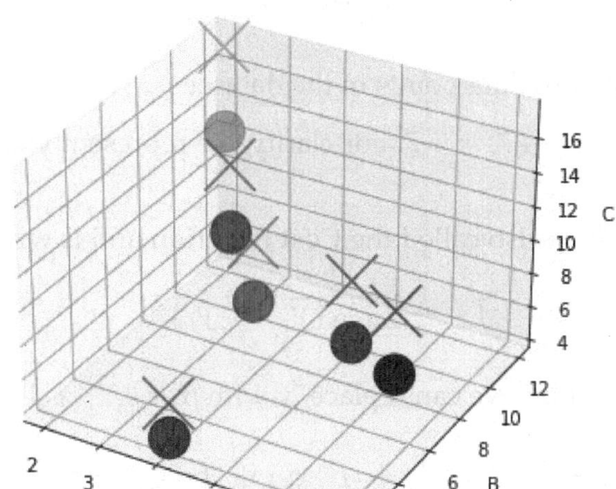

Figure 4.6*: First Estimate made by the machine shown using crosses*

The machine realizes that the estimates could be better; so, it determines the error in its estimates. The errors may be positive or negative. So, the net effect of the error may be lost. Realizing this, the machine takes the squares of the error so that there are only positive numbers. This is shown in *Figure 4.7*:

Engineered Features		**Engineered Target**	**Estimate at β0 = 2, β1 = 2, β2 = 2**	**Error**	
x1 = A^2	x2 = B^2	y = C^2	yhat = β0 + β1 * x1 + β2 * x2	e = y - yhat	e^2
16	4	19.8025	42	(22.20)	492.73
36	36	72.25	146	(73.75)	5,439.06
9	81	90.25	182	(91.75)	8,418.06
49	25	73.96	150	(76.04)	5,782.08
4	144	148.84	298	(149.16)	22,248.71
9	81	88.36	182	(93.64)	8,768.45
16	49	64	132	(68.00)	4,624.00
				Mean Square Error (MSE) =	**7,967.58**

Figure 4.7*: Calculation of the error in the estimate*

The machine needs to minimize the error. So, the machine calculates the mean of all the squared errors, that is., the mean of all . This is called the **Mean Square Error (MSE)**.

Cost function

We have established that we must minimize the MSE to get the best values for β_0, β_1 and β_2. Let us write the formula for MSE :

$$MSE = \frac{1}{m}\sum_{i=1}^{m}(\overline{y}_i - y_i)^2$$

Here, m is the number of data points in the dataset.

In the example in *Figure 4.7, m = 7*. For clarity, we represent yhat (as used in *Figure 4.7*) as ¯y.

This formula for MSE is also called the **Cost Function** and is written as follows.

$$J = \frac{1}{m}\sum_{i=1}^{m}(\overline{y}_i - y_i)^2/$$

In the preceding equation, we can replace ¯y with $\beta_0 + \beta_1 x_1 + \beta_2 x_2$ as follows.

$$J = \frac{1}{m}\sum_{i=1}^{m}((\beta_0 + \beta_1 x_{1i} + \beta_2 x_{2i}) - y_i)^2$$

In this equation, we can alter and to obtain the minimum value for J. To minimize the cost function, we use the **Gradient Descent algorithm**.

Note: We may use other measures like Mean Average Error (MAE) as a Cost Function instead of MSE.

Gradient Descent algorithm

We can write the cost function as a function of , and .

$$J = f(\beta_0, \beta_1, \beta_2)$$

Differential calculus states that a function *f(x)* is minimized when the function's derivative, *df/dx*, is ZERO. J is a function of multiple variables, so we must take the partial derivatives.

To obtain the minimum value of J, we must try different values of β_0, β_1, and β_2. The different values of β_0, β_1, and β_2, that we will try are determined using the following strategy:

1. We will set a threshold below which, if we get a value for J, we will consider that we have found the minimum. This is because we may never get to the point when the derivative is ZERO as we perform floating point operations. To demonstrate, let us say that the set threshold is 0.
2. We set an initial value for β_0, β_1, and β_2. Let us say we have each β_0, β_1, and β_2 to 2 as the initial value.
3. We compute the value of J for this set of β_0, β_1, and β_2.

4. If the value of J <= threshold, we stop and consider the values of β_0, β_1, and β_2 as the point where we have found the best estimates.

5. If J > threshold, we compute new values for β_0, β_1, and β_2.

   $\beta_0 = \beta_0 - \alpha \frac{\delta J}{\delta \beta_0}$, where $\frac{\delta J}{\delta \beta_0}$ is the partial derivative of J with respect to β_0, and α is a hyperparameter called the learning rate.

   $\beta_1 = \beta_1 - \alpha \frac{\delta J}{\delta \beta_1}$, where $\frac{\delta J}{\delta \beta_1}$ is the partial derivative of J with respect to β_1

   $\beta_2 = \beta_2 - \alpha \frac{\delta J}{\delta \beta_2}$, where $\frac{\delta J}{\delta \beta_2}$ is the partial derivative of J with respect to β_2

   We repeat steps 3, 4, and 5.

Let us understand the preceding strategy with some numbers.

Let us consider that we start with β_0, β_1, and β_2 set as 2.

We can compute J as follows. From *Figure 4.6*, we get *J = 7,967.58*.

As J > 0 (threshold), we need to calculate the new values of β_0, β_1, and β_2 and try again.

To compute the values of β_0, β_1, and β_2, we need the values for $\frac{\delta J}{\delta \beta_0}$, $\frac{\delta J}{\delta \beta_1}$ and $\frac{\delta J}{\delta \beta_2}$.

Now, $\frac{\delta J}{\delta \beta_0} = \frac{1}{m} * 2 * \sum_{i=1}^{m}\left(\left(2 * \left((\beta_0 + \beta_1 x_{1i} + \beta_2 x_{2i}) - y_i\right)\right) * \frac{\delta \beta_0}{\delta \beta_0}\right)$

$$= \frac{1}{m} * 2 * \sum_{i=1}^{m}\left(\left(2 * \left((\beta_0 + \beta_1 x_{1i} + \beta_2 x_{2i}) - y_i\right)\right) * 1\right)$$

$$= \frac{1}{m} * 2 * m * \sum_{i=1}^{m}\left(2 * \left((\beta_0 + \beta_1 x_{1i} + \beta_2 x_{2i}) - y_i\right)\right)$$

Similarly, we can compute $\frac{\delta J}{\delta \beta_1}$.

$$\frac{\delta J}{\delta \beta_1} = \frac{1}{m} * 2 * \sum_{i=1}^{m}((2 * ((\beta_0 + \beta_1 x_{1i} + \beta_2 x_{2i}) - y_i)) * (x_{1i} * \frac{\delta \beta_1}{\delta \beta_1}))$$

$$= \frac{1}{m} * 2 * \sum_{i=1}^{m}(2 * \left((\beta_0 + \beta_1 x_{1i} + \beta_2 x_{2i}) - y_i\right) * x_{1i})$$

Similarly, we can compute $\frac{\delta J}{\delta \beta_2}$.

$$\frac{\delta J}{\delta \beta_2} = \frac{1}{m} * 2 * \sum_{i=1}^{m}(2 * \left((\beta_0 + \beta_1 x_{1i} + \beta_2 x_{2i}) - y_i\right) * x_{2i})$$

As these are many calculations, the following is a Python program to do all the math and provide the result:

```
A = [4, 6, 3, 7, 2, 3, 4]
B = [2, 6, 9, 5, 12, 9, 7]
C = [4.45, 8.5, 9.5, 8.6, 12.2, 9.4, 8]

import pandas as pd

df = pd.DataFrame({'A':A, 'B':B, 'C':C})

b0 = 2
b1 = 2
b2 = 2
alpha = 0.001
threshold = 0

for c in range(1000):
    # Compute the Cost
    J = 0
    for i in range(len(df)):
        yhat = (b0 +
                (b1 * ((df.loc[i, 'A'])**2)) +
                (b2 * ((df.loc[i, 'B'])**2))
               )
        y = ((df.loc[i, ,C'])**2)
        J += ((yhat - y)**2)

    J *= (1 / (len(df)))

    print("Iteration: %d, Cost - %f" % (c, J))
    print("\tb0 - %f, b1 - %f, b2 - %f" % (b0, b1, b2))
    if abs(J) < threshold:
        break

    # Partial Derivatives
    sumdiff = 0
```

```
    sumdiff_x1 = 0
    sumdiff_x2 = 0
    for i in range(len(df)):
        yhat = (b0 +
                (b1 * ((df.loc[i, ‚A’])**2)) +
                (b2 * ((df.loc[i, ‚B’])**2))
               )
        y = ((df.loc[i, ‚C’])**2)
        sumdiff += (yhat - y)
        sumdiff_x1 += ((yhat - y) * df.loc[i, ‚A’])
        sumdiff_x2 += ((yhat - y) * df.loc[i, ‚B’])

    del_J_b0 = ((1 / (len(df))) * 2 * sumdiff) * len(df)
    del_J_b1 = ((1 / (len(df))) * 2 * sumdiff_x1)
    del_J_b2 = ((1 / (len(df))) * 2 * sumdiff_x2)

    # Update parameters
    b0 = b0 - (alpha * del_J_b0)
    b1 = b1 - (alpha * del_J_b1)
    b2 = b2 - (alpha * del_J_b2)
Iteration: 0, Cost - 7967.584401
     b0 - 2.000000, b1 - 2.000000, b2 - 2.000000
Iteration: 1, Cost - 602.639537
     b0 - 0.850925, b1 - 1.374269, b2 - 0.628136
Iteration: 2, Cost - 110.871596
     b0 - 1.044256, b1 - 1.431695, b2 - 0.938418
Iteration: 3, Cost - 88.755549
     b0 - 0.958279, b1 - 1.353157, b2 - 0.888774
Iteration: 4, Cost - 64.916981
     b0 - 0.937041, b1 - 1.311669, b2 - 0.913652
Iteration: 5, Cost - 50.580732
     b0 - 0.906735, b1 - 1.269448, b2 - 0.920929
…
```

```
Iteration: 996, Cost - 0.636261
        b0 - -0.028681, b1 - 0.994015, b2 - 0.999426
Iteration: 997, Cost - 0.636138
        b0 - -0.029208, b1 - 0.994028, b2 - 0.999430
Iteration: 998, Cost - 0.636016
        b0 - -0.029735, b1 - 0.994041, b2 - 0.999434
Iteration: 999, Cost - 0.635893
        b0 - -0.030261, b1 - 0.994054, b2 - 0.999438
```

So, by applying the Linear Regression algorithm to the input data:

$$y = -0.0302 + 0.9940\ x_1\ + 0.9994\ x_2$$

In other words, we get as follows:

$$c^2 = -0.0302 + 0.9940\ A^2\ + 0.9994\ B^2$$

Notice that this is nearly what Pythagoras' Theorem states about right-angled triangles:

$$C^2 = A^2 + B^2$$

Notice a few components of the code:

- The preceding code is just for demonstrating the gradient descent algorithm. The solution obtained is quite an optimum solution.
- Where the Gradient Descent will converge, depends on the starting values of the coefficients.
- α is set to 0.001. Setting the value of α is a critical component. If we set α to a very small value, the gradient descent will converge to the minima very slowly. If the value of α is large, we may never converge to minima as we may keep oscillating about the minima.

You could try the program with different values of α by changing the number of iterations and the initial values of β_0, β_1, and β_2.

Transitioning to the Logistic Regression algorithm

Linear Regression is used to predict the outcome of a target variable, which is a continuous variable. For classification problems, the target variable is categorical. We will now discuss a method using a linear model for predicting a categorical variable.

We will start our discussion with binary classification (that is, the target variable can assume two values – 0 and 1) and later extend this to multi-class classification.

When we use a linear model for predicting a categorical variable, it is called a Logistic Regression model. In other words, the algorithm to solve classification models using a linear method is called the Logistic Regression algorithm.

In the Logistic Regression algorithm, we convert the problem of predicting the target variable (which is categorical) into a problem of predicting the probability of occurrence of the target variable. Now, the probability is a value between 0 and 1, which makes the problem of predicting a categorical target variable a problem for predicting a continuous variable.

Let us understand this through an example. Suppose our problem is to predict whether an SMS is spam. We need to predict two classes: SPAM and NOT SPAM. Now, we label SPAM as 1 and NOT SPAM as 0. Our problem is to predict 1 or 0. However, we change the problem to predicting the probability of an SMS being SPAM. In other words, our target variable is $P_y(y = 1)$. $P_y(y = 1)$ can take a value between 0 and 1 as this is a probability. So, it is a continuous variable. On obtaining the $P_y(y = 1)$ value, we consider a threshold like a threshold = 0.5. If $P_y(y = 1) >$ threshold, we consider y = 1 (or SPAM in this case). If $P_y(y = 1) <= threshold$, $y = 0$ (or NOT SPAM in this case).

So, we are using a Linear Regression method to make a prediction. On obtaining the prediction, we compare the prediction against a threshold to get the predicted binary category.

Sigmoid function

For the Logistic Regression algorithm, we need a function that will output a value between 0 and 1. The function which does this is the Sigmoid Function. The Sigmoid Function is of the form as follows:

$$\sigma(t) = \frac{1}{1 + e^{-t}}$$

Here, t can assume a value between -∞ to +∞.

When t = -∞, $e^{-t} = e^{-(-\infty)} = e^{\infty} = \infty$. So, $\sigma(t) = \frac{1}{1+e^{-t}} = \frac{1}{1+\infty} = \frac{1}{\infty} = 0$.

When t = +∞, $e^{-t} = e^{-(+\infty)} = e^{-\infty} = 0$. So, $\sigma(t) = \frac{1}{1+e^{-t}} = \frac{1}{1+0} = \frac{1}{1} = 1$.

If we plot the values of σ(t) for different values of t, we get the graph shown in *Figure 4.8*:

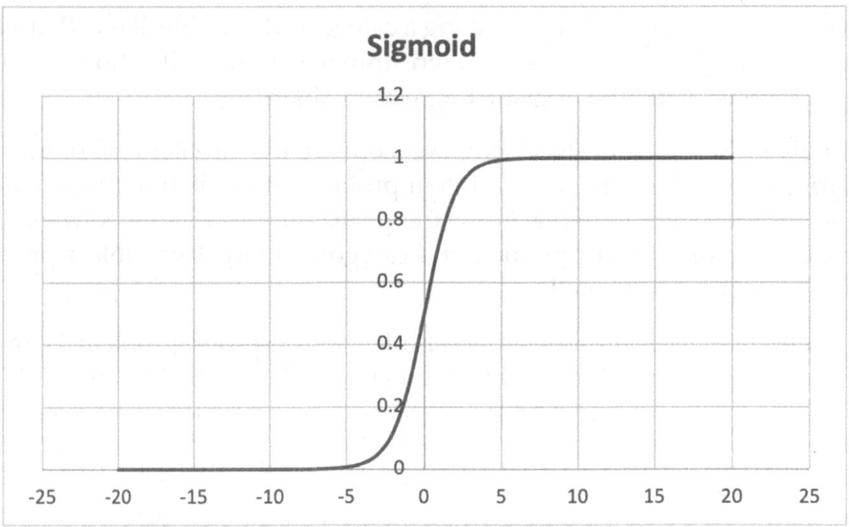

***Figure 4.8**: Graph of the Sigmoid Function*

So, the Sigmoid function always takes a value between 0 and 1.

The problem we will have for classification with one or more than 1 number of features (or independent variables) and 1 target variable (or dependent variable). So, the linear form of the problem will be as follows:

$$y = a_0 + a_1 x_1 + a_2 x_2 + \ldots + a_n x_n$$

Applying the Sigmoid function, we will get as follows:

$$\sigma(y) = \frac{1}{1+e^{-y}} = \frac{1}{1+e^{-(a_0+a_1x_1+\cdots+a_nx_n)}}$$

So, for every data point, we will get a value between 0 and 1. To make the prediction, we formulate as follows:

$$y = \begin{cases} 1, if\ \sigma(y) > 0.5 \\ 0, if\ \sigma(y) \leq 0.5 \end{cases}$$

Here, we have considered our threshold as 0.5. We could set the threshold to any other value between 0 and 1 depending on our problem.

Now we will have many data points, say m data points, in our dataset. For each data point, we will get as follows:

$\sigma(y_i) = \frac{1}{1+e^{-y_i}} = \frac{1}{1+e^{-(a_0+a_1x_{1i}+\cdots+a_nx_{ni})}}$, here i varies from 1 to m.

Cost function for Logistic Regression algorithm

Unlike the Linear Regression algorithm, we cannot use a measure like the MSE as the Cost Function for the Logistic Regression algorithm. We will need to engineer a cost function such that we get a measure of whether we are making a binary classification accurately. Once we establish the cost function, we can apply the gradient descent algorithm to minimize the cost function to obtain the optimum model.

We now know that the prediction for a data point is as follows:

$$\sigma(y_i) = \frac{1}{1+e^{-y_i}} = \frac{1}{1+e^{-(a_0+a_1x_{1i}+\cdots+a_nx_{ni})}}$$

Let us call $\sigma(y_i)$ as (p_i). So, we get as follows:

$$\overline{p_i} = \sigma(y_i) = \frac{1}{1+e^{-y_i}} = \frac{1}{1+e^{-(a_0+a_1x_{1i}+\cdots+a_nx_{ni})}}$$

The cost function for the Logistic Regression algorithm is given as follows:

$$J = \begin{cases} -\log(\overline{p_i}), if\ y_i = 1 \\ -\log(1-\overline{p_i}), if\ y_i = 0 \end{cases}$$

Let us understand this cost function. We note that probability can only take a value between 0 and 1. So, (p_i) and $(1 - p_i)$ will always be between 0 and 1. Log (x) is always a negative number when $0 < x < 1$. So, when log(x) is a negative number, -log(x) will always be a positive number. So, the first thing to note is that the cost function for the Logistic Regression algorithm will always output a positive number.

Next, if $= 1$ and p_i is close to 1, then $J = -log(p_i)$ is close to 0 as $log(1) = 0$. This means that if the actual class is 1 and my prediction shows a higher probability of the class being 1, we will attach a minimal cost. If $= 1$ and p_i is close to 0, then $J = -log(p_i)$ is a large number. This means that if the actual class is 1 and my prediction shows a lower probability of the class being 1, we will attach a very high cost.

Similarly, if $y_i = 0$ and p_i is close to 0 (or $(1 - p_i)$ is close to 1), then $J = -log(1 - p_i)$ is close to 0 as $log(1) = 0$. This means that if the actual class is 0 and my prediction shows a higher probability of the class being 0, we will attach a minimal cost. If $y_i = 0$ and p_i is close to 1 (or $(1 - p_i)$ is a large number), then $J = -log(1 - p_i)$ is a large number. This means that if the actual class is 0 and my prediction shows a lower probability of the class being 0, we will attach a very high cost.

So that we retain this characteristic of the cost function, we can write the cost function as follows:

$$J = \frac{1}{m} \sum_{i=1}^{m} [y_i \, log(\overline{p_i}) + (1 - y_i) log \, (1 - \overline{p_i})]$$

This can be expanded as follows:

$$J = \frac{1}{m} \sum_{i=1}^{m} [y_i \, log(\sigma(y_i)) + (1 - y_i) log \, (1 - \sigma(y_i))]$$

$$= \frac{1}{m} \sum_{i=1}^{m} \left[y_i \, log \left(\frac{1}{1 + e^{-y_i}} \right) + (1 - y_i) \, log \left(1 - \frac{1}{i + e^{-y_i}} \right) \right]$$

You can expand it further by replacing $y_i = a_0 + a_1 x_{1i} + a_2 x_{2i} + \ldots + a_n x_{ni}$.

This cost function is called the Log-Loss Function. The Sigmoid Function is called the Logistic Function. Using the Sigmoid Function and the Log-Loss Function, this algorithm gets the name Logistic Regression algorithm.

We have reached a formula like the one used for the Linear Regression algorithm.

We need to minimize J by altering the coefficients. We change the coefficients so that each iteration gives the coefficient as follows:

$a_i = a_i - \alpha \frac{\delta J}{\delta a_i}$, where α is the learning rate.

You may find it intimidating to find $\frac{\delta J}{\delta a_i}$. We have provided a simple method using the **sympy** library in Python, as shown in *Figure 4.9*:

```
from sympy import *
```

```
a0, a1, a2, x1, x2 = symbols('a0, a1, a2, x1, x2')
```

```
J = ((a0 + (a1*x1) + (a2*x2)) * log(1 / (1 + exp(0 - (a0 + (a1*x1) + (a2*x2)))))) + \
    ((1 - (a0 + (a1*x1) + (a2*x2))) * log(1 - (1 / (1 + exp(0 - (a0 + (a1*x1) + (a2*x2)))))))
J
```

$$(a_0 + a_1x_1 + a_2x_2)\log\left(\frac{1}{e^{-a_0-a_1x_1-a_2x_2}+1}\right) + (-a_0 - a_1x_1 - a_2x_2 + 1)\log\left(1 - \frac{1}{e^{-a_0-a_1x_1-a_2x_2}+1}\right)$$

```
diff(J, a0)
```

$$-\log\left(1 - \frac{1}{e^{-a_0-a_1x_1-a_2x_2}+1}\right) + \log\left(\frac{1}{e^{-a_0-a_1x_1-a_2x_2}+1}\right) + \frac{(a_0 + a_1x_1 + a_2x_2)\,e^{-a_0-a_1x_1-a_2x_2}}{e^{-a_0-a_1x_1-a_2x_2}+1}$$
$$- \frac{(-a_0 - a_1x_1 - a_2x_2 + 1)\,e^{-a_0-a_1x_1-a_2x_2}}{\left(1 - \frac{1}{e^{-a_0-a_1x_1-a_2x_2}+1}\right)\left(e^{-a_0-a_1x_1-a_2x_2}+1\right)^2}$$

```
diff(J, a1)
```

$$-x_1\log\left(1 - \frac{1}{e^{-a_0-a_1x_1-a_2x_2}+1}\right) + x_1\log\left(\frac{1}{e^{-a_0-a_1x_1-a_2x_2}+1}\right)$$
$$+ \frac{x_1(a_0 + a_1x_1 + a_2x_2)\,e^{-a_0-a_1x_1-a_2x_2}}{e^{-a_0-a_1x_1-a_2x_2}+1} - \frac{x_1(-a_0 - a_1x_1 - a_2x_2 + 1)\,e^{-a_0-a_1x_1-a_2x_2}}{\left(1 - \frac{1}{e^{-a_0-a_1x_1-a_2x_2}+1}\right)\left(e^{-a_0-a_1x_1-a_2x_2}+1\right)^2}$$

```
diff(J, a2)
```

$$-x_2\log\left(1 - \frac{1}{e^{-a_0-a_1x_1-a_2x_2}+1}\right) + x_2\log\left(\frac{1}{e^{-a_0-a_1x_1-a_2x_2}+1}\right)$$
$$+ \frac{x_2(a_0 + a_1x_1 + a_2x_2)\,e^{-a_0-a_1x_1-a_2x_2}}{e^{-a_0-a_1x_1-a_2x_2}+1} - \frac{x_2(-a_0 - a_1x_1 - a_2x_2 + 1)\,e^{-a_0-a_1x_1-a_2x_2}}{\left(1 - \frac{1}{e^{-a_0-a_1x_1-a_2x_2}+1}\right)\left(e^{-a_0-a_1x_1-a_2x_2}+1\right)^2}$$

Figure 4.9: *Calculation of* $\frac{\delta J}{\delta a_i}$

Applying the Logistic Regression algorithm

Let us dry run through a simple example of applying the Logistic Regression algorithm to a classification problem.

We have labeled data for temperatures at any place classified as 0 for HOT and 1 for COLD, as shown in *Figure 4.10*:

Temperature (x1)	Weather (y)
40	0
2	1
-3	1
10	1
20	0
30	0
4	1
7	1
22	0
50	0
60	0
-5	1
4	1
6	1
32	0

0 - HOT
1 - COLD

Figure 4.10*: Weather data for classification*

So, we have one independent variable (), and the dependent variable is y.

So, we need to form a linear relationship as follows:

$$y = a_0 + a_1x_1$$

As this is a classification problem, we will form the Sigmoid function as follows:

$$\sigma(y) = \frac{1}{1+e^{-y}} = \frac{1}{1+e^{-(a_0+a_1x_1)}}$$

You can follow the provided Python program to create the Logistic Regression model:

```
X = [40, 2, -3, 10, 20, 30, 4, 7, 22, 50, 60, -5, 4, 6, 32]
y = [0, 1, 1, 1, 0, 0, 1, 1, 0, 0, 0, 1, 1, 1, 0]

import pandas as pd
```

```
df = pd.DataFrame({'X':X, 'y':y})

from sympy import *
a0, a1, x1 = symbols('a0, a1, x1')

J = ((a0 + (a1*x1)) * log(1 / (1 + exp(0 - (a0 + (a1*x1)))))) + \
    ((1 - (a0 + (a1*x1))) * log(1 - (1 / (1 + exp(0 - (a0 +
(a1*x1)))))))
diff_a0 = diff(J, a0)
diff_a1 = diff(J, a1)

a0_val = 5
a1_val = 5
alpha = 0.001
threshold = 0
testList = []

for c in range(100):
    # Compute the Cost
    Cost = 0
    for i in range(len(df)):
        Cost += J.evalf(subs = {a0: a0_val, a1: a1_val, x1: df.loc[i,
'X']})

    Cost *= (1 / (len(df)))

    print("Iteration: %d, Cost - %f" % (c, Cost))
    print("\ta0 - %f, a1 - %f" % (a0_val, a1_val))
    testList.append({'Cost': Cost, 'a0': a0_val, 'a1': a1_val})
    if Cost < threshold:
        break

    # Partial Derivatives
    sumdiff = 0
    sumdiff_x1 = 0
    for i in range(len(df)):
```

```
        sumdiff += diff_a0.evalf(subs = {a0: a0_val, a1: a1_val, x1: 
df.loc[i, 'X']})
        sumdiff_x1 += diff_a1.evalf(subs = {a0: a0_val, a1: a1_val, x1: 
df.loc[i, 'X']})

    del_J_a0 = ((1 / (len(df))) * sumdiff) * len(df)
    del_J_a1 = ((1 / (len(df))) * sumdiff_x1)

    # Update parameters
    a0_val = a0_val - (alpha * del_J_a0)
    a1_val = a1_val - (alpha * del_J_a1)
Iteration: 0, Cost - 14766.723588
      a0 - 5.000000, a1 - 5.000000
Iteration: 1, Cost - 876.745616
      a0 - 3.053107, a1 - 1.037362
Iteration: 2, Cost - 170.045108
      a0 - 2.396249, a1 - -0.545897
Iteration: 3, Cost - 31.870917
      a0 - 2.633374, a1 - 0.148471
Iteration: 4, Cost - 6.492363
      a0 - 2.486089, a1 - -0.143966
Iteration: 5, Cost - 2.124769
      a0 - 2.499813, a1 - -0.026896
…
Iteration: 41, Cost - 0.049555
      a0 - 1.614739, a1 - -0.034913
Iteration: 42, Cost - 0.027046
      a0 - 1.596394, a1 - -0.034430
Iteration: 43, Cost - 0.005170
      a0 - 1.578308, a1 - -0.033954
Iteration: 44, Cost - -0.016089
      a0 - 1.560479, a1 - -0.033485
```

We can test the model as follows:

```
def testWeather(testResult):
    THRESHOLD = 0.8
    returnValue = "HOT"
    if test > THRESHOLD:
        returnValue = "COLD"

    return returnValue
Y = (1 / (1 + exp(0 - (a0 + (a1*x1)))))
test = Y.evalf(subs = {a0:testList[-2]['a0'], a1:testList[-2]['a1'], x1:
43})
testWeather(test)
'HOT'
test = Y.evalf(subs = {a0:testList[-2]['a0'], a1:testList[-2]['a1'], x1:
3})
testWeather(test)
'COLD'
```

Notice that we have used the threshold value of 0.8 for making the decision.

Note: The Gradient Descent algorithm and the Logistic Regression algorithm are the foundation of Neural Networks.

Decision boundary

Now that we have created the Logistic Regression model let us plot the values of the Sigmoid Function for all the data points. We have represented the Sigmoid Value as $\bar{p}_i = \sigma\,(y_i)$. So, p_i is the probability of classifying as class 1. So, $(1 - \bar{p}_i)$ is the probability of classifying as class 0.

We use the following code to compute the values of $\bar{p}_i$ and $(1 - \bar{p}_i)$ and add the values to the data frame containing the values of x_1:

```
s = (1 / (1 + exp(0 - (a0 + (a1*x1)))))
sList = []
tList = []
for i in range(len(df)):
    P = s.evalf(subs = {a0:testList[-2]['a0'], a1:testList[-2]['a1'], x1:
```

```
df.loc[i, 'X']})
    sList.append(P)
    tList.append(1 - P)

df['P'] = sList
df['1 - P'] = tList
df1 = df.sort_values('X')
df1
```

```
     X  y                 P             1 - P
11  -5  1  0.851710300213465  0.148289699786535
2   -3  1  0.842927108518952  0.157072891481048
1    2  1  0.819120502901119  0.180879497098881
6    4  1  0.808840258125458  0.191159741874542
12   4  1  0.808840258125458  0.191159741874542
13   6  1  0.798119738371053  0.201880261628947
7    7  1  0.792593493754922  0.207406506245078
3   10  1  0.775349423340448  0.224650576659552
4   20  0  0.710790601831251  0.289209398168749
8   22  0  0.696633699504311  0.303366300495689
5   30  0  0.636379925412218  0.363620074587782
14  32  0  0.620525203403658  0.379474796596342
0   40  0  0.554815166735906  0.445184833264094
9   50  0  0.470186599726776  0.529813400273224
10  60  0  0.387238278858741  0.612761721141259
```

Now, we plot the values of p_i, of and $(1 - \bar{p}_i)$, i.e., the columns "X", "P" and "1 – P" from the data frame df using the following code:

```
import matplotlib.pyplot as plt
ax = plt.axes()

ax.plot(df1.X, df1.iloc[:,-2].values)
ax.plot(df1.X, df1.iloc[:,-1].values)
ax.axvline(x = 46.5, c = 'red', linestyle = "dashed")
```

```
ax.axhline(y = 0.5, c = 'black', linestyle = "dashed")
plt.show()
```

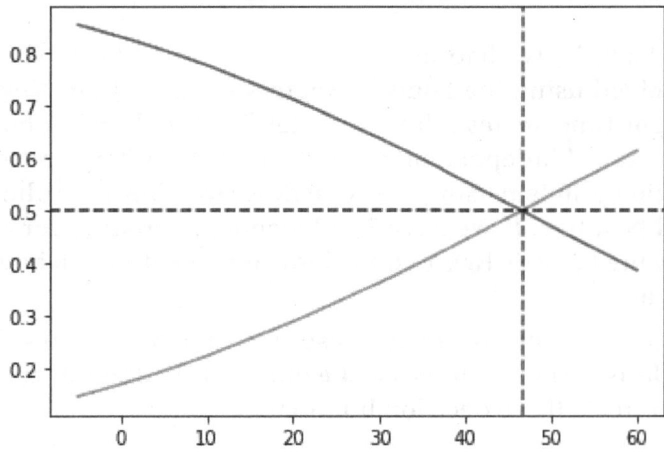

Figure 4.11: *Plot of , and (1 -)*

The significant thing to notice in *Figure 4.11* is that the plot of $\bar{p}_i$ and (1 - $\bar{p}_i$) crosses each other at y = 0.5. This will be the case no matter what data we provide to build the model (Also, this is the case when we have more than one independent variable). If we draw a vertical line at the point where plots of p_i and (1 - $\bar{p}_i$) crosses, like the red dashed line in *Figure 4.10,* we get the decision boundary. The decision is that for any value of $x_1 >$ decision boundary, the prediction will be class 1. And so, for any value of $x_1 <=$ decision boundary, the prediction will be class 0.

Using the following code, we can find the precise value of x_1 where we have the decision boundary.

```
import numpy as np


threshold = 0.0005

nums = np.arange(40.0, 50.0, 0.1)

for x in nums:

   S = s.evalf(subs = {a0:testList[-2]['a0'], a1:testList[-2]['a1'], x1:
x})

    if abs(S - 0.5) < threshold:

        print("X1 =", x, ", Sigmoid =", S)

X1 = 46.50000000000009 , Sigmoid = 0.499861003599472
```

An example of one independent variable was used so that it could be possible to visualize the decision boundary. Though it can be challenging to visualize, the concept is the same if we have more than one independent variable.

Note: In our example, we had one independent variable for the classification problem we solved using the Logistic Regression algorithm. Now, the Logistic Regression algorithm creates a linear model. So, the decision boundary was a point when we have 1 independent variable. If we have 2 independent variables for a classification problem using the Logistic Regression algorithm, the decision boundary will be a line. If we have 3 independent variables for a classification problem using the Logistic Regression algorithm, the decision boundary will be plane. And so on.

All classification algorithms create these decision boundaries. However, the shapes of the decision boundaries may be different. The task of any classification algorithm is to create these decision boundaries.

Multi-Class classification

We have seen that we can use the Logistic Regression algorithm for solving binary classification problems. When we have multi-class classification problems, we can modify the usage of the Logistic Regression algorithm.

The first such strategy is called **One-versus-Rest (OVR)** strategy. To understand the One-versus-Rest strategy, consider that we need to classify it into ten classes. For example, we have images of English Digits, and we need to identify whether it is 0 or 1 or 2 or 3 or 4 or 5 or 6 or 7 or 8, or 9. In the One-versus-Rest strategy, we will convert this into ten classifications to be solved by the Logistic Regression algorithm. The first classification problem would be to classify whether it is a 0 or anything else. The second classification problem would be to classify whether it is a 1 or anything else. And so on. After solving the ten classification problems, we would take the class with the maximum probability, which would be the class assigned to the data point.

The second strategy is called **One-versus-Others (OVO)** strategy. Suppose we have the same problem in classifying images of the English Digits. Then, using One-versus-Others, we will set up classification problems for classifying 0 versus 1, 0 versus 2, 0 versus 3, and so on. So, we would take each class and evaluate it against all the other classes. So, in the classification problem for classifying images of English Digits, we would have to set up ${}^{10}C_2$ classification problems. Then, we would take the class with the maximum probability from all these models, which would be the class assigned to the data point.

Note: For multi-class classification, we also have the SoftMax() function. However, the discussion on the SoftMax() function is beyond the scope of this book.

Hepatitis diagnosis prediction classifier

We take a problem from the medical space to discuss the implementation of the Logistic Regression algorithm in the Scikit-Learn library and see an application of the Logistic Regression algorithm.

The dataset we will use was provided by G. Gong of Carnegie Melon University in 1988. The dataset contains details regarding patients diagnosed with hepatitis. There are 19 features and one target variable in the dataset. Apart from the age and sex of the patient, dataset 17 contains different medical conditions, including the Bilirubin level, Albumin level, and whether the liver is big. The target variable has two values – 1 if the patient dies and 2 if the patient did not die. There are altogether 155 data points in the dataset. The model's objective is to predict whether the patient will die, given a patient's condition. The dataset can be found at **UCI Machine Learning Repository: Hepatitis Data Set (https://archive.ics.uci.edu/ml/datasets/Hepatitis)**.

Loading the data

First, we need to load the data. As the data is available in a **Comma Separated Values (CSV)** file, we can use the **read_csv()** function from the **pandas** library for loading the data. By opening the data file in a text editor, it is found that the data does not have any header.

```
import pandas as pd

df = pd.read_csv("hepatitis.data", header = None)

df
```

```
     0  1   2  3   4  5  6  7  8  9  10 11 12 13    14   15   16   17
18  19
0    2  30  2  1   2  2  2  2  1  2  2  2  2  2  1.00   85   18  4.0
?   1
1    2  50  1  1   2  1  2  2  1  2  2  2  2  2  0.90  135   42  3.5
?   1
2    2  78  1  2   2  1  2  2  2  2  2  2  2  2  0.70   96   32  4.0
?   1
3    2  31  1  ?   1  2  2  2  2  2  2  2  2  2  0.70   46   52  4.0
80   1
```

```
4      2  34   1  2   2  2  2  2  2  2  2  2  2  2  1.00     ?  200  4.0
?  1
..   ..  ..  .. ..  .. .. .. .. .. .. .. .. .. ..   ...   ...   ...   ...
..  ..
150    1  46   1  2   2  1  1  1  2  2  2  1  1  1  7.60     ?  242  3.3
50   2
151    2  44   1  2   2  1  2  2  2  1  2  2  2  2  0.90   126  142  4.3
?  2
152    2  61   1  1   2  1  1  2  1  1  2  1  2  2  0.80    75   20  4.1
?  2
153    2  53   2  1   2  1  2  2  2  2  1  1  2  1  1.50    81   19  4.1
48   2
154    1  43   1  2   2  1  2  2  2  2  1  1  1  2  1.20   100   19  3.1
42   2

[155 rows x 20 columns]
```

We notice 155 data points with 20 columns.

The first column contains the target variable, that is, whether the patient died. We will rename this column and leave the rest of the column names as it is:

```
df.rename(columns = {0:"target"}, inplace = True)
df.head()
```

```
   target   1  2  3  4  5  6  7  8  9 10 11 12 13     14    15    16    17
18  19
0         2  30  2  1  2  2  2  2  1  2  2  2  2  2  1.00    85    18  4.0
?  1
1         2  50  1  1  2  1  2  2  1  2  2  2  2  2  0.90   135    42  3.5
?  1
2         2  78  1  2  2  1  2  2  2  2  2  2  2  2  0.70    96    32  4.0
?  1
3         2  31  1  ?  1  2  2  2  2  2  2  2  2  2  0.70    46    52  4.0
80   1
4         2  34  1  2  2  2  2  2  2  2  2  2  2  2  1.00     ?   200  4.0
?  1
```

Imputing the missing values

In the dataset, the number of "?" appears in the attribute values. These are the missing values in the dataset.

From the authors, we gather the following:

- Column number 1 contains the age of the patient.
- Column numbers 2, 3, 4, 5, 6, 7, 8, 9,10, 11, 12, 13, and 19 contain a "Yes"/"No" value. We say that the values in these columns are categorical.
- Column numbers 14, 15, 16, 17, and 18 contain a continuous value.

Imputing the missing values means putting a value in places where the value is missing.

For the columns containing categorical values, we will impute the missing values using the modal value of the column. Modal value means the value occurring the maximum number of times in the column.

For the columns containing continuous values, we will impute the missing values using the median value of the column. Median value means the value which divides the data in the column into two halves.

Before imputing the data, we must replace all the "?" with a symbol used in Python – Nan – representing a NULL value. The following code is used for this purpose.

```
df.replace('?', np.nan, inplace = True)
df.head()
```

```
   target  1  2    3  4  5  6  7  8  9 10 11 12 13    14   15   16   17
18  \
0       2 30  2    1  2  2  2  2  1  2  2  2  2  2  1.00   85   18  4.0
NaN
1       2 50  1    1  2  1  2  2  1  2  2  2  2  2  0.90  135   42  3.5
NaN
2       2 78  1    2  2  1  2  2  2  2  2  2  2  2  0.70   96   32  4.0
NaN
3       2 31  1  NaN  1  2  2  2  2  2  2  2  2  2  0.70   46   52  4.0
80
4       2 34  1    2  2  2  2  2  2  2  2  2  2  2  1.00  NaN  200  4.0
NaN

    19
```

```
0   1
1   1
2   1
3   1
4   1
```

We can see that the "?" has been replaced with NaN.

Now, we treat the missing values in the columns containing continuous data. For imputing a data frame containing data, we use the **SimpleImputer** available in Scikit-Learn.

```
from sklearn.impute import SimpleImputer


# Fill the missing values of the continuous variables with the Median of that column
columns_to_impute_with_median = [15, 16, 17, 18, 19]
impMedian = SimpleImputer(missing_values = np.nan, strategy = 'median')
arrMedianImputed    =    impMedian.fit_transform(df[columns_to_impute_with_median])


df.drop(columns_to_impute_with_median, axis = 1, inplace = True)
df = pd.concat((df.reset_index(drop = True),
                pd.DataFrame(arrMedianImputed, columns = columns_to_impute_with_median).reset_index(drop = True)),
                 axis = 1)
df.head()
   target   1  2    3  4  5  6  7  8  9 10 11 12 13     14     15     16
17  \
0       2  30  2    1  2  2  2  2  1  2  2  2  2  2  1.00   85.0   18.0  4.0
1       2  50  1    1  2  1  2  2  1  2  2  2  2  2  0.90  135.0   42.0  3.5
2       2  78  1    2  2  1  2  2  2  2  2  2  2  2  0.70   96.0   32.0  4.0
3       2  31  1  NaN  1  2  2  2  2  2  2  2  2  2  0.70   46.0   52.0  4.0
4       2  34  1    2  2  2  2  2  2  2  2  2  2  2  1.00   85.0  200.0  4.0


    18   19
```

```
0  61.0  1.0
1  61.0  1.0
2  61.0  1.0
3  80.0  1.0
4  61.0  1.0
```

Next, we treat the missing values in the columns containing categorical data.

```
# Fill the missing values of the categorical variables with the Modal of that column
columns_to_impute_with_mode = [8, 9, 10, 11, 12, 13, 14]
impMode = SimpleImputer(missing_values = np.nan, strategy = 'most_frequent')
arrModeImputed = impMode.fit_transform(df[columns_to_impute_with_mode])


df.drop(columns_to_impute_with_mode, axis = 1, inplace = True)
df = pd.concat((df.reset_index(drop = True),
               pd.DataFrame(arrModeImputed, columns = columns_to_impute_with_mode).reset_index(drop = True)),
               axis = 1)
df.head()
   target   1  2    3  4  5  6  7      15     16   17    18   19  8  9 10
11  \
0       2  30  2    1  2  2  2  2    85.0   18.0  4.0  61.0  1.0  1  2  2  2
1       2  50  1    1  2  1  2  2   135.0   42.0  3.5  61.0  1.0  1  2  2  2
2       2  78  1    2  2  1  2  2    96.0   32.0  4.0  61.0  1.0  2  2  2  2
3       2  31  1  NaN  1  2  2  2    46.0   52.0  4.0  80.0  1.0  2  2  2  2
4       2  34  1    2  2  2  2  2    85.0  200.0  4.0  61.0  1.0  2  2  2  2


  12 13    14
0  2  2  1.00
1  2  2  0.90
2  2  2  0.70
3  2  2  0.70
4  2  2  1.00
```

After imputing the data, let us check whether more rows with missing values exist:

```
df.isnull().sum()
target    0
1         0
2         0
3         1
4         0
5         1
6         1
7         1
15        0
16        0
17        0
18        0
19        0
8         0
9         0
10        0
11        0
12        0
13        0
14        0
dtype: int64
```

We see a few missing values. As the number of missing values is minimal, we will drop these rows (containing the missing values) from the dataset:

```
df.dropna(inplace = True)
df.isnull().sum()
target    0
1         0
2         0
3         0
4         0
```

```
5       0
6       0
7       0
15      0
16      0
17      0
18      0
19      0
8       0
9       0
10      0
11      0
12      0
13      0
14      0
dtype: int64
print(df.shape)
(153, 20)
```

We have 153 data points to create our model.

Let us check the characteristics of the data in terms of the number of data points for the different classes:

```
df['target'].value_counts()
2    121
1     32
Name: target, dtype: int64
```

We see that we have 32 data points for class 1, whereas we have 121 data points for class 2. So, our dataset is imbalanced.

Building and testing the model

Let us now create the training dataset and the test dataset. We will keep 80% of the available data in the training dataset, and the rest 20% will be used in the test dataset:

```
X = df.drop(["target"], axis = 1, inplace = False)
y = df["target"]
from sklearn.model_selection import train_test_split

XTrain, XTest, yTrain, yTest = train_test_split(X, y, test_size = 0.1,
random_state = 42)
print("Shape of Training Data:", XTrain.shape)
print("\nDistribution of Target Variable in Training Dataset\n", yTrain.
value_counts())
Shape of Training Data: (137, 19)

Distribution of Target Variable in Training Dataset
 2     109
1     28
Name: target, dtype: int64
```

As the columns with continuous data have data in a wide range, we will scale the data so that all the data are in the same range. Refer to the discussion on *Standard Scaler* in *Chapter 3, K-Nearest Neighbor Algorithm:*

```
from sklearn.preprocessing import StandardScaler

columns_to_scale = [1, 15, 16, 17, 18, 19]

sc = StandardScaler()
arrTrainScaled = sc.fit_transform(XTrain[columns_to_scale])
arrTrainScaled[:5]
array([[ 0.06306606, -0.84976737, -0.21832346, -0.01053376, -1.83085539,
         1.05246962],
       [ 0.46680671,  1.41670315, -0.63177997, -1.93470076, -1.71650518,
         1.05246962],
       [ 1.274288  , -0.3485287 , -0.43593215, -1.93470076,  0.68484926,
        -0.95014619],
       [ 0.46680671, -0.37032169, -0.70794301,  0.63085524,  0.28462352,
         1.05246962],
```

```
[-0.58291898, -1.54714292, -0.69706258,  0.31016074,  0.85637457,
 -0.95014619]])
```

After scaling the date, we will remove the original columns (that were scaled) and add the columns containing the scaled data.

```
# Drop the Columns that were scaled and add the scaled-valued columns
XTrain = XTrain.drop(columns_to_scale, axis = 1, inplace = False)
XTrain = pd.concat((XTrain.reset_index(drop = True),
                    pd.DataFrame(arrTrainScaled,
                                 columns = columns_to_scale).reset_index(drop
= True)),
                   axis = 1)
```

Now that the data is ready for creating the model, we will make the Logistic Regression Model:

```
from sklearn.linear_model import LogisticRegression

lr = LogisticRegression(solver = "liblinear",
                        class_weight = "balanced",
                        max_iter = 10000,
                        random_state = 42)
lr.fit(XTrain, yTrain)
LogisticRegression(class_weight='balanced',   max_iter=10000,   random_
state=42,
                   solver='liblinear')
```

Notice the parameters used for creating the **LogisticRegression** class instance:

- The parameter **solver** sets the algorithm, which will be used to obtain the coefficients' best values. The "liblinear" solver used here is most suitable for small datasets.
- The parameter **class_weight = "balanced"** gives the class with fewer data points more weight. This way, we counter the problem of the imbalanced dataset.

Now that the Logistic Regression model is ready, we can make predictions using the model and check the accuracy of the model on the Training Dataset. We also create the Confusion Matrix to check where the model is performing well and where it is faltering.

```
from sklearn.metrics import confusion_matrix, accuracy_score,
ConfusionMatrixDisplay


yTrainPred = lr.predict(XTrain)


print("Accuracy = %7.5f%s" % (accuracy_score(yTrain, yTrainPred) * 100,
"%"))
cm = confusion_matrix(yTrain, yTrainPred)
ConfusionMatrixDisplay(cm, display_labels = lr.classes_).plot()
Accuracy = 86.86131%
<sklearn.metrics._plot.confusion_matrix.ConfusionMatrixDisplay at
0x7f991175b700>
```

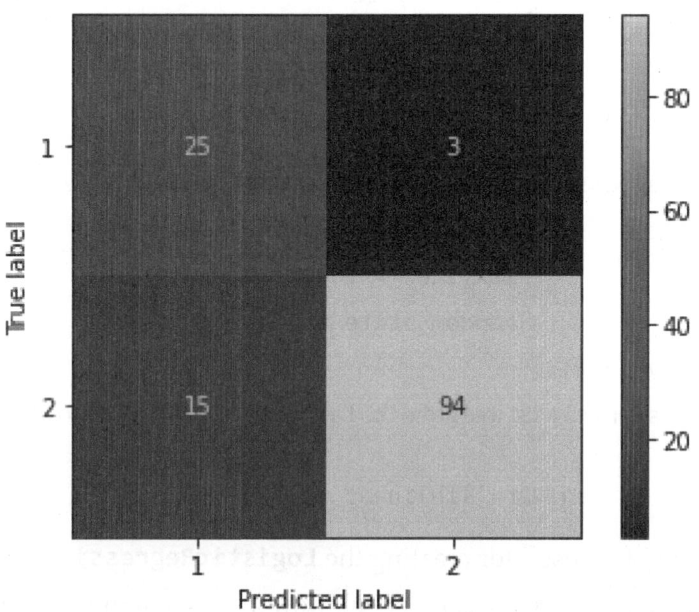

***Figure 4.12**: Confusion Matrix of predictions made on the Training Dataset*

So, we have a Training Accuracy of 86.86%.

Lastly, let us test the model on the Test Dataset and check the Accuracy.

As we did for the test in the Training Data, we also created the Confusion Matrix to check where the model is performing well and where it is faltering.

```
arrTestScaled = sc.transform(XTest[columns_to_scale])
XTest.drop(columns_to_scale, axis = 1, inplace = True)
```

```
XTest = pd.concat((XTest.reset_index(drop = True),
                   pd.DataFrame(arrTestScaled,
                          columns = columns_to_scale).reset_index(drop
= True)),
                axis = 1)


yTestPred = lr.predict(XTest)


print("Accuracy = %7.5f%s" % (accuracy_score(yTest, yTestPred) * 100,
"%"))
cm = confusion_matrix(yTest, yTestPred)
ConfusionMatrixDisplay(cm, display_labels = lr.classes_).plot()
Accuracy = 68.75000%
<sklearn.metrics._plot.confusion_matrix.ConfusionMatrixDisplay at
0x7f99310807c0>
```

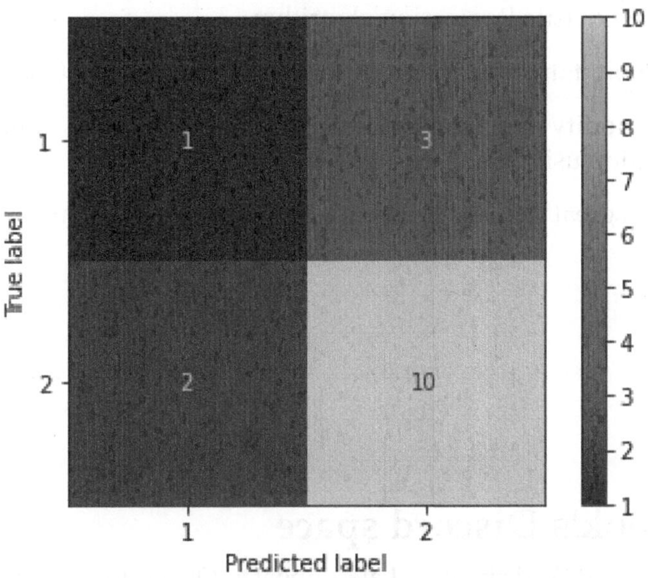

***Figure 4.13**: Confusion Matrix of predictions made on the Test Dataset*

So, we have a Test Accuracy of 68.75%.

Conclusion

In this chapter, we discussed that we built a cost function based on the model parameters to minimize the cost function. Then, we devised a way to update the model parameters and test the cost function. We repeated the process of updating the model parameters and finding the value of the cost function until we reached minima. At the minimum, we would get the values of the model parameters which are the most optimum. This is the generic way most of the algorithms are built.

The next chapter discusses another very powerful algorithm – the Decision Tree Algorithm.

Points to remember

- Using the Logistic Regression algorithm, we create a linear classification model.
- The Logistic Regression algorithm is a binary classification algorithm.
- We modify the Linear Regression algorithm using the Sigmoid Function to create the Logistic Regression algorithm.
- The Sigmoid Function always returns a value between 0 and 1.
- We can modify the Logistic Regression algorithm to conduct multi-class classification using strategies like OVR and OVO.
- `sympy` is a great Python library for Symbolic Programming.

CHAPTER 5
Decision Tree Algorithm

One of the popular mathematical models for creating classification models is the **Decision Tree algorithm**. The Decision Tree algorithm by itself is rarely used. However, variations of the Decision Tree algorithm, like the Random Forest algorithm, are heavily used. Decision Trees can be used for both Regression and Classification tasks. We will focus on applying Decision Trees for Classification tasks in this chapter.

Decision Trees are created by computing **Gini index** or based on **Entropy**. We will discuss the Gini index implementation in detail. The understanding of the Entropy implementation will be evident from the discussion on Gini index implementation.

Figure 5.1

Structure

In this chapter, we will discuss the following topics:

- Creating a Decision Tree
    - Using Gini index to form a Decision Tree
        - Understanding Gini index
        - Forming the Decision Tree using the CART algorithm
- Malware detection in JPEG files
    - The need
    - About JPEG files
    - The strategy
    - Building the model
        - Extracting EXIF tags from JPEG files
        - Cleaning the data
        - Forming the TF-IDF vectors
        - Reducing the number of features
        - Balancing the dataset
        - Building the Decision Tree model
    - Testing the model
        - Finding the training accuracy score
        - Finding the test accuracy score

Objectives

After reading this chapter, you will understand how decision trees are formed using Gini Index. The complete mathematics has been explained. We apply the Decision Tree algorithm to classify good and bad JPEG files in this chapter. You will also understand how to extract features from JPEG files.

Creating decision tree

We mainly use two techniques to create decision trees. They are using **Gini index** and using **Entropy**. We will discuss both methods. However, we will make the decision tree using the Gini index. The technique used to create decision trees using Gini index can be replicated by Entropy to create decision trees.

Using Gini index to form a decision tree

We will discuss the concept using an example.

Consider that we have a dataset of 10 records with two independent and one dependent variable. Let the independent variables be **x1** and **x2**. Let the dependent variable be **y**. Refer to the following table:

x1	x2	y
1	4	0
7	6	0
1	6	0
1	2	1
5	2	1
7	2	1
5	4	0
2	4	0
1	7	1
2	7	1

Table 5.1: *The raw data*

The data in *Table 5.1* shows that the dependent variable y has two values – 0 and 1. So, the data has been classified into two classes – 0 and 1.

If we plot the data in *Table 5.1,* we will get the graph as shown in *Figure 5.1:*

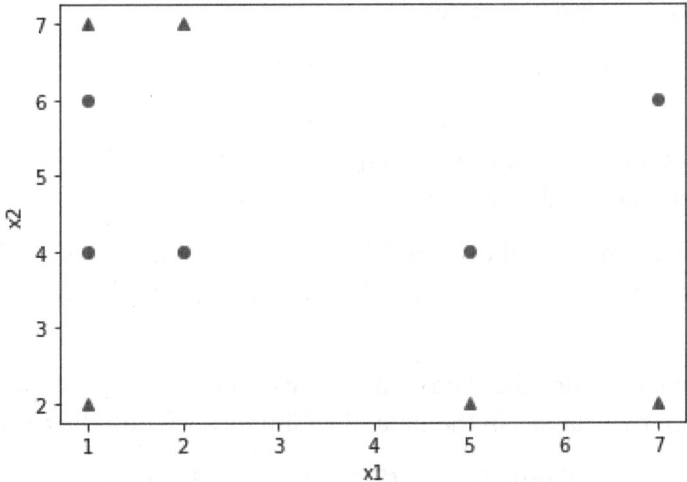

Figure 5.2: *Graph of the data in Table 5.1*

In *Figure 5.1,* the green triangles are for the data points where *y = 1,* and the red circles are for the data points where *y = 0.*

The decision tree we want to form is to be able to decide the class of the data point (i.e., y) based on the values of the variables x_1 and x_2. So, we must make decisions based on what values of x_1 or x_2 we must take in which direction. To understand this, consider a dummy decision tree, as shown in *Figure 5.2:*

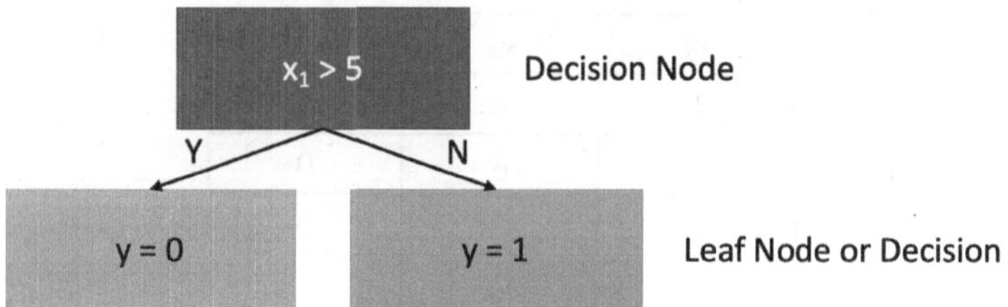

Figure 5.3: *Dummy Decision Tree*

In *Figure 5.2,* we are deciding whether the class for the data point (i.e., y) is 1 or 0 based on whether $x_1 > 5$. So, to form the decision tree, we need to figure out all these questions which lead us to the decisions.

Now, the question is how we decide the conditions for which we will split the decision tree. We will use the **Classification and Regression Tree** (**CART**) algorithm. To apply the CART Algorithm, we use the **Gini index**.

Understanding Gini index

Gini index is the measure of the impurity of a dataset.

Mathematically, Gini index is stated as.

$$Gini(t) = 1 - \sum P(i|t)^2$$

Where i is all the unique classes in the dataset, and t refers to the dataset. So, i varies from 1 to the total number of classes in the dataset. P(i | t) is the probability of class i occurring given that the dataset is t.

For example, in the dataset shown in *Table 5.1,* the unique classes are 0 and 1. So, for calculating Gini index, i would have values 0 and 1. So, in this case, i varies from 1 to 2.

For example, we consider the dataset as given in *Table 5.1* (we will call this dataset d1). As there are two classes in the data, the Gini index would be calculated as

$$Gini(d1) = 1 - (P(0|d1)^2 + P(1|d1)^2)$$

In dataset d1, we see 10 data points. 5 are for class 0, and 5 are for class 1. So:

$$P(0 \mid d1) = 5/10 = 0.5$$

$$P(1 \mid d1) = 5/10 = 0.5$$

So, Gini index for dataset $d1 = 1 - (0.5^2 + 0.5^2) = 1 - (0.25 + 0.25) = 1 - 0.5 = 0.5$

Notice that the term $\sum \boldsymbol{P(i|t)^2}$ can vary from 0 to 1. This is because P(i | t) is a probability and thus can assume a value between 0 and 1. The term $\sum \boldsymbol{P(i|t)^2}$ is a sum of probabilities of all classes in a sample space. So, the one extreme scenario is that only one class occurs in the dataset; its probability would be 1, and all other classes would have a probability of 0. In this case, $\sum \boldsymbol{P(i|t)^2}$ would be 1. In this case, Gini index would be 0.

The other extreme would be that Gini index would be 1.

A Gini index of 0 implies that the dataset is perfectly pure. A Gini index of 1 means the dataset contains all the randomly distributed points. A Gini index of 0.5 indicates that all the classes in the dataset are equally represented.

Forming the decision tree using the CART algorithm

CART forms binary trees using features and thresholds which yield the minimum Gini index.

Let us first go through the mechanics of forming the decision tree using the CART algorithm.

1. First, we calculate the Gini index of the dataset. If the Gini index of the dataset is 0, then the dataset is pure and thus needs not to do anything else.
2. If the Gini index of the dataset in step 1 is not 0, we decide the possible points from our dataset where a decision can be made. These points are called **thresholds**. This implies that we analyze the independent variables and make a list of values from the data from the independent variables where we can decide.
3. We will calculate the loss for each of the thresholds decided in Step 2.
4. From the loss calculated in step 3, the threshold(s) for which the loss is minimum, we would decide the data point where we would split.
5. From step 4, we would get two datasets (as CART forms a binary tree). For both datasets, we will repeat all the steps.

So, now we need to establish a loss function for the algorithm. The **loss function** (J) used in CART is as follows:

$$J = \frac{(m_{left} * Gini(left)) + (m_{right} * Gini(right))}{m}$$

To form a decision tree using CART, we find the points where the data can be split into two branches. The dataset on the left-hand side of the split is represented in the loss function as ***left,*** and the dataset on the right-hand side of the split is defined in the loss function as ***right***. In the loss function, m_{left} is the number of data points in the dataset on the left-hand side of the split, and m_{right} is the number of data points in the dataset on the right-hand side of the split. **Gini(left)** is the dataset's Gini index on the split's left-hand side, and **Gini(right)** is the dataset's Gini index on the split's right-hand side. **m** is the total number of data points in the complete dataset before splitting. So, $\mathbf{m} = m_{left} + m_{right}$.

The technique establishes a list of data points from the feature variables where we will evaluate the loss function. The data point where the loss is the minimum would be used to split the data.

To make the decision tree, we need to try various points for the features x_1 and x_2, where we can split the decision. So, we compute the possible values of x_1 and x_2 where there could be a split. We will understand this concept using the data we have in *Table 5.1*.

To compute the different values of x_1, we consider the range from the minimum value of x_1 to the maximum value of x_1. Then, we take points at equal intervals in this range. We see that the minimum(x_1) = 1 and maximum(x_1) = 7. To avoid edge conditions, we will consider the upper limit of the range as the *maximum(x1) + 1*. So, the range for x_1 is 1 to 8. We will consider intervals of 0.5 in our range. So, the values of x_1 that we will try to use for splitting the decision are as follows:

1.00, 1.50, 2.00, 2.50, 3.00, 3.50, 4.00, 4.50, 5.00, 5.50, 6.00, 6.50, 7.00, 7.50

Similarly, we consider the points of the variable x_2 for splitting the decision. We see that the minimum(x_2) = 2 and maximum(x_2) = 7. So, the range for x_2 is 2 to 8. The values of x_2 that we will try to use for splitting the decision are as follows:

2.00, 2.50, 3.00, 3.50, 4.00, 4.50, 5.00, 5.50, 6.00, 6.50, 7.00, 7.50

The points we will consider for splitting the decision tree are called **thresholds**.

Let us compute the loss for the threshold $x_1 = 1.00$. So, we split the dataset for $x_1 <=$ 1.00, then the dataset on the left-hand side of the split and the dataset on the right-hand side of the split would look as shown in *Table 5.2:*

$x_1 \leq 1.00$			$x_1 > 1.00$		
x1	x2	y	x1	x2	y
1	4	0	2	4	0
1	6	0	2	7	1
1	2	1	5	2	1
1	7	1	5	4	0
			7	2	1
			7	6	0

***Table 5.2**: The m_{left} and m_{right} dataset at split point $x_1 \leq 1.00$*

From *Table 5.2*, we get that the number of data points on the left-hand side of the split is four, and thus, $m_{left} = 4$. Similarly, we get that, $m_{right} = 6$. Also, we get that m = 10.

We must calculate Gini(*left*) and Gini(*right*).

To calculate Gini(*left*), we get the following from *Table 5.2*.

$$P(0 \mid left) = 2/4 = 0.5$$

$$P(1 \mid right) = 2/4 = 0.5$$

So, $Gini(left) = 1 - (0.5^2 + 0.5^2) = 1 - (0.25 + 0.25) = 1 - 0.5 = 0.5$

To calculate Gini(right), we get the following from *Table 5.2*.

$$P(0 \mid right) = 3/6 = 0.5$$

$$P(1 \mid right) = 3/6 = 0.5$$

So, $Gini(right) = 1 - (0.5^2 + 0.5^2) = 1 - (0.25 + 0.25) = 1 - 0.5 = 0.5$

Now, we can calculate the loss at the threshold $x_1 = 1.00$.

$$J(x_1 = 1.00) = \frac{4*0.5+6*0.5}{10} = \frac{2+3}{10} = \frac{5}{10} = 0.5$$

Let us try one more example to understand the technique. Let us calculate the loss at the threshold $x_2 = 2.50$. So, we split the dataset for $x_2 <= 2.50$, then the dataset on the left-hand side of the split and the dataset on the right-hand side of the split would look as shown in *Table 5.3:*

$x_2 \leq 2.50$			$x_2 > 2.50$		
x1	**x2**	**y**	**x1**	**x2**	**y**
1	2	1	1	4	0
5	2	1	1	6	0
7	2	1	1	7	1
			2	4	0
			2	7	1
			5	4	0
			7	6	0

Table 5.3: *The m_{left} and m_{right} dataset at split point $x_2 \leq 2.50$*

From *Table 5.3*, we get that the number of data points on the left-hand side of the split is three, and thus, $m_{left} = 3$. Similarly, we get that $m_{right} = 7$. Also, we get that m = 10.

To calculate Gini(left), we get the following from *Table 5.3*.

$$P(0 \mid left) = 0/3 = 0.0$$

$$P(1 \mid left) = 3/3 = 1.0$$

So, $Gini(left) = 1 - (0.0^2 + 1.0^2) = 1 - (0.00 + 1.00) = 1 - 1.0 = 0$

To calculate Gini(right), we get the following from *Table 5.3*.

$$P(0 \mid right) = 5/7 = 0.7143$$

$$P(1 \mid right) = 2/7 = 0.2857$$

So, $Gini(right) = 1 - (0.7143^2 + 0.2857^2) = 1 - (0.5102 + 0.0816) = 1 - 0.5918 = 0.4082$

Now, we can calculate the loss at the threshold $x_2 = 2.50$.

$$J(x_2 = 2.50) = \frac{3*0+7*0.4082}{10} = \frac{0+2.8571}{10} = \frac{2.8571}{10} = 0.28571$$

We need to perform similar calculations for all the thresholds that we have established. I leave it to you to complete all the calculations manually or using a program. Provided in *Table 5.4* is the loss for all the thresholds:

Feature	Threshold	Loss
x_1	1.0	0.5000
x_1	1.5	0.5000
x_1	2.0	0.5000

Feature	Threshold	Loss
x_1	2.5	0.5000
x_1	3.0	0.5000
x_1	3.5	0.5000
x_1	4.0	0.5000
x_1	4.5	0.5000
x_1	5.0	0.5000
x_1	5.5	0.5000
x_1	6.0	0.5000
x_1	6.5	0.5000
x_1	7.0	0.5000
x_1	7.5	0.5000
x_2	2.0	0.2857
x_2	2.5	0.2857
x_2	3.0	0.2857
x_2	3.5	0.2857
x_2	4.0	0.5000
x_2	4.5	0.5000
x_2	5.0	0.5000
x_2	5.5	0.5000
x_2	6.0	0.5000
x_2	6.5	0.5000
x_2	7.0	0.5000
x_2	7.5	0.5000

***Table 5.4**: Loss for all the thresholds*

Table 5.4 shows the thresholds for which we get the minimum loss given in *Table 5.5*:

Feature	Threshold	Loss
x_2	2.0	0.2857
x_2	2.5	0.2857
x_2	3.0	0.2857

Feature	Threshold	Loss
x_2	3.5	0.2857

***Table 5.5**: Thresholds with minimum loss*

Table 5.5 shows that we have more than one threshold value where we have the minimum loss. So, we could consider any of these thresholds for splitting the decision tree. For programming purposes, we need a rule. So, we will establish that we will consider the maximum threshold value when we have the same minimum loss value. So, we will split our decision tree at $x_2 = 3.5$.

The dataset at the split $x_2 = 3.5$ looks as shown in *Table 5.6:*

$x_2 \leq 3.50$			$x_2 > 3.50$		
x1	x2	y	x1	x2	y
1	2	1	1	4	0
5	2	1	1	6	0
7	2	1	1	7	1
			2	4	0
			2	7	1
			5	4	0
			7	6	0

***Table 5.6**: The and dataset at split point*

At each split of the decision tree, we get a **node**. At this point, we have obtained our first node. This node is called the **root node** of the decision tree. We start building our decision tree with this node, as shown in *Figure 5.4:*

x_2 <= 3.5
Gini Index = 0.5
Samples = 10
Values = {0:5, 1:5}

***Figure 5.4**: Root Node of our Decision Tree*

Next, let us consider the dataset on the left-hand side of the root node, as shown in *Figure 5.3*. In other words, we consider only the data points (as shown in *Table 5.1*) where x_2 <= 3.5. We have the dataset as shown in *Table 5.7:*

x1	x2	y
1	2	1
5	2	1
7	2	1

***Table 5.7**: The data points in the dataset (as shown in Table 5.1) where $x_2 \leq 3.50$*

Let us calculate the Gini index for the dataset, as shown in *Table 5.7*. Let us call the dataset shown in *Table 5.7* d2. So, we get as follows:

$$P(0 \mid d2) = 0/3 = 0 \text{ and } P(1 \mid d2) = 3/3 = 1$$

$$Gini(d2) = 1 - (+) = 1 - 1 = 0$$

From our understanding of the Gini index, we know that the Gini index of 0 means that the dataset is pure and has no impurity. So, this dataset need not be split any further.

So, we have one more node for our decision tree. However, this node cannot be split any further. Such nodes are called **Leaf Nodes**. Leaf Nodes provide a decision. In this example, we get the decision that when x_2 <= 3.5, the value of y should be 1.

The updated decision tree is shown in *Figure 5.5:*

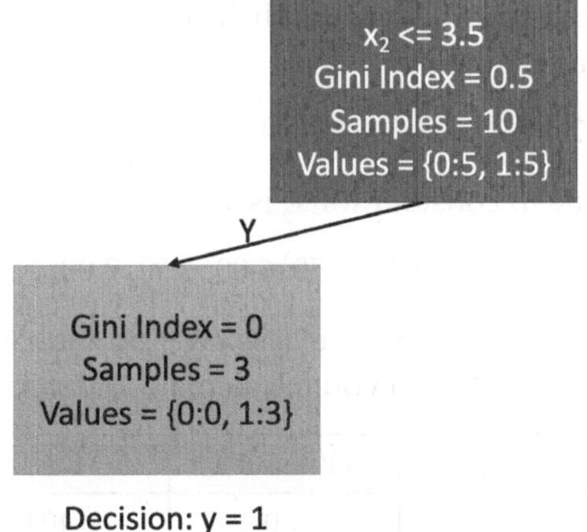

***Figure 5.5**: Updated Decision Tree with a Leaf Node (shown in orange color)*

Now, let us consider the dataset on the right-hand side of the root node, as shown in *Figure 5.4*. In other words, we consider only the data points (as shown in *Table 5.1*) where $x_2 > 3.5$. We have the dataset as shown in *Table 5.8:*

x1	x2	y
1	4	0
7	6	0
1	6	0
5	4	0
2	4	0
1	7	1
2	7	1

***Table 5.8**: The data points in the dataset (as shown in Table 5.1) where* $x_2 > 3.50$

Let us call the dataset, as shown in *Table 5.8* d3. By now, we know we need to calculate the Gini index for the dataset d3. We get as follows.

$$P(0 \mid d3) = 5/7 = 0.7143 \text{ and } P(1 \mid d3) = 2/7 = 0.2857$$

$$Gini(d3) = 1 - (+) = 1 - (0.5102 + 0.0816) = 1 - 0.5918 = 0.4082$$

As the Gini index of the dataset d3 is not 0, dataset d3 is impure, and thus we need to split this dataset to find decision points or leaf nodes. So, we will need to calculate the loss for all the thresholds. As the range of values of x_1 and x_2 may change, we must reestablish the thresholds. Using the same logic of using the minimum and maximum values of the features to establish the threshold, we get the threshold value to consider for as follows.

1.00, 1.50, 2.00, 2.50, 3.00, 3.50, 4.00, 4.50, 5.00, 5.50, 6.00, 6.50, 7.00, 7.50

And the threshold value to consider for x_2 is as follows:

4.00, 4.50, 5.00, 5.50, 6.00, 6.50, 7.00, 7.50

As we have discussed calculating the loss, we provide the loss values for the thresholds in *Table 5.9*, leaving it to you to calculate and verify:

Feature	Threshold	Loss
x_1	1.0	0.4048
x_1	1.5	0.4048
x_1	2.0	0.3429
x_1	2.5	0.3429
x_1	3.0	0.3429
x_1	3.5	0.3429

Feature	Threshold	Loss
x_1	4.0	0.3429
x_1	4.5	0.3429
x_1	5.0	0.3810
x_1	5.5	0.3810
x_1	6.0	0.3810
x_1	6.5	0.3810
x_1	7.0	0.4082
x_1	7.5	0.4082
x_2	4.0	0.2857
x_2	4.5	0.2857
x_2	5.0	0.2857
x_2	5.5	0.2857
x_2	6.0	0.0000
x_2	6.5	0.0000
x_2	7.0	0.4082
x_2	7.5	0.4082

***Table 5.9**: Loss for all the thresholds*

Table 5.9 shows that the thresholds with minimum thresholds are as shown in *Table 5.10*.

Feature	Threshold	Loss
x_2	6.0	0.0000
x_2	6.5	0.0000

***Table 5.10**: Thresholds with a minimum loss for the dataset we have called d3*

As was our strategy to consider the maximum threshold value when we have more than one threshold having the same value for the minimum loss, we will consider the data point $x_2 = 6.5$ for splitting the decision tree. So, our updated decision tree looks as shown in *Figure 5.6:*

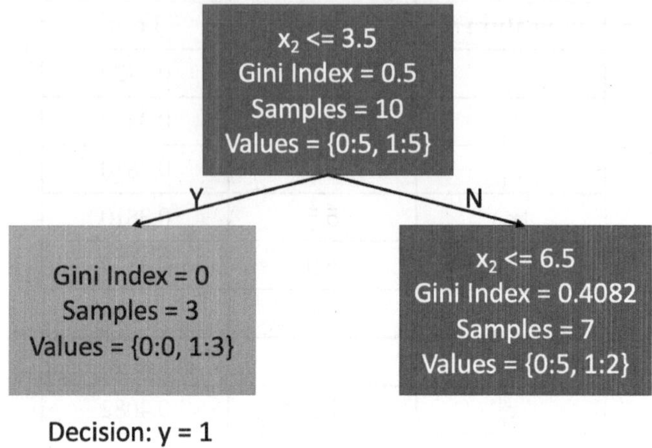

***Figure 5.6**: Updated Decision Tree with a new Node at x_2 <= 6.5*

As we have done before, we will split the dataset, as shown in *Table 5.8*, based on the new decision node we created, as shown in *Figure 5.6*, i.e., based on $x_2 <= 6.5$. Based on this, the dataset on the left-hand side is shown in *Table 5.11*, and the dataset on the right-hand side is shown in *Table 5.12:*

x1	x2	y
1	4	0
7	6	0
1	6	0
5	4	0
2	4	0

***Table 5.11**: The data points in the dataset (as shown in Table 5.8) where $x_2 \leq 6.50$*

We will call the dataset, as shown in *Table 5.11* d4:

x1	x2	y
1	7	1
2	7	1

***Table 5.12**: The data points in the dataset (as shown in Table 5.8) where $x_2 > 6.50$*

We will call the dataset, as shown in *Table 5.12* d5.

Let us calculate the Gini index for dataset d4. We get as follows:

$$P(0 \mid d4) = 5/5 = 1 \text{ and } P(1 \mid d4) = 0/5 = 0$$

$$Gini(d4) = 1 - (+) = 1 - (1 + 0) = 1 - 1 = 0$$

So, the dataset d4 is pure; thus, we get a leaf node.

Now, let us calculate the Gini index for dataset d5. We get as follows:

$$P(0 \mid d5) = 0/2 = 0 \text{ and } P(1 \mid d5) = 2/2 = 1$$

$$Gini(d5) = 1 - (+) = 1 - (0 + 1) = 1 - 1 = 0$$

So, the dataset d5 is pure; thus, we get a leaf node.

As both the datasets d4 and d5 are pure, we need not further split either of the datasets d4 or d5.

So, we get the final decision tree for the dataset we stated in *Table 5.1,* as shown in *Figure 5.7:*

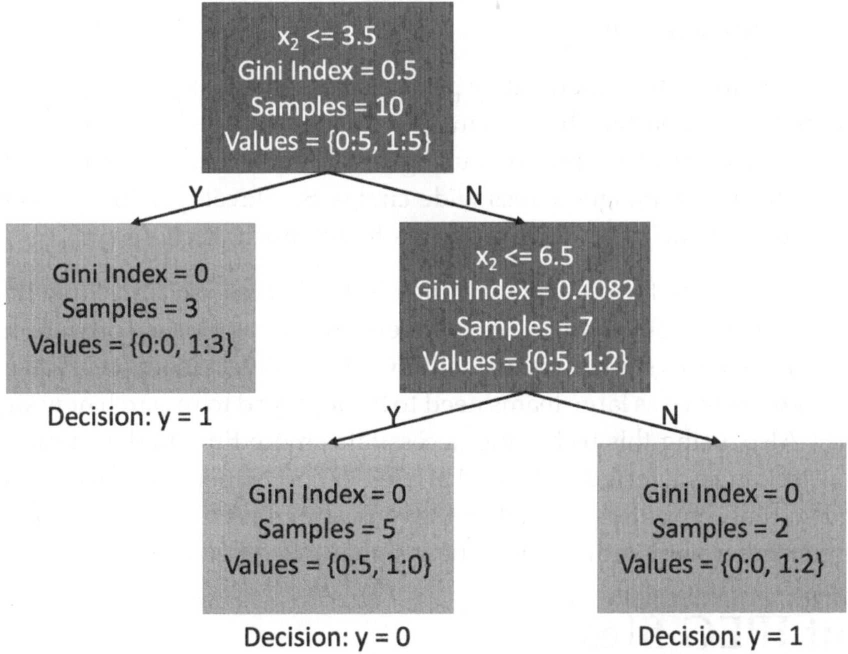

Figure 5.7: *Final Decision Tree based on the data in Table 5.1*

In the decision tree, we developed, as shown in *Figure 5.6,* both decisions are being made based on the feature x_2. However, this will not be the case when we use real data. Most of the nodes will be different features.

Malware detection in JPEG files[1]

Now we apply the Decision Tree algorithm to detect malware in JPEG files.

The need

Cybersecurity is paramount in the modern world for any government and any enterprise. Governments and enterprises are under constant cyber-attacks from all kinds of adversaries. It is said that the next war will be fought in the Cyber Space. So, it is of utmost importance to develop products and strategies to deal with the threat of cyber-attacks.

One of the means of cyber-attacks is through malware. Malware is malicious computer programs embedded in the software of regular use. For example, an email may carry malware that can infect the machine of the receiver of the email and then spread across an enterprise.

One very ubiquitous file exchanged by people across the globe is images. The advent of social media has boosted the exchange of images. Images can be exchanged not only between 2 computers: but also using devices like mobile phones, etc. Also, people tend to spread images across wide circles. So, developers of malware target embedding their malicious code into images to get much traction.

One of the prevalent forms of image files is JPEG files. So, infecting JPEG files has lots of incentives for malware developers. So far, antivirus software has been developed that studies signatures inside JPEG files to detect malware. However, this technique is expensive as large teams need to be deployed to research new signatures constantly. Also, using this technique necessitates more time to detect malware. So that malware can be detected faster and at a lesser cost, supervised machine learning is needed so that computers can detect the malware in JPEG files without having to feed the computer with knowledge of new signatures constantly.

About JPEG files

JPEG is the acronym for **Joint Photographic Experts Group,** which developed this standard for storing photographs in 1992. JPEG stores digital images in a compressed format. JPEG has its format. We will not get into the format of the JPEG Files in this chapter as we focus on machine learning. However, it is essential to note that in 2010 JPEG included a feature called EXIF Tags which enabled adding additional information about the images in a JPEG File. Using EXIF Tags, it is now possible to

1 Implementing Enterprise Cybersecurity with Open-Source Software and Standard Architecture – River Publishers (Chapter 3)

have information about the JPEG images like the brightness of the image, aperture of the image, owner of the camera, lens make, image width & height, date when the image was created, date when the image was compressed and much more information. Each mentioned information is stored as an EXIF Tag in the JPEG Files.

A significant thing about EXIF Tags is that most of the EXIF Tags can be altered using suitable software. The malware creators exploit this feature of JPEG Files and change the EXIF Tags to embed malicious code.

One of the ways to remove malware from JPEG Files is to convert the JPEG Files to BIT MAP Image Files (also called BMP Files). BMP Files only store the image information and do not carry any EXIF Tags from the JPEG Files. So, significant information about the images is lost in converting JPEG Files to BMP Files.

In summary, if we analyze the EXIF Tags in JPEG Files, we can determine whether the JPEG File is clean or malicious.

The strategy

EXIF Tags in the JPEG Files can contain values that are strings or numbers. While hackers also manipulate the numbers, the more interest is in the strings, which generally have some code that the hackers want to be executed in the user's machine. We now know that to make machine learning models; we must represent the strings as numbers using some vectorizer. So, what we will do is we will collate all the EXIF Tags present in a JPEG File as a single string, and then we will vectorize this string.

In *Chapter 4, Logistics Regression Algorithm*, we have discussed the TF-IDF Vectorizer. We will use the TF-IDF Vectorizer to vectorize the string formed from the EXIF Tags extracted from each JPEG File in our dataset. Once we have the TF-IDF vectors, we will use them to create the Decision Tree model.

Building the model

We will now discuss all the steps required for building the model for detecting malware in JPEG files.

We start with defining constants. These constants will be required in the program units that follow. Using constants is a good programming practice as it allows for making changes to the program without having to make changes at multiple locations in the program.

```
# Constants

FILE_NAME_COLUMN_NAME = 'FileName'
```

```
FILE_TYPE_COLUMN_NAME = 'FileType'

TAG_STRING_COLUMN_NAME = 'TagString'

NUMERIC_COLUMN_IDENTIFIER = 'AAA'

BENIGN_FILE = 0

FILE_WITH_MALWARE = 1
```

Extracting EXIF tags from JPEG files

The following functions can extract EXIF Tags from JPEG files.

We start with writing a function to determine whether the input file is a JPEG File. JPEG Files have a signature of 0xFFD8 at the beginning of the file. We will use the function **verify()** available in the Python library **Image** to determine whether the provided file is a JPEG file.

```
from PIL import Image


def isImageFile(imageFileName):

    returnValue = True


    try:

        img = Image.open('./' + imageFileName) # open the image file

        img.verify() # verify that it is an image

    except (IOError, SyntaxError) as e:

        returnValue = False


    return returnValue
```

The function **isImageFile()** returns TRUE if the input file name provided as input is a JPEG File. Else, it returns FALSE.

We will write a function named **JPEGFileFeatureExtractorToDictionary()** to read a JPEG file and extract all the EXIF Tags in the JPEG File. The function returns a dictionary where the keys are the name of the EXIF Tag, and the associated values are the values of the EXIF Tags as present in the JPEG File.

```
from PIL import Image

from PIL.ExifTags import TAGS


def JPEGFileFeatureExtractorToDictionary(imageFile):

    #Declare an empty Dictionary

    returnValue = {}


    # read the image data using PIL

    image = Image.open(imageFile)


    # extract EXIF data

    exifdata = image.getexif()


    # iterating over all EXIF data fields

    for tag_id in exifdata:

        # get the tag name

        tag = TAGS.get(tag_id, tag_id)

        data = exifdata.get(tag_id)

        # decode bytes

        if isinstance(data, bytes):

            data = data.decode('iso8859-1')


        returnValue[tag] = data


    return returnValue
```

Now we have a function to extract all the EXIF Tags from a single JPEG File.

Next, we will write a function named **`extractTagsFromADirectory()`** to extract the EXIF tags from all the files in a directory. This function will read all the files in a directory and, for each file, call the function **`JPEGFileFeatureExtractorToDictionary()`**.

This file will consolidate all the dictionaries returned by the function **`JPEGFileFeatureExtractorToDictionary()`** into a list and return the list.

```
import glob


def extractTagsFromADirectory(inputDirectory):
    # Declare Counters
    numberOfValidFiles = 0
    numberOfInvalidFiles = 0
    numberOfFilesWithoutTags = 0

    # Create an Empty List to hold all the features of all the files
    returnValue = []

    n = 0

    # Loop through all the files in the Input Directory
    for file in glob.glob(inputDirectory):
        # Create an empty Dictionary
        oneFileFeatures = {}

        try:
            # Read the file and extract the features
            fileFeatures = JPEGFileFeatureExtractorToDictionary(file)

            # If the File had some features, then create an entry for
            the file
            if len(fileFeatures.keys()) > 0:
                # Write the File Name
                oneFileFeatures[FILE_NAME_COLUMN_NAME] = file
```

```
            # Add the File Features to the main Dictionary
            oneFileFeatures.update(fileFeatures)

            # Add the entry to the return value
            returnValue.append(oneFileFeatures)

            numberOfValidFiles = numberOfValidFiles + 1
        else:
            # Check if the file is a valid Image File
            if isImageFile(file):
              numberOfFilesWithoutTags = numberOfFilesWithoutTags + 1
            else:
                numberOfInvalidFiles = numberOfInvalidFiles + 1

    except:
        # Check if the file is a valid Image File
        if isImageFile(file):
            numberOfFilesWithoutTags = numberOfFilesWithoutTags + 1
        else:
            numberOfInvalidFiles = numberOfInvalidFiles + 1

return (returnValue, numberOfValidFiles, numberOfInvalidFiles,
numberOfFilesWithoutTags)
```

The function **`extractTagsFromADirectory()`** returns a list of dictionaries containing the EXIF tags from all the files available in the directory (provided as input). This function also returns the number of input files that were valid JPEG files and contained EXIF tags, the number of input files that were not valid JPEG files, and the number of input files that were valid JPEG files but did not contain any EXIF tag.

Here, we need to consider that if a JPEG File does not contain any EXIF tags, then such JPEG files cannot have any malware.

Now that we have the functions needed to extract the EXIF tags from JPEG files, we must use them. Here we use a strategy to store all the clean JPEG files in a directory and all the JPEG files containing malware in a different directory. This way, we know which files clean JPEG files and which JPEG files contain malware. This way, we label our data as required for building Supervised Learning models.

Below is the code to extract EXIF tags from clean JPEG files.

```
benignFileFeatures, numValidFiles, numInvalidFiles, numFilesWithoutTags
= extractTagsFromADirectory(“./Data/clean_jpeg/*.j*”)

print(“Valid JPEG Files = %d\nInvalid Image Files = %d\nJPEG Files without
Tags = %d” % (numValidFiles, numInvalidFiles, numFilesWithoutTags))

Valid JPEG Files = 4582

Invalid Image Files = 0

JPEG Files without Tags = 816
```

So, we have 4,582 JPEG Files that contain EXIF tags in our dataset. We will consider only these files for training our model.

Next, we extract EXIF tags from JPEG files containing malware.

```
malwareFileFeatures, numValidFiles, numInvalidFiles, numFilesWithoutTags
= extractTagsFromADirectory(“./Data/malicious_files/*”)

print(“Valid JPEG Files = %d\nInvalid Image Files = %d\nJPEG Files without
Tags = %d” % (numValidFiles, numInvalidFiles, numFilesWithoutTags))

Valid JPEG Files = 400

Invalid Image Files = 12

JPEG Files without Tags = 3
```

So, we have 400 JPEG Files containing EXIF tags and malware in our dataset. We will consider only these files for training our model.

Notice that three files have been marked as JPEG files containing malware and have no EXIF tags. Typically, these are cases for further research. I tried to load these three files to Google Drive, and they were successfully uploaded to Google Drive. Google Drive has a powerful malware detector, and usually, files containing malware cannot be uploaded to Google Drive. So, for the moment, it is safe to assume that these three files have been wrongly labeled as JPEG files containing malware.

Now that we have the EXIF tags from all the JPEG files in our dataset, we will form a string of all the EXIF tags in a JPEG and store it as a record in a data frame. Once we finish this exercise, we will have a data frame containing a string of all the EXIF tags in each JPEG file. Also, we will label each record as whether it is from a clean JPEG file or a JPEG file containing malware. This way, we will create our labeled data which can be used for building a supervised learning model.

The function **fillDataInDataFrame()** takes a list of dictionaries as returned by the function **extractTagsFromADirectory()** and creates a data frame. The data frame will contain two columns – one having all the EXIF tags in a JPEG file and another stating whether the associated string is from a clean JPEG file or a JPEG file containing malware.

```
import pandas as pd

from tqdm import tqdm


def fillDataInDataFrame(featureDictionary, extractionDescription,
fileType):

    # Create an Empty DataFrame object

    df = pd.DataFrame()


    for record in tqdm(featureDictionary, desc = extractionDescription):

        # Create an empty Dictionary

        oneRecord = {}


        # Create an empty string

        recordString = “”


        # Loop through all the features in a record

        for k in record.keys():

            # Extract the value for the key and append it to the record
            string
```

```
            # This will be used for TFID
            # Add a SPACE between each tag value
            # Do not include File Name
            if k != FILE_NAME_COLUMN_NAME:
                recordString = recordString + str(record[k]) + " "

        # Add the record string as a separate column in the record
        oneRecord[TAG_STRING_COLUMN_NAME] = recordString[:-1]

        # Add column to mark Dependent Column as Benign File
        oneRecord[FILE_TYPE_COLUMN_NAME] = pd.to_numeric(fileType,
        downcast = 'integer')

        # Add the Record to the Data Frame
        df = pd.concat([df,
                        pd.DataFrame(oneRecord,
                                     columns = [TAG_STRING_COLUMN_NAME,
                                     FILE_TYPE_COLUMN_NAME],
                                     index = [0])])

    return df
```

Now we will call the function **fillDataInDataFrame()** with the list of dictionaries containing EXIF tags of clean JPEG files. And then, we will call the same function with the list of dictionaries containing EXIF tags of JPEG files containing malware. This way, we will get two data frames. We need a single data frame containing all the input data to build a machine-learning model. So, we will concatenate **benignFileDF** and **malignantFileDF** into a single data frame.

```
df = pd.concat([benignFileDF, malignantFileDF], ignore_index = True)
df['FileType'] = pd.to_numeric(df['FileType'], downcast='integer')
```

So now we have a data frame containing all the data which can be used for creating a supervised learning model for detecting malware in JPEG files. Let us check the distribution of the data points.

```
df[FILE_TYPE_COLUMN_NAME].value_counts()

0    4582

1     400

Name: FileType, dtype: int64
```

We have 4,582 data points for clean JPEG files and 400 data points for JPEG files containing malware.

Cleaning the data

During the experiment, I found that JPEG files containing malware can contain chr(0) in the EXIF Tags. chr(0) or ASCII character 0 is the end of the file indicator. When any program encounters chr(0), it stops reading further information. So, removing all the chr(0) from the data is required.

```
dfTFID = df[[TAG_STRING_COLUMN_NAME, FILE_TYPE_COLUMN_NAME]].copy()

dfTFIDClean = pd.DataFrame()

for i in dfTFID.index:

    dfTFIDClean.loc[i, TAG_STRING_COLUMN_NAME] = dfTFID.iloc[i,
    0].replace(chr(0), '')

    dfTFIDClean.loc[i, FILE_TYPE_COLUMN_NAME] = dfTFID.iloc[i, 1]

dfTFIDClean.shape

(4982, 2)
```

We now have the data frame dfTFIDClean, which can be used for further processing.

Forming the TF-IDF vectors

We can now vectorize the data, and we will use TF-IDF Vectorizer for vectorization.

```
from sklearn.feature_extraction.text import TfidfVectorizer


tfidfconverter = TfidfVectorizer(max_features = 90000, ngram_range = (1,4))
```

```
X = tfidfconverter.fit_transform(dfTFIDClean.TagString).toarray()

y = dfTFID.FileType

y.value_counts()

0    4582

1     400

Name: FileType, dtype: int64

X.shape

(4982, 39747)
```

After vectorization, we see that we have 39,747 features.

Reducing the number of features

We see that we have nearly 40,000 features. This can be overwhelming. Also, this can cause the model to take much time to be built. The most important fact is that so many features cannot contribute effectively to the model.

So, we need several features to retain only the essential features for building the model. We can achieve this by applying **Principal Component Analysis (PCA)**. PCA is a technique where we create linear combinations of the features and arrange the features in the order of influence of the features. In other words, we arrange the features such that the most influential is kept first, followed by the next most influential feature.

We will use the PCA implementation available in the Scikit-Learn library. The PCA implementation in Scikit-Learn uses **Singular Value Decomposition** (**SVD**). *For more details on SVD, refer to Appendix 3.*

After applying PCA, we can determine how many variables explain how much variability in the data. It usually is sufficient to retain all the features which can explain about 95% of the variability in the data. So, first, we apply PCA and check how many variables explain 95% of the variability in the data. *Figure 5.7* shows that about 4,800 principal components explain about 95% variability in the data. So, we will retain only 4,800 principal components from our dataset using PCA.

```
pca = PCA(n_components = 4800, random_state = 42)

X = pca.fit_transform(X)

print(X.shape)
```

```
(4982, 4800)
```

So, now we have 4,982 data points in 4,800 features.

Balancing the dataset

We noticed 4,582 data points for clean JPEG files and 400 data points for JPEG files containing malware. So, the number of JPEG files containing malware is less than 10% of the clean JPEG files. Such datasets are called **Imbalanced datasets**.

Generally, any dataset regarding fraud is imbalanced. This is because the number of instances of fraud is always very few compared to the number of cases of clean transactions. In the credit card fraud scenario, we may get less than 1% of the data regarding fraudulent transactions from a dataset of all the transactions.

Imbalanced datasets pose a problem: The class or classes of data with less representation may get less weightage by the algorithm. As a result, the classification generally becomes inaccurate. So, in most cases, we balance the dataset.

There are two ways to balance a dataset. The first way is called **over-sampling**. In the over-sampling technique, we try to create artificial data points for the class with fewer data points so that the data points in this class with fewer data points become the same (or almost the same) as the class with more data points. The other way is called **under-sampling**. In the under-sampling technique, we reduce the data points in the class with more data points such that the number of data points in all the classes becomes nearly the same.

In our case, we have only about 5,000 data points; we cannot afford to reduce the number of data points. So, we will use the over-sampling technique.

An imbalanced dataset can be over-sampled using the algorithm **Synthetic Minority Over-Sampling Technique (SMOTE)**. We will apply SMOTE to our dataset.

```
import imblearn as ib


# Transform the dataset

oversample = ib.over_sampling.SMOTE(random_state = 42)

X, y = oversample.fit_resample(X, y)

X.shape

(9164, 4800)

y.value_counts()
```

```
0    4582
1    4582
Name: FileType, dtype: int64
```

So, now we have an equal number of data points for both the classes, i.e., clean JPEG files and JPEG files containing malware.

Building the decision tree model

We have completed all the steps required to extract and pre-process the data. We can now build the decision tree model.

```
from sklearn.tree import DecisionTreeClassifier


modelDT = DecisionTreeClassifier(random_state = 42)
modelDT.fit(X, y)
DecisionTreeClassifier(random_state=42)
```

The model is now ready.

Testing the model

We will now test the model. To test the model, we will check how the model performs on the Training data. Once we get the model's accuracy on the training data, we will test the model on the test data.

If the training and the test accuracy are high, we can be sure that the built model is good for the purpose.

If the training accuracy is high and the test accuracy is low, then we have a concern as we can conclude that the model learned the training data too well and thus does not perform well when data unseen by the model is provided to the data. This can happen when the model is too complex. By complex model, it is implied that the model has too many variables and does not generalize well. A common practice is to make the model less complex by reducing the number of variables. We call such models overfitting models.

Though rare, we can have situations where the training accuracy is low, and the test accuracy is high. Under this circumstance, the model may be too simple. We call such models underfitting models. We need to add more variables to the model in this case.

Finding the training accuracy score

We will first test the model on training data.

```
from sklearn import metrics

import matplotlib.pyplot as plt

import seaborn as sns


y_pred = modelDT.predict(X)


cm = metrics.confusion_matrix(y, y_pred)


ax = plt.subplot()

sns.heatmap(cm, annot = True, fmt = 'g', ax = ax);


# labels, title and ticks

ax.set_xlabel('Predicted labels');

ax.set_ylabel('True labels');

ax.set_title('Confusion Matrix');

ax.xaxis.set_ticklabels(['Benign', 'Malware']);

ax.yaxis.set_ticklabels(['Benign', 'Malware']);


print(«\n\nConfusion Classification Report\n»)

print(metrics.classification_report(y, y_pred))


print("\n\nAccuracy: %5.5f%s" % (metrics.accuracy_score(y, y_pred) * 100,
"%"))


Confusion Classification Report
```

```
              precision    recall  f1-score   support

           0       1.00      1.00      1.00      4582
           1       1.00      1.00      1.00      4582

    accuracy                           1.00      9164
   macro avg       1.00      1.00      1.00      9164
weighted avg       1.00      1.00      1.00      9164

Accuracy: 99.96726%
```

Add

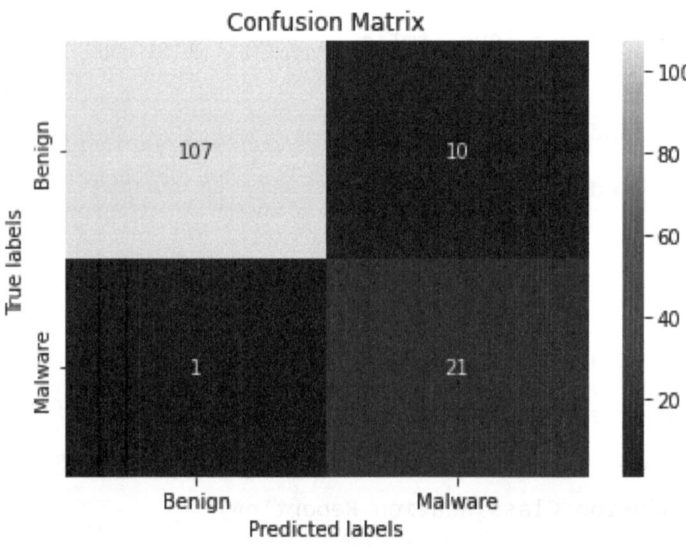

***Figure 5.8**: Confusion Matrix generated by applying the model to the Training Dataset*

We see a training accuracy 99.96726%.

Finding the test accuracy score

We will now perform a test of the model on the test dataset. Note that the model has not seen the test dataset in this case. So, it is as good as a live dataset for making predictions from the model. The only difference is that we have labels for the test data.

Before we can apply the model to the test data, we need to preprocess the test data. The steps to preprocess the test data are as follows:

1. We need to extract the EXIF tags from the JPEG files in the test dataset. We need to form a data frame of the concatenated EXIF tags.
   a. We now have the clean JPEG files for the test dataset in one directory and the JPEG files containing malware for the test dataset in another.
   b. So, after forming the individual data frames for the EXIF tags of the clean JPEG files and the JPEG files containing malware, we will need to concatenate the data frames into a single data frame.
2. Then, we must remove the chr(0) from the data.
3. Once we have the clean data, we will form the TF-IDF vectors.
4. On the TF-IDF vectors, we will apply PCA to reduce the number of features.

Once the above steps have been performed, we can apply the model to the resultant data to make predictions. The test accuracy is 92.08633%. As the training accuracy was above 99.9%, the model is **overfitting**. However, it can still be said that the model is good, mainly because the model reported just 1 in 139 JPEGs as a False Negative.

> *Note:* The notebook containing the code discussed in this chapter for building a decision tree model for detecting malware in JPEG files can be found at https://drive.google.com/file/d/1f-gpDLBZCHZSQHYJuAX0uLmsZkmgbupA/view?usp=share_link. However, to use this notebook, one would have to collect clean JPEG files and JPEG files containing malware. This is because it is not possible for me to upload the data available with me to any cloud storage for 2 reasons.
>
> 1. No cloud storage will allow me to upload any file containing malware.
> 2. The size of the data is too large.

Conclusion

The Decision Tree algorithm is a *greedy* algorithm. This is because the Decision Tree algorithm tries to find an optimal split at the root node and continues to find optimal splits at each subsequent node until it cannot further reduce the impurity. Because of this approach, the Decision Tree algorithm tends to overfit the data. When the model is overfitting, it cannot generalize well on the new data it provides for making predictions.

In this chapter, apart from discussing the decision tree model, we also discussed how to balance the dataset when the dataset is imbalanced. For balancing the dataset, we discussed the SMOTE algorithm. We also discussed **Principal Component Analysis**

(**PCA**), which reduces the number of features to use in making a model without suffering from significant loss of information.

In the next chapter, we will discuss ensemble models, which is one way of making models which do not overfit.

Points to remember

- Decision trees can be built using the CART algorithm.
- CART algorithm uses the Gini index or Entropy to form the Decision Tree.
- Imbalanced can be balanced using SMOTE.
- We can reduce the number of features in a dataset by applying PCA.

CHAPTER 6
Ensemble Models

In the previous chapter, we understood that models built using the Decision Tree algorithm tend to overfit. Like the Decision Tree Algorithm, all algorithms have some weaknesses. One way to overcome this problem is to make a prediction using multiple models and then decide based on the collective intelligence of all these models. When we have numerous models working together to make decisions, we call such models Ensemble models.

In this chapter, we will explore different types of Ensemble Models:

Figure 6.1

Structure

In this chapter, we will discuss the following topics:

- Ensemble Models
  - The Intuition Behind Ensemble Models
  - Different Types of Ensemble Models
- Ensemble Model implementation in Scikit-Learn
  - VotingClassifier
  - BaggingClassifier
  - StackingClassifier
- Building Speech Emotion Analysis Model Using Bagging Algorithm
  - About the Data Set
  - Librosa library
  - Building a Speech Emotion Analysis Model
- Work for readers

Objectives

After reading this chapter, the nuances of the Ensemble model will be clear. Also, you will learn how to use the implementation of different Ensemble models from the Scikit-Learn library. Lastly, by the end of this chapter, you will learn how to solve a classification problem for extracting emotions from speech using Bagging model. We will discuss how to extract information from audio files and use it for machine learning as well.

Ensemble models

When faced with a very complex question, we can pose the question to one expert and get an opinion to form our conclusion. Here we will depend on the knowledge and intelligence of the expert. Every individual likely has some biases. So, the expert we contacted could answer based on their preferences. It is likely that the solution we conclude could have a limited chance of being accurate.

Suppose we change our approach and pose the question to several experts. Then, we collate the answers from all the experts and choose the solution that most experts agree with. In most cases, such a conclusion could be more accurate than one expert's opinion.

The idea of ensembles is to ask several experts about a given problem. In simple ensemble models, we provide the data to several models and get the answers from each model. Then, if it is a regression problem, we take the average of the answers obtained from all the models as the answer to the solution. If it is a classification problem, we take the answers from all the models, and the answer provided by the maximum number of models is taken as the answer.

To understand this more clearly, suppose we have a classification problem to determine whether an SMS is spam (that is, we need to classify it into two classes – SPAM and NOT SPAM). We will provide our labeled data to several algorithms and create all the models. When we want to predict a given data instance, we will pose the question to all the models. Some of the models may classify the case as SPAM, and some of the models may classify the case as NOT SPAM. We will count how many models predicted SPAM and how many predicted NOT SPAM. If the count of prediction as SPAM is greater than the count of the predictions as NOT SPAM, we will conclude that the case is of a SPAM SMS; else, we will conclude that the case is of a NOT SPAM SMS.

However, we need not always create models with multiple algorithms. Generally, we take a single algorithm like the Decision Tree algorithm. We know that the Decision Tree algorithm tends to overfit. Overfitting means the algorithm learns the data too well; thus, when new data is provided, the model tends to make mistakes. So, what we do is that we create subsets of the data. For simplicity to understand, suppose we have 1,000 data points. We create ten subsets of this data of 100 data points each. In each subset, we select 100 data points by randomly picking them from the original data set of 1,000. Now, we provide each of the ten subsets of 100 data points to create ten separate models using the Decision Tree algorithm. Now, each model sees only part of the data, and none of the models can see the complete data set. When the ten models make the predictions, we take our prediction as the decision made by the maximum number of models. We will always consider the prediction based on the predictions of all the models.

Such a technique of creating a model is called the ensemble technique, and such models are called Ensemble models.

The intuition behind Ensemble models

Suppose we have a biased coin with a probability of obtaining a head being 51% (and thus the probability of obtaining a tail is 49%). If we toss this coin once, the chance of getting a head or a tail will likely be equally likely. However, if we toss this coin 100 times, the chance is that we will obtain heads 51 times and obtain tails 49 times. However, if we toss this coin 10,000 times, the chance of getting heads is 5,100 times, and the chance of obtaining tails is 4,900 times. Notice that our conclusion is clearly distinguished as we increase the number of times we toss the coin.

Ensembles work in the same way. Suppose we have several classifiers that produce better results than the random guess. Then, when we create ensembles with sufficient data points using these classifiers and take the majority from the results, the ensembles generally provide more than 75% accuracy. The critical point to note is that we need to have sufficient data points. In statistics, this is called the **Law of large numbers**.

Different types of Ensemble models

There are many types of ensemble models. We will focus on four types of ensemble models, that is, Voting, Bagging, Boosting, and Stacking.

Voting ensemble model

In the **Voting** ensemble model, we subject the same data to several models built using different algorithms. Then, we make predictions from each model separately and take the decision provided by the maximum number of models.

In *Figure 6.2*, we see how Voting ensemble models work. We can build 3 different models on the same input data:

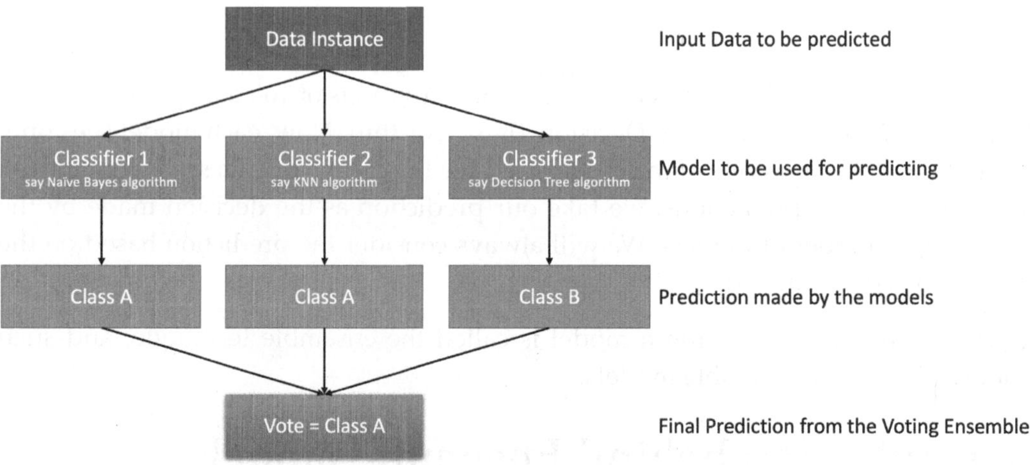

***Figure 6.2**: Simplified example of Voting ensemble*

As shown in *Figure 6.2*, we could build the three models using the Naïve Bayes, KNN, and Decision Tree algorithms. Then, when we have a data instance for which we need to make a prediction, we will subject the data instance to each of the three models and take the prediction from each. The prediction made by the maximum number of models is considered the final prediction from the Voting Ensemble model.

> ***Note:*** As we are discussing the classification algorithm, we will consider the decision as the class predicted by the maximum number of models.
>
> If the problem was for regression, we would take the output from each of the models and then (generally) take the average of the predictions made by each of the models.

> ***Note:*** In the illustration in Figure 6.1, we have considered three models. This is just for example. We could use as many numbers of models as we desire.

Let us say that each of the classifiers used in the Voting Ensemble model, as shown in *Figure 6.2*, has an accuracy of 80%, 85%, and 82%. The Voting classifier usually has an accuracy greater than the best models used in building the Voting ensemble model.

The theory is that if each of the classifiers in the Voting ensemble model is a "weak learner" (a "weak learner" is a model whose predictions are just better than a random guess), and there is a diverse set of "weak learners", the Voting Ensemble model can be "strong learner" (that is, a model with high accuracy).

For the best results, all the classifiers in the Voting Ensemble model should be independent. How we can make the classifiers in the Voting Ensemble Model independent by using classifiers that use different algorithms. Also, the accuracy of the Voting ensemble models increases if each of the classifiers in the Voting ensemble model makes different errors.

Bagging ensemble model

In Bagging ensemble models, we use the same algorithm to create multiple models. However, we provide a different subset of the data for each model. So, none of the models sees the complete data set. To provide different subsets of the data to each of the models, we create random subsets of the original data set. Then, we train each of the models on one of the subsets of the data set and consider the decision made by the maximum number of models.

Now to make the subsets of data, we have two options. The first option is to create the subsets by sampling the original data set with replacement. When we create ensemble models using this technique of creating subsets of data and using the same algorithm for creating the models, it is called **Bagging ensemble models**.

The second option is to create subsets by sampling the original data set without replacement. Ensemble models created by using such a technique for creating subsets of the original data set and using the same algorithm for creating the models are called **Pasting ensemble models**.

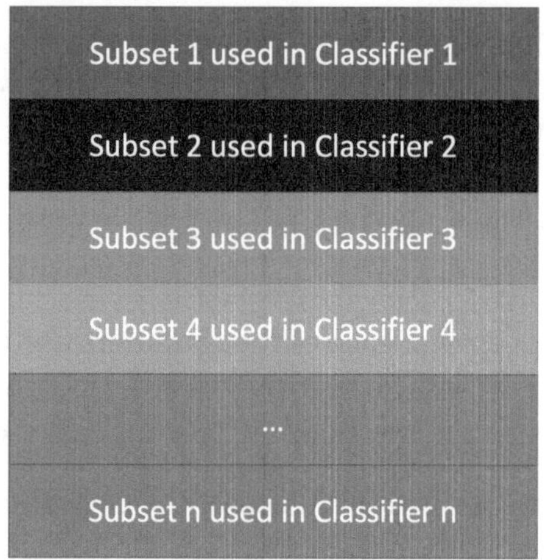

Each of the subsets are created by randomly picking the data from the original data set. In Bagging/Pasting Ensemble Models, the same algorithm is used to create models by using the data from one of the subsets

***Figure 6.3**: Illustration of how data sets are formed for Bagging/Pasting ensemble models*

Note: Let us understand sampling with replacement and sampling without replacement.

Suppose we have a data set that contains the elements 1, 2, 3, 4, and 5. From this data set, let us say that we need to draw a sample with two elements.

Suppose we pick 2 elements from this data set, and the elements are 1 and 4. Now, before we pick the next sample of 2 elements, if we put the elements 1 and 4 back in the data set and then sample, this would be called sampling with replacement. In other words, each time we sample from this data set, we would always make a selection from the original 5 elements in the data set.

On the other hand, after we have picked our first sample containing 1 and 4, we do not put these elements back in the data set. Then, for the next sample, we have to select from elements 2, 3, and 5. This is called sampling without replacement.

Bagging ensemble models can be created using any algorithm on different subsets of the original data set. However, the algorithm used primarily is the Decision Tree algorithm. When we make several decision tree models, we get many decision trees; thus, we call it a forest. *Chapter 7, Random Forest Algorithm* will explain a particular case of such Bagging ensemble models. Random Forest Algorithm is an extremely powerful and widely used algorithm that provides high accuracy without overfitting the data.

In the Bagging ensemble models, each classifier is a weak classifier. This is primarily because each classifier is trained on limited data. Each classifier has a higher bias as they are trained on a smaller data set, and thus each classifier learns its data very well. However, when the results of these classifiers are aggregated, the ensemble model has low bias and thus provides higher accuracy.

> *Note:* One of the several advantages of the Bagging/Pasting ensemble model is that for building these models we can easily use parallel computing. Thus, these modelling scales very easily.

As we create subsets of data by sampling at random with replacement, it is generally the case that several data points from the original data set do not make it to any of the subsets. About 63% of the data points make it to one of the subsets. So, we have about 37% of data points that are not used for creating the Bagging ensemble models. These data points are called **Out-of-Bag** data points. We can use the Out-of-Bag data points to test the Bagging models. Now, as the Out-of-Bag data points of the classifiers are never seen by the models, we can evaluate the Bagging Ensemble Models by assessing the accuracy of the predictions made.

Boosting ensemble model

Unlike Voting ensemble models and similar to Bagging ensemble models, Boosting ensemble models use the same algorithm to train the model.

Unlike Bagging Ensemble Models and similar to Voting ensemble models, Boosting ensemble models train the model on the complete data set.

Boosting ensemble models are trained in sequence. The idea is that the model is trained on the data set, and the model finds out the mistakes it made in the predictions. Now, the model trains for a second time, trying to eliminate the mistakes it made the last time. After the second round of training, the model again finds out the errors in the predictions and trains a third time to eliminate these mistakes. This cycle is repeated until the model can no longer eliminate mistakes.

We will discuss Boosting models in detail in *Chapter 8, Boosting*.

Stacking ensemble model

The idea behind the Stacking Ensemble Model is that if we have multiple models built using different algorithms that produce good predictions, why not have a mechanism to choose the model that can make the best prediction? In other words, after training the model using multiple algorithms, we devise a means to select the model which can be trusted.

Unlike in Bagging Ensemble Models, where we use subsets of the original data set to train the models, in Stacking Ensemble Models, we use the complete data set to train the models. Unlike in Boosting Ensemble Model, where we use the same algorithm to train the models in a sequence, we use multiple algorithms to build the different models. Once the models have been constructed in the Stacking Ensemble Models, the algorithm uses another model to make the final prediction.

In essence, the philosophy of the Stacking Ensemble Models is that instead of simple aggregation (like voting for classification or taking the average for regression) of the results from the different models created, we train an altogether separate model to make the prediction. The models used to train on the training data are called the **Base models** or **Level 0 models**. The model used for prediction is called the **Meta Model** or the **Level 1 model**.

We train the Base Models on the complete data set to meet this objective of the Stacking Ensemble Models. Then we take the predictions from these Base models and form a second data set (We sometimes combine this second data set with the original data set). We then train the Meta model on this second data set and make predictions from the Meta Model.

Stacking Ensemble Models are appropriate when multiple algorithms have skills on a particular data set; however, each has different skills on the data set. What is meant is that different algorithms produce models which make different errors on the training data, and the mistakes made by the different models are not much correlated. In Stacking Ensemble Models, the Base Models are generally built using complex algorithms like the Decision Trees algorithm, Random Forest algorithm, and so on. The Meta Model is usually made using simple algorithms like the Logistic Regression algorithm.

The mechanics of the Stacking Ensemble Model are provided in *Figure 6.4*:

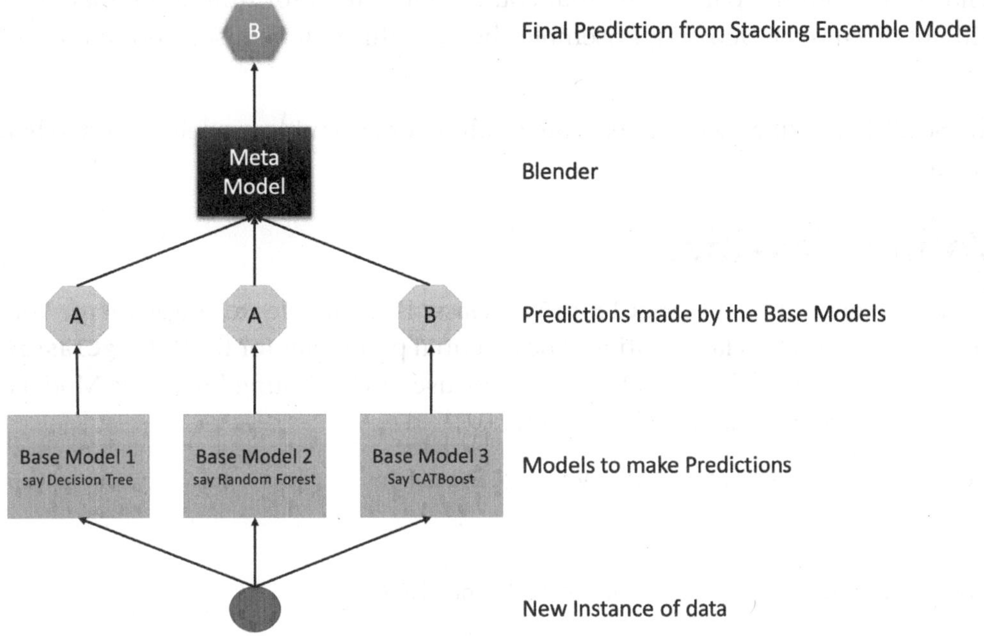

***Figure 6.4**: Illustration of the Stacking ensemble model*

We will not discuss Stacking ensemble model further in this book since it is not much used in the Machine learning world.

Ensemble Model implementation in Scikit-Learn

All the algorithms we discussed before this chapter (namely, the Naïve Bayes algorithm, K-Nearest Neighbor algorithm, Logistic Regression algorithm, and Decision Tree algorithm) could be understood by manual illustration. Also, the predictions made by these algorithms are easy to interpret. These kinds of models are called **White Box Models**.

However, in the Ensemble models (and Neural networks), it is difficult to explain why a particular data instance was classified in a specific class. That is why these models are called **Black Box Models**. We cannot walk through the Ensemble models using a data set. However, you can still program such models by yourself. We have included all the essential details to program the ensemble models.

The following are the details of the ensemble model implementations available in Scikit-Learn and the parameters that could be modified for tuning the models. We will not discuss the Boosting Ensembles here, as this will be discussed in *Chapter 8, Boosting*.

The Scikit-Learn library has a separate module for ensemble models, called **sklearn.ensemble**.

VotingClassifier

In sklearn.ensemble, **`VotingClassifier`** class is available to implement Voting ensemble models for classification. The essential parameter for the **`VotingClassifier`** class is **estimators**. Different estimators to be used in the Voting Ensemble Model can be provided in the estimators' parameter:

```
from sklearn.ensemble import VotingClassifier

...

from sklearn.naive_bayes import MultinomialNB

from sklearn.neighbors import KNeighborsClassifier

from sklearn.tree import DecisionTreeClassifier


...


nbCls = MultinomialNB()

knnCls = KNearestClassifier()

dtCls = DecisionTreeClassifier()


...


votingClf = VotingClassifier(estimators=[('nb', nbCls), ('knn', knnCls), ('dt', dtCls)])

...
```

BaggingClassifier

In sklearn.ensemble, **BaggingClassifier** class is available for implementing Bagging Ensemble Models for classification. *Table 6.1* lists the essential parameters for the **BaggingClassifier** class:

Parameter	Explanation
`estimator`	The estimator is to be used by the Bagging Classifier class. By default, the estimator is DecisionTreeClassifier. This parameter needs to be provided as an instance of the estimator class. In some versions of Scikit-Learn, this parameter may be available as `base_estimator`.
`n_estimators`	The number of estimator instances to be created. This means that the Bagging Classifier will create a number of models equal to the value of `n_estimators` using the estimator class and will create n_estimators number of data sets from the provided data set.
`bootstrap`	This is a Boolean parameter, that is, this parameter takes values of True and False. If the value of the bootstrap parameter is set to True, the samples are drawn with replacement. If the value of the bootstrap parameter is set to False, the samples are drawn without replacement.
`max_samples`	The maximum number of data points to be drawn from the original data set is to be provided for each instance of the estimators.
`oob_score`	This is a Boolean parameter, that is, this parameter takes values of True and False. This parameter is applicable only if the bootstrap parameter is set to True. When this parameter is set to True, the out-of-bag data points are used to check for the generalization error.

***Table 6.1**: Parameters for Bagging Classifier*

In the following code, we see how the BaggingClassifier from Scikit-Learn package can be used:

```
from sklearn.ensemble import BaggingClassifier

...

from sklearn.tree import DecisionTreeClassifier

...

baggingClf = BaggingClassifier(estimator=DecisionTreeClassifier(), n_
estimators = 1000, bootstrap=True, max_samples=500, oob_score=True)

...
```

StackingClassifier

In sklearn.ensemble, **StackingClassifier** class is available to implement Stacking Ensemble Models for classification. There are two essential parameters for the StackingClassifier class. The first essential parameter is **estimators,** which take a list of the different classifiers for building the base models. The second essential parameter is **final_estimator** which takes the class to construct the meta-model.

Another important parameter for **StackingClassifier** is the passthrough. It takes a Boolean value (that is, we must set this parameter to True or False). When passthrough is set to False, **StackingClassifier** uses the predictions from the Base Models as the input to build the Meta Model. When passthrough is set to True, **StackingClassifier** will use the prediction from the Base Model and the original data set to construct the Meta Model as shown in the following code:

```
from sklearn.ensemble import StackingClassifier

...

from sklearn.naive_bayes import MultinomialNB

from sklearn.neighbors import KNeighborsClassifier

from sklearn.tree import DecisionTreeClassifier

from sklearn.linear_model import LogisticRegression


...


nbCls = MultinomialNB()

knnCls = KNearestClassifier()

dtCls = DecisionTreeClassifier()

lrCls = LogisticRegression()


...


stackingClf  =  StackingClassifier(estimators=[('nb',  nbCls),  ('knn',
knnCls), ('dt', dtCls)], final_estimator=lrCls)

...
```

Building speech emotion analysis model using Bagging algorithm

Emotion analysis is widely used in many industries. Companies providing online services use emotion analysis to analyze customer feedback. In a clinical investigation, it is used to predict the state of the patients. The human resources department uses it for applications like attrition prediction, and so on. In the Insurance industry, it is used for detecting fraud. There are many more use cases for emotion analysis.

Emotion analysis is generally conducted on Text data. This is a field of **Natural Language Processing** (**NLP**). The different words are analyzed in this field to determine the sentiment and emotion. We will discuss emotion analysis from speech. In a speech, the aspects like pitch, tone, speaking pace, loudness, and so on., are analyzed to decide the emotion expressed in a speech.

This field of using machine learning for emotion analysis from the speech is still nascent, as few reliable data sets are available for building good machine learning models. We will discuss the mechanics of building such models. The models can be improved by supplying better quality data to the model and improving the model itself.

Regarding the data set

As discussed in this chapter, the datasets used in emotion analysis from speech have been obtained from Kaggle. The data is available from 2 sources. The first source is the University of Toronto, and the data set is called Toronto Emotional Speech Set or TESS.[1] The second data set is The Ryerson Audio-Visual Database of Emotional Speech and Song or Ravdess.[2]

TESS dataset

TESS dataset contains 2880 files. Each file contains an audio recording. A set of 200 target words were spoken in the carrier phrase "Say the word ____' by two actresses, and the sets were recorded in seven different emotions (anger, disgust, fear, happiness, pleasant surprise, sadness, and neutral). Both actresses spoke English as their first language, were university educated, and had musical training. Audiometric testing indicated that both actresses had thresholds within the normal range.

1 https://borealisdata.ca/dataset.xhtml?persistentId=doi:10.5683/SP2/E8H2MF

2 https://zenodo.org/record/1188976#.Y_RMYuxBzA1

Ravdess dataset

Ravdess dataset contains 1440 files: 60 trials per actor x 24 actors = 1440. The Ravdess data set includes 24 professional actors (12 female, 12 male), vocalizing two lexically-matched statements in a neutral North American accent. Speech emotions include calm, happy, sad, angry, fearful, surprised, and disgusted expressions. Each expression is produced at two levels of emotional intensity (normal, strong), with an additional neutral expression.

Each of the 1440 files has a unique filename. The filename consists of a 7-part numerical identifier (for example, 03-01-06-01-02-01-12.wav). These identifiers define the stimulus characteristics:

- Modality (01 = full-AV, 02 = video-only, 03 = audio-only).
- Vocal channel (01 = speech, 02 = song).
- Emotion (01 = neutral, 02 = calm, 03 = happy, 04 = sad, 05 = angry, 06 = fearful, 07 = disgust, 08 = surprised).
- Emotional intensity (01 = normal, 02 = strong). NOTE: There is no strong intensity for the 'neutral' emotion.
- Statement (01 = "Kids are talking by the door", 02 = "Dogs are sitting by the door").
- Repetition (01 = 1st repetition, 02 = 2nd repetition).
- Actor (01 to 24. Odd-numbered actors are male, even-numbered actors are female).

An example of a Ravdess file name is 03-01-06-01-02-01-12.wav

- Audio-only – 03
- Speech - 01
- Fearful - 06
- Normal intensity - 01
- Statement "dogs" - 02
- 1st Repetition - 01
- 12th Actor - 12 Female, as the actor ID number is even

Librosa package

Librosa[3] is a Python package for speech and audio analytics. It provides modular functions that simplify working with audio data and help achieve a wide range of applications, such as identifying the personal characteristics of different individuals' voice samples, the detection of emotions from audio samples, and so on.

Building a speech emotion analysis model

Having covered the background, we start building the speech emotion analysis model by following these steps:

Loading and exploring the dataset

We start by loading the datasets. One would get zipped files containing the audio files using the links provided in the preceding section. The ZIP files need to be unzipped before proceeding to the next step.

We use the **glob** library in Python to load the files. The appropriate path where the files in the dataset have been downloaded will need to be provided to the **glob()** function. In my case, the files are stored in the same directory where my Jupyter Notebook is stored:

```
import glob


tessFiles = glob.glob('./Ravdess_Tess/Tess/**/*.wav', recursive = True)

ravdessFiles = glob.glob('./Ravdess_Tess/ravdess/**/*.wav', recursive =
True)


print("Number of Tess Files loaded:", len(tessFiles))

print("Number of Ravdess Files loaded:", len(ravdessFiles))

Number of Tess Files loaded: 2679

Number of Ravdess Files loaded: 1168
```

Note that there are 2,679 files loaded from the TESS data set and 1,168 from the Ravdess data set.

3 https://librosa.org/doc/latest/index.html

Once the data set has been loaded, the audio files can be played using the following code:

```
import IPython.display as ipd

sampleAudio1 = ravdessFiles[0]
ipd.Audio(sampleAudio1)
<IPython.lib.display.Audio object>
sampleAudio2 = tessFiles[100]
ipd.Audio(sampleAudio2)
<IPython.lib.display.Audio object>
```

An audio player will appear when you run this code, as shown in *Figure 6.5*. Upon clicking the start button on the audio clip, the audio clip will start playing as shown in the following figure:

***Figure 6.5**: Audio Player as provided by IPython library*

From the dataset, we first need to establish the data distribution. Distribution of the data is a key aspect of building a good model. We know that the data contains audio clips of 8 different emotions. We need to check whether the number of audio files in the dataset for each emotion is similar or dissimilar. If the number of audio files for each emotion is similar, then we would say that the dataset is balanced. Otherwise, the dataset would be termed unbalanced.

If the dataset is balanced, the model will give almost equal weight to each emotion. If not, the model could be biased towards the emotion where more audio clips are available. Having a balanced data set helps in building good classification models.

We first establish how many audio clips we have for each emotion. Here, the emotion expressed in the audio clips is our label. We will tell the machine that a particular audio clip expresses a specific emotion. Based on this knowledge provided to the machine, the machine would be expected to learn how to determine the emotion expressed in a new audio clip supplied to the machine.

The emotion associated with every audio clip is encoded in the file name of the audio clip. The following code extracts the text related to the emotion from the file name and associates it with the audio clip. Please note that the file naming conventions for the TESS files and the Ravdess files are different. Also, note that the variables **tessFiles** and **ravFiles** contain the full path of all the audio clip files:

```
emotionsInTessFiles = [fileName.split("/")[-1].split("_")[-1].split(".")
[0].lower() for fileName in tessFiles]


emotionsInRavdessFiles = [fileName.split("/")[-1].split("_")[-1].
split(".")[0].lower() for fileName in ravdessFiles]
```

We now check that the emotions are available in the TESS and Ravdess files:

```
print('Audio Clips of Emotions available in Tess Files:',
set(emotionsInTessFiles))

print('Audio Clips of Emotions available in Ravdess Files:',
set(emotionsInRavdessFiles))

Audio Clips of Emotions available in Tess Files: {'disgust', 'neutral',
'fear', 'angry', 'sad', 'happy', 'surprised'}

Audio Clips of Emotions available in Ravdess Files: {'disgust', 'neutral',
'fear', 'angry', 'sad', 'happy', 'surprised'}
```

Notice that we have no samples are the emotion **calm**. We cannot determine the emotion **calm** from the model we will build using this data set.

Next, let us count how many audio files for each emotion are available in the two datasets:

```
import pandas as pd


print('Number of Audio Clips available for each Emotion in the Tess
Files')

dfTessEmotions = pd.DataFrame(emotionsInTessFiles, columns = ['Emotion'])

dfTessCount = dfTessEmotions.value_counts().reset_index(name = 'count')

dfTessCount
```

```
Number of Audio Clips available for each Emotion in the Tess Files
     Emotion  count
0    disgust    391
1  surprised    387
2      happy    383
3      angry    382
4       fear    379
5        sad    379
6    neutral    378
```

```
print('Number of Audio Clips available for each Emotion in the Rav Files')
dfRavdessEmotions = pd.DataFrame(emotionsInRavdessFiles, columns = ['Emotion'])
dfRavdessCount = dfRavdessEmotions.value_counts().reset_index(name = 'count')
dfRavdessCount
```

```
Number of Audio Clips available for each Emotion in the Rav Files
     Emotion  count
0        sad    183
1       fear    182
2  surprised    182
3    disgust    180
4      angry    179
5      happy    174
6    neutral     88
```

```
print('Number of Audio Clips available for each Emotion in both the Tess and Rav Files combined together')
dfCombined = dfTessEmotions.append(dfRavdessEmotions)
dfCombinedCount = dfCombined.value_counts().reset_index(name = 'count')
```

```
dfCombinedCount

Number of Audio Clips available for each Emotion in both the Tess and Rav
Files combined together

     Emotion  count

0    disgust    571

1  surprised    569

2        sad    562

3      angry    561

4       fear    561

5      happy    557

6    neutral    466
```

As we build the model by combining the TESS and Ravdess datasets, let us see the distribution of audio clips across the different emotions for the combined data set:

```
from matplotlib import pyplot as plt

%matplotlib inline

import seaborn as sb


sb.barplot(x = dfCombinedCount['Emotion'], y = dfCombinedCount['count'])

plt.show()
```

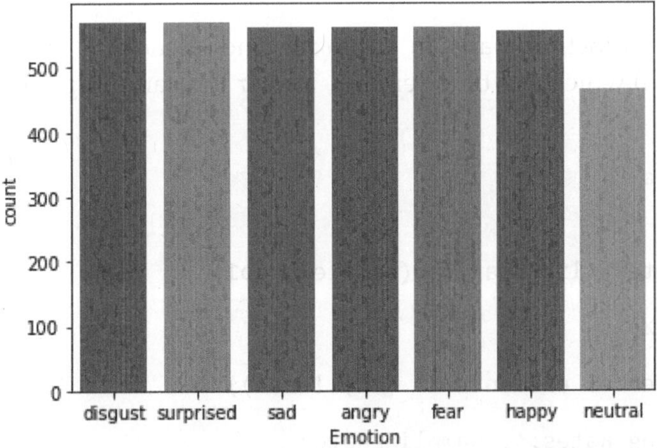

***Figure 6.6**: Distribution of emotions in the combined data set*

We see that we have almost the same number of files for all emotions except the neutral emotion. We can consider this data set to be balanced.

Visualizing audio signals

We will now visualize audio signals in the audio files. To do this, we will use the **librosa** library.

In most cases, the librosa library may need to be installed. Use the following code to install the librosa library on your machine. To install the librosa library on your machine, you would need the **numba** library in a version of at least 0.53 (This is when writing this chapter). Check whether the appropriate version of the numba library is installed on your machine. The following code installs the numba library and then installs the librosa library for safety.

```
!pip -qq install numba

!pip -qq install librosa
```

Now, we can use the librosa library to visualize the waveform in the audio files.

Before we can visualize the waveform, we need to load the audio clip. Audio clips are a time series with frequencies at different points in time.

An audio time series is in the form of a 1-dimensional array for mono or in the form of a 2-dimensional array for stereo, along with a time sampling rate (which defines the length of the array), where the elements within each of the arrays represent the amplitude of the sound waves is returned by librosa.load() function.

For Physics enthusiasts, the frequency and amplitude of a waveform are inversely proportional.

`librosa.load()` function loads an audio file and decodes it into a 1-dimensional array (for mono) which is a time series X, and sr is a sampling rate of X. Default sr is 22kHz:

```
import librosa


X, samplingRate = librosa.load(sampleAudio1)

print('X\n', X)

print('\nNumber of elements in X:', len(X))

print('Sampling Rates:', samplingRate)
```

```
X
 [ 0.0000000e+00  0.0000000e+00  0.0000000e+00 ... -2.3070108e-05
 -3.5594071e-06  0.0000000e+00]

Number of elements in X: 91231
Sampling Rates: 22050
```

Now we plot the waveform for the sample audio clip:

```
import librosa.display

plt.figure(figsize=(15, 5))
librosa.display.waveshow(X, sr = samplingRate)
plt.show()
```

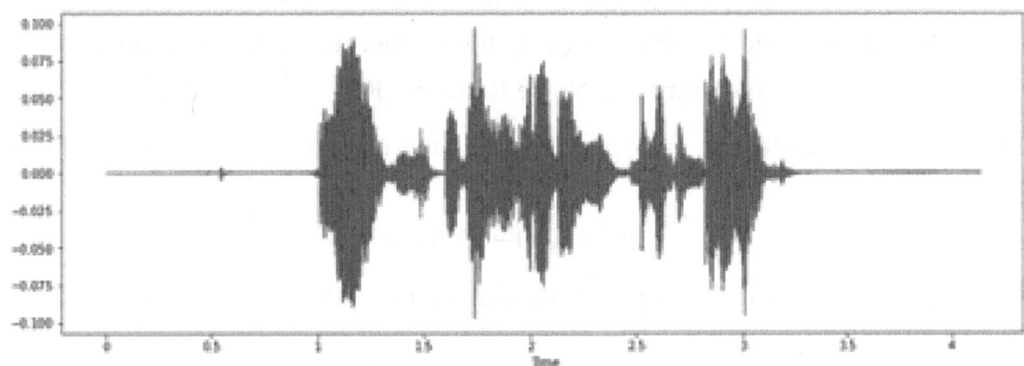

Figure 6.7: *Waveform of an Audio Clip*

Extracting features from the audio clips

Next, we need to extract the features from the audio clips. For extracting the features from the audio files, we will use the librosa library. We will take one audio clip and apply individual functions in the librosa library to see what features to extract.

The first step is to load the audio clip using the **`librosa.load()`** function:

```
import librosa

X, samplingRate = librosa.load(sampleAudio1)
```

```
print('X\n', X)
print('\nNumber of elements in X:', len(X))
print('Sampling Rates:', samplingRate)
X
 [ 0.0000000e+00  0.0000000e+00  0.0000000e+00 ... -2.3070108e-05
 -3.5594071e-06  0.0000000e+00]

Number of elements in X: 91231
Sampling Rates: 22050
```

The next step is to apply a **pre-emphasis filter** on the signal to amplify the high frequencies. A pre-emphasis filter is useful in several ways:

- Balances the frequency spectrum since high frequencies usually have smaller magnitudes compared to lower frequencies,
- Avoids numerical problems during the Fourier transform operation, and
- May improve the **Signal-to-Noise Ratio** (**SNR**).

The pre-emphasis filter can be applied to a signal X using the first-order filter in the following equation:

$$y(t) = X(t) - \alpha X(t-1)$$

This can be implemented using the following code: the typical values for the filter coefficient (α) are 0.95 or 0.97:

```
import numpy as np


preEmphasis = 0.97
emphasizedSignal = np.append(X[0], X[1:] - preEmphasis * X[:-1])
print('Emphasized Signal\n', emphasizedSignal)
print('Number of elements:', len(emphasizedSignal))


plt.figure(figsize=(15, 5))
librosa.display.waveshow(emphasizedSignal, sr = samplingRate)
plt.show()
```

```
Emphasized Signal

 [0.0000000e+00 0.0000000e+00 0.0000000e+00 ... 1.2685145e-05 1.8818599e-
05

 3.4526249e-06]

Number of elements: 91231
```

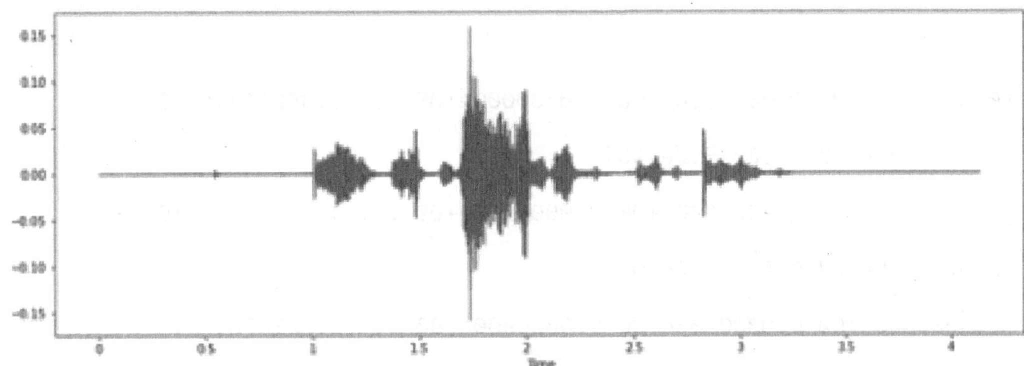

Figure 6.8: Waveform of the Emphasized signal

Next, we apply the **Soft-Time Fourier-Transformation** (**STFT**) to the audio signal. It is a Fourier-related transform used to determine the sinusoidal frequency and phase content of local sections of a signal as it changes over time. In practice, the procedure for computing STFTs is to divide a longer time signal into shorter segments of equal length and then compute the Fourier transform separately on each shorter segment. This reveals the Fourier spectrum in each shorter segment.

The parameter **`n_fft`** is the length of the windowed signal after padding with zeros. The number of rows in the STFT matrix D is *(1 + n_fft/2)*. The default value, *n_fft = 2048* samples, corresponds to a physical duration of 93 milliseconds at a sample rate of 22050 Hz, that is, the default sample rate in librosa. This value is well adapted for music signals. However, the recommended value in speech processing is 512, corresponding to 23 milliseconds at a sample rate of 22050 Hz:

```
stft = np.abs(librosa.stft(emphasizedSignal, n_fft = 512))


print('STFT\n', stft)

print('\nSTFT Shape:', stft.shape)

STFT

 [[0.0000000e+00 0.0000000e+00 0.0000000e+00 ... 2.7251832e-05
```

```
 3.9635463e-05 1.7816286e-05]
[0.0000000e+00 0.0000000e+00 0.0000000e+00 ... 4.9780392e-05
 7.5606654e-06 3.2048592e-05]
[0.0000000e+00 0.0000000e+00 0.0000000e+00 ... 6.8415793e-05
 3.0560906e-05 4.4785582e-05]
...
[0.0000000e+00 0.0000000e+00 0.0000000e+00 ... 3.3986405e-10
 1.6158309e-07 2.5879692e-06]
[0.0000000e+00 0.0000000e+00 0.0000000e+00 ... 4.2882733e-10
 1.6229825e-07 2.5878842e-06]
[0.0000000e+00 0.0000000e+00 0.0000000e+00 ... 1.2256726e-10
 1.6183600e-07 2.5879510e-06]]

STFT Shape: (257, 713)
```

Next, we extract **Mel-frequency cepstral coefficients** (**MFCCs**).

In sound processing, the **mel-frequency cepstrum** (**MFC**) represents the short-term power spectrum of a sound based on a linear cosine transform of a log power spectrum on a nonlinear mel scale of frequency.

MFCCs collectively make up an MFC. They are derived from a cepstral representation of the audio clip (a nonlinear "spectrum-of-a-spectrum"). The difference between the cepstrum and the mel-frequency cepstrum is that in the MFC, the frequency bands are equally spaced on the mel scale, which approximates the human auditory system's response more closely than the linearly spaced frequency bands used in the normal spectrum. This frequency warping can allow for a better representation of sound.

Even though higher order coefficients represent increasing levels of spectral detail, depending on the sampling rate and estimation method, 12 to 20 cepstral coefficients are typically optimal for speech analysis. The parameter **`n_mfcc`** is the length of the **Fast Fourier Transformation** (**FFT**) window.

MFCCs are features that can be used for our model:

```
# Compute MFCCs

mfccs = np.mean(librosa.feature.mfcc(y = emphasizedSignal, sr =
samplingRate, n_mfcc = 20).T,axis=0)


print('MFCCs\n', mfccs)

print('\nShape of MFCCs:', mfccs.shape)

MFCCs

 [-689.4513       13.136131   -38.444023    28.491467   -36.779255

    9.32245     -34.116608    -1.4327488  -19.810574     4.656265

  -11.9879      -10.639513     4.917104   -14.493996     1.9685546

  -12.012225      3.0940394  -10.074612    -1.8482265   -6.0479755]


Shape of MFCCs: (20,)
```

Let us plot the Spectrogram of the MFCCs:

```
plt.specgram(mfccs, Fs = samplingRate)

plt.xlabel('Time')

plt.ylabel('Frequency')

plt.show()
```

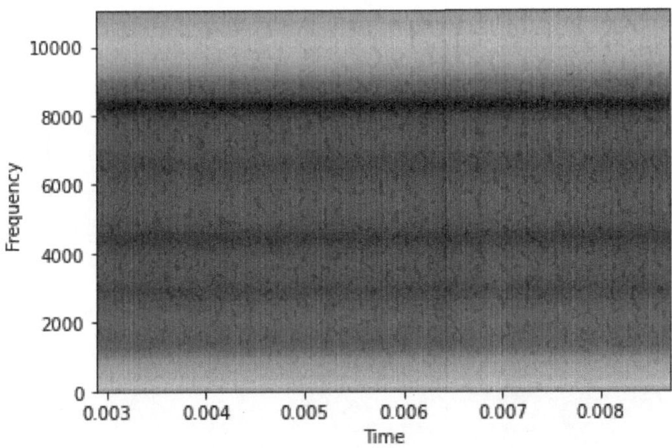

***Figure 6.9**: Spectrogram of the MFCCs*

Now we will compute the **Chroma features.**

In Western music, chroma feature or chroma gram closely relates to the twelve pitch classes. Chroma-based features, also called "pitch class profiles", are a powerful tool for analyzing music whose pitches can be meaningfully categorized (often into twelve categories) and whose tuning approximates the equal-tempered scale. One main property of chroma features is that they capture harmonic and melodic characteristics of music while being robust to changes in timbre and instrumentation.

We can extract chroma from speeches to gather information about the pitch.

The parameter **n_fft** is the length of the FFT window.

The parameter **hop_length** is the number of samples between successive frames.

Chroma features are the features that can be used in our model:

```
chroma = np.mean(librosa.feature.chroma_stft(S = stft, sr = samplingRate,
                                               n_fft = 2048, hop_length =
                                               1024).T, axis = 0)

print('Chroma Features\n', chroma)

print('\nShape of Chroma Features:', chroma.shape)

Chroma Features

 [0.51026803 0.4963213  0.49816346 0.51692945 0.5742091  0.6114398

 0.64996433 0.7051374  0.7605585  0.79590446 0.73575807 0.574072  ]


Shape of Chroma Features: (12,)
```

Let us plot the Spectrograms of the chroma features:

```
plt.specgram(chroma, Fs = samplingRate)

plt.xlabel('Time')

plt.ylabel('Frequency')

plt.show()
```

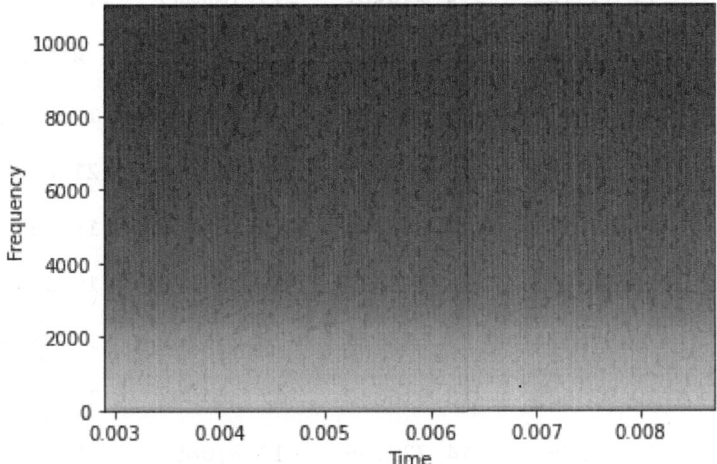

***Figure 6.10**: Spectrogram of Chroma features*

Lastly, we compute the Mel Spectrogram.

In 1937, Stevens, Volkmann, and Newmann proposed a unit of pitch such that equal distances in pitch sounded equally distant to the listener. This is called the **mel scale**.

Mel Spectrograms are features of our Model:

```
mel = np.mean(librosa.feature.melspectrogram(y = emphasizedSignal,
                                             sr = samplingRate,
                                             n_fft = 2048, hop_length =
                                             1024).T,axis=0)

mel = librosa.power_to_db(mel, ref = np.max)

print('Mel Features\n', mel)

print('\nShape of Mel Features:', mel.shape)

Mel Features

 [-62.29589    -55.944923   -51.42813    -49.577095   -36.52014
 -20.505787   -17.008743   -11.825571   -13.846834   -23.155426
 -31.581066   -23.514423   -13.599155   -12.581316    -7.536886
  -4.568012    -7.3826084  -11.508095   -15.077692   -13.694248
 -10.892952    -8.349024    -7.7596455   -8.25111     -8.282166
```

```
 -7.4645004  -11.132153   -18.039593   -17.104042   -16.618618
-14.429581    -9.146317    -2.1230888   -1.833271    -8.294319
-16.557907   -20.145111   -21.30455    -22.422905   -14.90712
-13.183041   -13.53274    -10.864588   -17.803444   -21.807007
-22.206394   -17.357193   -16.585354   -15.534296   -15.985748
-14.982983   -18.545902   -21.243832   -19.022278   -19.113834
-18.046383   -20.975574   -23.683514   -20.231289   -17.454521
-17.251965   -19.933525   -18.916237   -17.384598   -16.033215
-16.760536   -17.24545    -14.729155   -17.01065    -16.850792
-18.18747    -22.2695     -22.106583   -18.122662   -20.153107
-20.045021   -18.92778    -19.219032   -17.791103   -16.543953
-12.767435   -12.977457   -14.692564   -14.171074   -11.944859
 -9.595242    -9.698883   -10.716244    -9.285278   -10.026995
-10.549688   -12.03039    -11.083176   -13.272942   -15.013399
-14.728907   -13.327648   -12.561974   -15.392506   -12.369511
 -8.754185    -7.717781    -7.853283    -4.5001583   -1.8436794
 -0.49430084  -2.2715492   -1.8720245   -1.1360512   -1.535614
 -0.9676609   -0.6364498    0.          -3.2611046   -6.5593185
-16.590225   -50.712784   -80.         -80.         -80.
-80.         -80.         -80.         -80.         -80.
-80.         -80.         -80.        ]

Shape of Mel Features: (128,)
```

Let us plot the Spectrograms:

```
plt.specgram(mel, Fs = samplingRate)
plt.xlabel('Time')
```

```
plt.ylabel('Frequency')

plt.show()
```

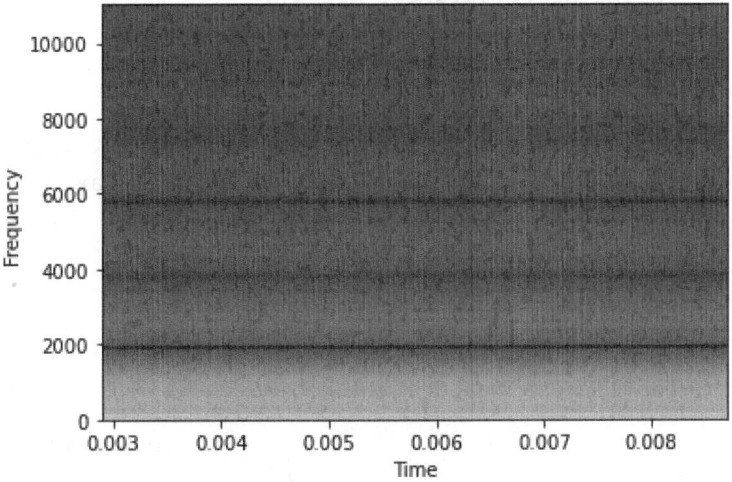

Figure 6.11*: Mel Spectrogram*

Now that we have discussed what features we could collect from the audio clips, let us write a function to collect all the features from an audio clip:

```
def extractFeatures(fileName):

    features = np.array([]) # Variable to store all the features


    # Load the Audio Clip

    X, samplingRate = librosa.load(fileName)


    # Pre Emphasise

    preEmphasis = 0.97

    emphasizedSignal = np.append(X[0], X[1:] - preEmphasis * X[:-1])


    # Apply Soft-Time Fourier-Transformation (STFT) to the signal

    stft = np.abs(librosa.stft(emphasizedSignal, n_fft = 512))


    # Compute mfcc and collect features
```

```
    mfccs = np.mean(librosa.feature.mfcc(y = emphasizedSignal, sr =
    samplingRate, n_mfcc = 20).T,axis=0)
    features = np.hstack((features, mfccs))

    # Compute chroma features and collect features
    chroma = np.mean(librosa.feature.chroma_stft(S = stft, sr =
    samplingRate, n_fft = 2048, hop_length = 1024).T, axis = 0)
    features = np.hstack((features, chroma))

    # Compute melspectrogram and collect features
    mel = np.mean(librosa.feature.melspectrogram(y = emphasizedSignal,
                                                  sr = samplingRate,
                                                  n_fft = 2048, hop_length
                                                  = 1024).T,axis=0)
    mel = librosa.power_to_db(mel, ref = np.max)
    features = np.hstack((features, mel))

    return features
```

Let us test our function to collect features from our sample audio clip:

```
features = extractFeatures(sampleAudio1)
print('Features\n', features)
print('\nNumber of Features:', len(features))
Features
 [-6.89451294e+02  1.31361313e+01 -3.84440231e+01  2.84914665e+01
 -3.67792549e+01  9.32244968e+00 -3.41166077e+01 -1.43274879e+00
 -1.98105736e+01  4.65626478e+00 -1.19878998e+01 -1.06395130e+01
  4.91710377e+00 -1.44939957e+01  1.96855462e+00 -1.20122252e+01
  3.09403944e+00 -1.00746117e+01 -1.84822655e+00 -6.04797554e+00
  5.10268033e-01  4.96321291e-01  4.98163462e-01  5.16929448e-01
```

```
 5.74209094e-01  6.11439824e-01  6.49964333e-01  7.05137372e-01
 7.60558486e-01  7.95904458e-01  7.35758066e-01  5.74072003e-01
-6.22958908e+01 -5.59449234e+01 -5.14281311e+01 -4.95770950e+01
-3.65201416e+01 -2.05057869e+01 -1.70087433e+01 -1.18255711e+01
-1.38468342e+01 -2.31554260e+01 -3.15810661e+01 -2.35144234e+01
-1.35991554e+01 -1.25813160e+01 -7.53688622e+00 -4.56801224e+00
-7.38260841e+00 -1.15080948e+01 -1.50776920e+01 -1.36942482e+01
-1.08929520e+01 -8.34902382e+00 -7.75964546e+00 -8.25111008e+00
-8.28216553e+00 -7.46450043e+00 -1.11321526e+01 -1.80395927e+01
-1.71040421e+01 -1.66186180e+01 -1.44295807e+01 -9.14631653e+00
-2.12308884e+00 -1.83327103e+00 -8.29431915e+00 -1.65579071e+01
-2.01451111e+01 -2.13045502e+01 -2.24229050e+01 -1.49071198e+01
-1.31830406e+01 -1.35327396e+01 -1.08645878e+01 -1.78034439e+01
-2.18070068e+01 -2.22063942e+01 -1.73571930e+01 -1.65853539e+01
-1.55342960e+01 -1.59857483e+01 -1.49829826e+01 -1.85459023e+01
-2.12438316e+01 -1.90222778e+01 -1.91138344e+01 -1.80463829e+01
-2.09755745e+01 -2.36835136e+01 -2.02312889e+01 -1.74545212e+01
-1.72519646e+01 -1.99335251e+01 -1.89162369e+01 -1.73845978e+01
-1.60332146e+01 -1.67605362e+01 -1.72454491e+01 -1.47291546e+01
-1.70106506e+01 -1.68507919e+01 -1.81874695e+01 -2.22695007e+01
-2.21065826e+01 -1.81226616e+01 -2.01531067e+01 -2.00450211e+01
-1.89277802e+01 -1.92190323e+01 -1.77911034e+01 -1.65439529e+01
-1.27674351e+01 -1.29774570e+01 -1.46925640e+01 -1.41710739e+01
-1.19448586e+01 -9.59524155e+00 -9.69888306e+00 -1.07162437e+01
-9.28527832e+00 -1.00269947e+01 -1.05496883e+01 -1.20303898e+01
-1.10831757e+01 -1.32729416e+01 -1.50133991e+01 -1.47289066e+01
-1.33276482e+01 -1.25619736e+01 -1.53925056e+01 -1.23695107e+01
```

```
 -8.75418472e+00 -7.71778107e+00 -7.85328293e+00 -4.50015831e+00
 -1.84367943e+00 -4.94300842e-01 -2.27154922e+00 -1.87202454e+00
 -1.13605118e+00 -1.53561401e+00 -9.67660904e-01 -6.36449814e-01
  0.00000000e+00 -3.26110458e+00 -6.55931854e+00 -1.65902252e+01
 -5.07127838e+01 -8.00000000e+01 -8.00000000e+01 -8.00000000e+01
 -8.00000000e+01 -8.00000000e+01 -8.00000000e+01 -8.00000000e+01
 -8.00000000e+01 -8.00000000e+01 -8.00000000e+01 -8.00000000e+01]

Number of Features: 160
```

We get 160 features for each of the audio clips.

Forming the Dataset

Now that we have the function to extract features from audio clips, we will extract the features from all the audio clips:

```
!pip -qq install tqdm
from tqdm import tqdm

def extractFeaturesFromFiles(files):
    X = []
    for file in tqdm(files):
        features = extractFeatures(file)

        X.append(features)

    return X

XTess = extractFeaturesFromFiles(tessFiles)
XRavdess = extractFeaturesFromFiles(ravdessFiles)
100%|██████████| 2679/2679 [05:43<00:00,  7.79it/s]
```

```
100%|██████████| 1168/1168 [03:28<00:00,  5.60it/s]
```

We will combine two sets of features (one from the TESS files and one from the Ravdess files) to form our data set:

```
X = np.vstack((XTess, XRavdess))


print('Shape of X:', X.shape)

Shape of X: (3847, 160)
```

We have the labels for the files in the data frame dfCombined. However, the labels are stored as strings. We cannot use these strings to train a model. We need to convert these strings into numbers. We will use a **LabelEncoder** to convert these string labels to numeric labels:

```
from sklearn.preprocessing import LabelEncoder


le = LabelEncoder()

dfCombined['EmotionLabel'] = le.fit_transform(dfCombined['Emotion'])


y = dfCombined['EmotionLabel']
```

So, now we have the features in the variable X and the labels in the variable y.

Building a Bagging classifier model

We will create a multi-class Bagging classification model.

First, we need to create the training set on which the model will be created and the test set is used to test the model.

```
from sklearn.model_selection import train_test_split


XTrain, XTest, yTrain, yTest = train_test_split(X, y, test_size = 0.05,
random_state = 42)


print('XTrain - Shape:', XTrain.shape, ' XTest - Shape:', XTest.shape)

print('yTrain - Shape:', yTrain.shape, ' yTest - Shape:', yTest.shape)

XTrain - Shape: (3654, 160)  XTest - Shape: (193, 160)
```

```
yTrain - Shape: (3654,)  yTest - Shape: (193,)
```

Now, we create the Bagging Model on the Training set:

```
from sklearn.ensemble import BaggingClassifier
from sklearn.tree import DecisionTreeClassifier

bc = BaggingClassifier(base_estimator = DecisionTreeClassifier(),
                       n_estimators = 10,
                       oob_score = True,
                       random_state = 42)

bc.fit(XTrain, yTrain)
BaggingClassifier(base_estimator=DecisionTreeClassifier(), oob_score=True,
                  random_state=42)
```

We make the predictions using the model on the training set and check the metrics. For the metrics, we will check the accuracy score, precision, recall, and f-score:

```
from sklearn.metrics import accuracy_score, precision_score, recall_
score, f1_score

# Make the predictions
yPredTrain = bc.predict(XTrain)

# Compute the metrics
accuracy = accuracy_score(yTrain, yPredTrain)
precision = precision_score(yTrain, yPredTrain, average = 'weighted')
recall = recall_score(yTrain, yPredTrain, average = 'weighted')
f1Score = f1_score(yTrain, yPredTrain, average = 'weighted')
```

```
print('Accuracy:', accuracy)
print('Precision:', precision)
print('Recall:', recall)
print('F1 Score:', f1Score)
Accuracy: 0.9956212370005474
Precision: 0.9956359773638089
Recall: 0.9956212370005474
F1 Score: 0.9956214486226791
```

We now make the predictions on the Test Set and check the metrics:

```
# Make the predictions
yPredTest = bc.predict(XTest)

# Compute the metrics
accuracy = accuracy_score(yTest, yPredTest)
precision = precision_score(yTest, yPredTest, average = 'weighted')
recall = recall_score(yTest, yPredTest, average = 'weighted')
f1Score = f1_score(yTest, yPredTest, average = 'weighted')

print('Accuracy:', accuracy)
print('Precision:', precision)
print('Recall:', recall)
print('F1 Score:', f1Score)
Accuracy: 0.8238341968911918
Precision: 0.8273995176996665
Recall: 0.8238341968911918
F1 Score: 0.8245289984658447
```

Applying the Bagging classifier model on live data

The purpose of building the model is to make predictions on live data. For this purpose, we demonstrate the mechanics of applying the model to the live data. The following code loads the live data and makes predictions on the same.:

```
# Set the model to Random Forest Model we just developed
MODEL = bc

# Load the Kaggle Files
kaggleFiles    =    glob.glob('./Kaggle_Testset/Kaggle_Testset/*.wav',
recursive = False)

# Extract features from the Kaggle Files
XKaggle = extractFeaturesFromFiles(kaggleFiles)

# Make predictions for the emotions in the Kaggle Files
dfKaggle = pd.DataFrame(columns = ['Id', 'Label'])
predKaggle = MODEL.predict(XKaggle)
predictedEmotions = le.inverse_transform(predKaggle)
for ctr in range(len(kaggleFiles)):
    fileNumber = kaggleFiles[ctr].split("/")[-1].split(".")[0]
    dfKaggle = dfKaggle.append({'Id':fileNumber,
    'Label':predictedEmotions[ctr]}, ignore_index=True)

print(dfKaggle.head())
100%|██████████| 201/201 [00:19<00:00, 10.38it/s]
    Id    Label
0   16    happy
1  103  neutral
2  117    angry
```

```
3  116  neutral

4  102  disgust
```

Work for readers

For the Emotion extraction from the speech model, we used the Bagging classifier, which used many models developed using the Decision Tree algorithm. Now, check whether the Bagging classifier's accuracy is better than that obtained from a single model built using the Decision Tree algorithm.

Conclusion

Ensemble models harness the power of using many weak or complex models and use the collective strength of each of the models to provide a powerful model. Ensemble models generally have less bias than the individual models. We observed many techniques for forming the ensemble, like using multiple algorithms to build individual models and then aggregating the results or building models using the same algorithm on different subsets of the data and then aggregating the results, and so on.

In the next chapter, we will discuss the Random Forest algorithm. The Random Forest algorithm is an ensemble model, a particular case of the Bagging ensemble model.

Points to remember

- When we combine many models to form a single model, such models are called Ensemble Models.
- There are four Ensemble models: the Voting Ensemble Model, Bagging Ensemble Model, Boosting Ensemble Model, and Stacking Ensemble Model.
- In the Voting Ensemble Model, we make predictions from multiple models built using different algorithms and aggregate the individual models' results to make predictions.
- We divide the original data set into many subsets in the Bagging Ensemble Model. We apply a model built using the same algorithm on each subset. Then we aggregate the results from each of the models to make predictions.
    - In Bagging ensemble models, we create the subsets of the data set using sampling with replacement.

- When we create the subsets of the data set using sampling without replacement and apply multiple models built using the same algorithm, the model is called Pasting Ensemble Model.
- Boosting ensemble models apply a model built using one algorithm on the complete data set and learns in a sequence by trying to eliminate the errors made in the previous iteration.
- In Stacking ensemble models, we apply multiple models built using different algorithms and then take the predictions of each of these models and use this as the data for a final model to make the prediction.

Join our book's Discord space

Join the book's Discord Workspace for Latest updates, Offers, Tech happenings around the world, New Release and Sessions with the Authors:

https://discord.bpbonline.com

Chapter 7
Random Forest Algorithm

In the previous chapter, we discussed combining many models to form an ensemble. The decisions from the ensembles are better than those from the individual models. One type of ensemble model we discussed was the Bagging Ensemble Model, where we made multiple models using a single algorithm and trained each model on a different subset of the original dataset. This way, each model sees only a part of the data while learning, and thus the collective decision of the ensemble is less biased and therefore makes better decisions on the new data instances.

A particular case of the Bagging Ensemble Model is the Random Forest algorithm, where we make subsets of the original dataset by vertical and horizontal partitioning.

Figure 7.1

Structure

In this chapter, we will discuss the following topics:

- The algorithm
  - o The idea behind the Random Forest algorithm
- Random Forest implementation in Scikit-Learn
- Detecting malware in ELF files
  - o About ELF files
  - o About the data
  - o Building and testing the model

Objectives

After reading this chapter, the nuances of the Random Forest algorithm will be clear. Further, we apply the Random Forest algorithm for classifying malware in ELF files. The details of extracting information from ELF files will be clear, and how to convert the information into a form that can be used for machine learning will be clear.

The algorithm

Random Forest algorithm was created by *Leo Breiman* of the *University of California, Berkeley*, in 2001. Random Forest algorithm was initially made to solve classification problems. However, it can be used for solving regression problems as well. The Random Forest algorithm remains a very powerful and popular algorithm. The following is the abstract of the paper by *Breiman*.

Random forests are a combination of tree predictors such that each tree depends on the values of a random vector sampled independently and with the same distribution for all trees in the forest. The generalization error for forests converges to a limit as the number of trees in the forest becomes large. The generalization error of a forest of tree classifiers depends on the strength of the individual trees in the forest and the correlation between them. Using a random selection of features to split each node yields error rates that compare favorably to Adaboost (Freund and Schapire [1996]) but are more robust with respect to noise. Internal estimates monitor error, strength, and correlation and these are used to show the response to increasing the number of features used in the splitting. Internal estimates are also used to measure variable importance. These ideas are also applicable to regression.

The idea behind the Random Forest algorithm

The Random Forest algorithm is a modification of the Bagging Ensemble Model. In *Chapter 6, Ensemble Model,* we discussed that in Bagging Ensemble Model, we divide the original dataset into many subsets, selecting samples at random with replacement. On each subset, we train a model using the same algorithm. Then, to make the prediction, we take the predictions from each model and select the class suggested by most models as the prediction.

In Random Forest algorithm, we use Decision Tree algorithm to train the models on many subsets of the original dataset. There is a difference in creating the subsets of the original dataset. In Random Forest algorithm, we create subsets such that each subset contains not only some of the data points from the original dataset but also each subset contains only some of the features from the original dataset. Further, the subsets are created such that each subset has the same label distribution as the labels in the original dataset.

Figure 7.1 illustrates how subsets from the original dataset are created in the Random Forest algorithm:

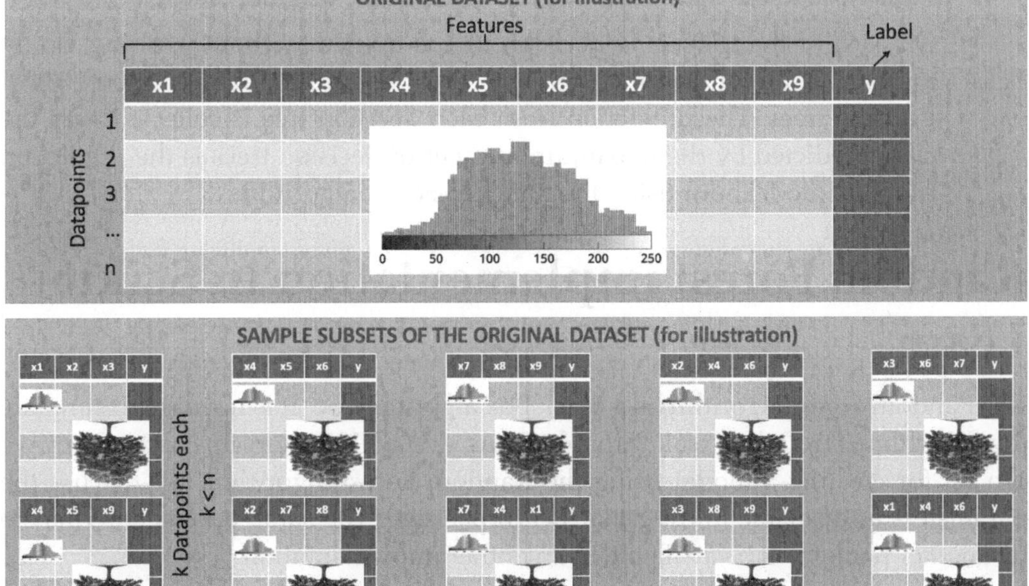

***Figure 7.2**: Illustration of how subsets are created from the original dataset in the Random Forest Algorithm*

A few important points to note regarding the illustration in *Figure 7.1*:

- In the illustration, there are nine features in the original dataset. From 9 features, we are creating subsets containing three features each. So, there can be ${}^9C_3$ ways to get three features from different combinations of 9 features. ${}^9C_3 = \frac{9!}{6! * 3!} = \frac{9 * 8 * 7}{3 * 2 * 1} = 84$. So, the random forest algorithm can create 84 subsets containing three features from the original dataset containing nine features. Now, it is optional that to create this model; we create 84 subsets. We can control how many subsets we want the algorithm to use. This point is highlighted because the Random Forest algorithm creates 100s of subsets from the datasets in real-world applications. Each of such models created is called an **estimator**.
- Each subset contains k data points where $k < n$ (n being the number of data points in the original dataset). The k data points in each subset are selected at random with replacement.
- Note that the picture of the data distribution in the original dataset is repeated in each subset in the illustration. This is because when the subsets are created in the Random Forest algorithm, the distribution of the labels in each should be as close to the distribution of the labels in the original dataset.
- On each of the subsets, a decision tree is trained **without pruning**. So, in a model created using the Random Forest algorithm, there will be 100s of decision trees. The prediction from each decision tree is collected, and the class predicted by the maximum number of decision trees is the prediction from the model built using the Random Forest algorithm.

Random Forest implementation in Scikit-Learn

The Random Forest algorithm is a Black Box algorithm. So, it is not easy to simulate the algorithm through a walkthrough. Thus, we will discuss the parameters we can set for creating a model using the Random Forest algorithm. We discuss the parameters as available in the Scikit-Learn package. The same parameters (maybe by another name) will be available in any other implementation.

To solve classification models using the Random Forest algorithm, Scikit-Learn has provided the class `sklearn.ensemble.RandomForestClassifier`.

The following are the important parameters of this class:

- `n_estimators`: This parameter defines how many trees to form in the forest. We know that for each subset, one decision tree model is created (we refer to these models as trees). Also, from the illustration in *Figure 7.1*, we know that based on the number of features in the original dataset and our choice of several features to use in each decision tree model, the number of subsets can be different. As discussed, we must create only some possible subsets (or decision trees). We can control the number of trees of form using this parameter. By default, the value of this parameter is 100. This parameter states the number of models that will be trained on subsets of the original dataset. The votes will be collected from all these models to make the final prediction from the model created using the Random Forest algorithm.
- `max_features`: This parameter controls how many features from the original dataset will be used to form each subset of the original dataset. By default, this parameter is set to the $\sqrt{n}$, n being the number of features in the original dataset. Based on this parameter, features are selected randomly from the original dataset (this number limits the number of features chosen) and assigned to each subset of the original dataset.
- **Criterion**: We know that the algorithm applied to each subset of the original dataset in the Random Forest algorithm is the Decision Tree algorithm. This parameter states the method to use for forming the Decision Trees. The decision trees are formed by default using the 'Gini Index'. However, we could also set this parameter to 'entropy' or 'log_loss' to use 'Information Gain' to decide splits in the decision trees.
- `min_sample_split`: When the decision tree is formed, we know that we start by splitting the root node and keep moving down the tree until we have only leaves left. However, using this parameter, we can stop splitting the nodes when a node has samples that are less than or equal to the value of this parameter.
- `max_depth`: By default, this parameter is set to None. Setting this parameter to None implies that each decision tree will be split until only leaf nodes remain.
- `bootstrap`: This parameter takes a value of either True or False. By default, the value of this parameter is True. When this parameter is set to True, each decision tree is created on a sample of the data from the original dataset. When this parameter is set to False, the original dataset trains each decision tree.

- `max_samples`: This parameter is applicable only if bootstrap is set to True. This parameter controls how many samples to use for training each decision tree. If this parameter is set to None, all the data points from the original dataset are used to train each decision tree.
- `oob_score`: When the bootstrap parameter is set to True, subsets of the original dataset are used to train each decision tree. We know that subsets are created by randomly selecting data points with replacements. This implies that we will have about one-third of the data points from the original dataset, which will not be used to train decision trees. These data points are called **out-of-box** samples or **oob**. The out-of-box samples can be used to check for the generalization of the model created using the Random Forest algorithm. This parameter takes a Boolean value, i.e., True or False. When this parameter is set to True, the out-of-box samples are used to check for generalization and generate a generalization score of the resultant model.

Detecting malware in ELF files[1]

An increasingly exploitable attack surface in today's rapidly evolving malware landscape is that of Linux-based **Internet of Things (IoT**) devices and, thus, Linux binary files. **Executable and Linkable Format** (**ELF**) files are the executable files used in any Unix operating system, including Linux systems. The rise of connected objects with the evolution and revolution of IoT has led to a massive influx of Linux-based malware and attacks targeting IoT devices. The increasing number of Linux malware can be attributed to the infrequent patching, use of default passwords, and almost negligible isolation of these devices, making them highly vulnerable to exploitation. Manual malware analysis is ineffective due to many such cases, so detection models based on machine learning approaches could serve valuable results.

Malware can be defined as any malicious program that intends to cause damage to a computer, server, client, or computer network. Malware can be categorized and classified into different types depending on its functionality.

The five malware categories classified by the model discussed in this chapter are listed as follows:

- **Backdoor**: Malicious software capable of opening unauthorized access to remote systems.
- **Botnet**: A botnet is a compromised system network allowing hackers to control them remotely and execute commands.

1 Implementing Enterprise Cybersecurity with Open-Source Software and Standard Architecture – River Publishers (Chapter 3)

- **DDOS**: A DDOS malware can launch Distributed-Denial-of-Service attacks by bombarding victim machine(s) with unnecessary packets and thus rendering the machines unresponsive to legitimate requests.
- **Trojan**: A trojan is any malware that disguises itself as something legitimate and misleads users of its true intent.
- **Virus**: Malicious code capable of replicating itself by inserting its code into other programs is termed a virus.

About ELF files

The information in the ELF files can be broadly classified into three types:

- Data in the File Header
- Data in the Program Header
- Data in the Sections

The ELF Files have 1 File Header, 1 Program Header, and many Sections of information.

The Structure of the ELF Files is shown in the following figure:

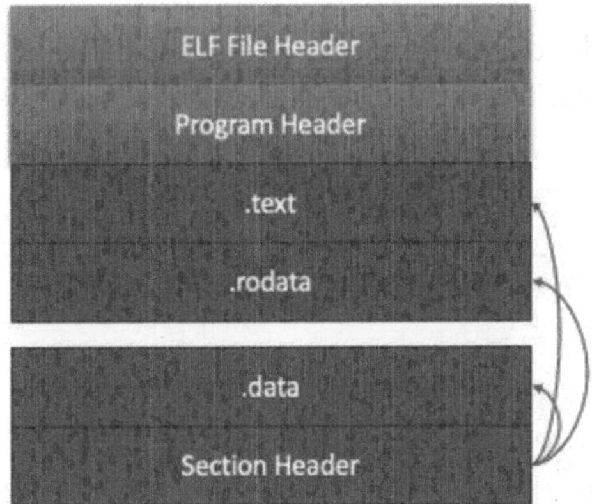

The illustration on the left shows the structure of the ELF Files in the memory of a machine when an ELF File is loaded for execution.

Every ELF File has only 1 File Header and only 1 Program Header. However, an ELF File can have many sections and each section has a Section Header.

.text is the program text of the program.

.rodata is the Read Only data of the program.

.data are the sections where all the transient data of the program are loaded.

***Figure 7.3**: Structure of the ELF Files (Source: Wikipedia)*

ELF File Header

Every ELF File has the first 2 bytes as 0x7F. By checking these 2 bytes, we can determine whether a file is a valid ELF File or not.

The ELF File Header defines whether to use 32- or 64-bit addresses. The header contains three fields affected by this setting and offsets others that follow them. The ELF header is 52 or 64 bytes long for 32-bit and 64-bit binaries, respectively.

The ELF File Header contains information on the target operating system. This information is stored in 1-byte. The target operating system can be any flavor of Unix, like Solaris, HP-UX, NetBSD, Linux, etc. There is also a byte in the ELF File Header that states the version of the target operating system.

There is a 2-byte information on the type of ELF File in the ELF File Header. The ELF file types can be Executable, Dynamic Linked Library, Core Dump, and so on.

There is 2-byte information on the type of machine for which the ELF File has been built. The information can be SPARC, Intel 80860, NEX, Power PC, Digital Alpha, Hitachi, and so on.

After all this information, there is a 4-byte pointer where the process should start execution. This is a very vulnerable point in the ELF File. The malware designers try to alter this pointer to point the program to the memory location where the malware developers induct their code.

Then, there is a 4-byte pointer to the Program Header. This is also a vulnerable point in the ELF Files for the same reason discussed earlier.

There is a 4-byte pointer to the Section Header table. This is also a vulnerable point in the ELF Files for the same reason discussed earlier.

Then there is a 4-byte pointer to the Section Header table. Following that, there is a 2-byte pointer to the size of the ELF File Header. This value must be 64 bytes for the 64-bit format and 52 bytes for the 32-bit format.

There is more information like the number of entries in the Program Header, the size of the Section Header, etc.

Program Header

The program header table tells the system how to create a process image. It is found in the file offset **`e_phoff`**, and consists of **`e_phnum`** entries, each with size **`e_phentsize`**. The layout is slightly different in 32-bit ELF vs. 64-bit ELF because the **`p_flags`** are in a different structure location for alignment reasons.

The first information in the Program Header is the type of the segment, whether the segment is loadable, dynamically linkable, interpretable, auxiliary information, etc.

The rest of the information in the Program Header are flags of 1 byte or 2 bytes. One can assume that tampering with this information will not interest the malware developers.

Section information

There are many sections in the ELF File. Each Section is for a specific type of information. The types of sections can be program data, symbol table, string table, symbol hash table, dynamic linking information, dynamic linker symbol table, array of constructors, array of destructors, etc.

For each section, there is information regarding whether the section is writable or executable, might be merged, contains null-terminated strings, etc.

Then, there is information regarding the various addresses for the different information.

So, this is a section where malware makers can alter various information.

About the data

The dataset contains types of files, as provided in *Table 7.1*:

File type		Number of files
Benign		**2,315**
Malicious	Backdoor	744
	Botnet	782
	DDOS	799
	Trojan	508
	Virus	595
	TOTAL	**3,428**

***Table 7.1**: Distribution of Input ELF Files*

So, the data set contained 2,315 benign ELF Files and 3,428 malicious ELF files. We see that there are a reasonable number of files in each category. Based on this data, 90% of the data will be used as the training and 10% as the test sets. The distribution of files used for training and testing the model is given in *Table 7.2*. To create training and test datasets, files are picked at random.

File type		Training set	Test set
Benign		2,078	237
Malicious	Backdoor	676	68
	Botnet	713	69
	DDOS	725	74
	Trojan	461	47
	Virus	539	56
	TOTAL	3,114	314

***Table 7.2**: Distribution of ELF Files after creating the Training Set and Test Set*

Building and testing the model

Before we can build the model for malware detection from ELF Files, we need to be able to read the ELF Files and extract features based on which the model will be made. To read ELF Files using Python programming, we can use the library **`pyelftools`**. We will have to install this package on our machine before we can proceed. The following code installs the **`pyelftools`** package:

```
!python3 -m pip install pyelftools
```

The following is the code for declaring the constants we will use to build this model. The use of these constants will become clear as we discuss the rest of the code. Avoid using literal values in my programs as much as possible because using literal values makes maintaining the program difficult.

```
# Constants

EMPTY_SECTION_NAME_SUBSTITUTE = "S"

FILE_NAME_COLUMN_NAME = "FileName"

FILE_TYPE_COLUMN_NAME = 'FileType'

NUMERIC_COLUMN_IDENTIFIER = "N"

MALWARE_SECTION_NAME_PREFIX = "M"


BENIGN_FILE = 0

BACKDOOR_FILE = 1

BOTNET_FILE = 2
```

```
DDOS_FILE = 3

TROJAN_FILE = 4

VIRUS_FILE = 5
```

Extracting data from ELF files

We will write a series of functions to extract information from the ELF Files. The first function **extractInformationFromADirectory()** is used for extracting details of all the ELF Files stored in a directory. Note that we have six types of files, 1 type of file is the benign ELF file, and the other five are the malicious ELF files containing different types of malwares. So, the strategy is to keep all the files of one type in a separate directory, and we will read the files from this directory, and based on what type of files the directory contains, we will label the records accordingly.

This function calls the function **isELFFile()**, which detects whether a file provided to this function is a valid ELF file.

This function calls the **ExtractFileDetails()**, which extracts the details from a single ELF file.

```
import glob


def extractInformationFromADirectory(inputDirectory):

    # Declare Counters

    numberOfValidFiles = 0

    numberOfInvalidFiles = 0

    numberOfFilesWithNoFileHeader = 0

    numberOfFilesWithNoProgramHeader = 0

    numberOfFilesWithNoSections = 0


    # Create an Empty List to hold all the features of all the files

    returnValue = []


    # Loop through all the files in the Input Directory

    for file in glob.glob(inputDirectory):
```

```
# Create an empty Dictionary

oneFileFeatures = {}


try:

    # Read the file and extract the features

    fileFeatures, validFlag, hasFileHeader, hasProgramHeader,
    hasSections = ExtractFileDetails(file)

    if(validFlag and len(fileFeatures.keys()) > 0):

        numberOfValidFiles += 1


        # Add the File Features to the main Dictionary

        oneFileFeatures.update(fileFeatures)


        # Add the entry to the return value

        returnValue.append(oneFileFeatures)

    else:

        if hasFileHeader == False:

            numberOfFilesWithNoFileHeader += 1

        else:

            if hasProgramHeader == False:

                numberOfFilesWithNoProgramHeader += 1

            else:

                if hasSections == False:

                    numberOfFilesWithNoSections += 1

                else:

                    numberOfInvalidFiles += 1


except:
```

```
        # Check if the file is a valid ELF File

        if isELFFile(file):

            pass

        else:

            numberOfInvalidFiles += 1


    return (returnValue,

            numberOfValidFiles,

            numberOfInvalidFiles,

            numberOfFilesWithNoFileHeader,

            numberOfFilesWithNoProgramHeader,

            numberOfFilesWithNoSections)
```

The following function is **ExtractFileDetails()**. This function is used to extract the details of an ELF File's information. An ELF file's information is stored as File Header, Program Header, and Section Information. There is one set of information for the File Header and Program Header. However, there can be many sections in an ELF File.

This function calls the function **ExtractFileHeader()** to extract the information of the File Header of an ELF File. The function **ExtractSegmentDetails()** is called to extract information about the program header of an ELF File. **ExtractSectionDetails()** is called to extract the information from all the sections in an ELF File.

```
def ExtractFileDetails(file):

    returnValue = {}

    validELFFile = True

    hasFileHeader = True

    hasProgramHeader = True

    hasSections = True


    try:

        with open(file, 'rb') as elffile:
```

```
try:
    eFile = ELFFile(elffile)

    # Extract the File Header Information
    fileHeader = ExtractFileHeader(eFile)
    if(len(fileHeader) > 0):
        returnValue.update(fileHeader) # Add the attributes
        to dictionary
    else:
        hasFileHeader = False
        raise Exception()

    # Extract the Program Header Information
    segmentDetails = ExtractSegmentDetails(eFile)
    if(len(segmentDetails) > 0):
        returnValue.update(segmentDetails) # Add the
        attributes to dictionary
    else:
        hasProgramHeader = False
        raise Exception()

    sectionDetails = ExtractSectionDetails(eFile)
    if(len(sectionDetails) > 0):
        returnValue.update(sectionDetails) # Add the
        attributes to dictionary
    else:
        hasSections = False
        raise Exception()
```

```
        except:

            validELFFile = False


        finally:

            elffile.close()

    except:

        pass


    return (returnValue, validELFFile, hasFileHeader, hasProgramHeader,
    hasSections)
```

The function **`ExtractFileHeader()`** is used to extract all the information from the File Header of an ELF File.

```
from elftools.elf.elffile import ELFFile


def ExtractFileHeader(elffile):

    returnValue = {} # Dictionary to hold the unique attributes of the
    header


    # The header information can be obtained as a dictionary.

    # However, there are some dictionaries inside this dictionary.

    # So, we create a flat structure taking out all the unique attributes
    and forming a dictionary.

    for key, value in elffile.header.items():

        # If the value for the key is a dictionary, then loop through
        all the attributes of this dictionary to collect the features.

        # The approach is simplistic as I do not go for a recursive
        function as it is known that there can be only one additional
        level of the dictionary.

        if key == "e_ident":

            for insideKey, insideValue in value.items():
```

```
                if insideKey == "EI_MAG":
                    pass
                else:
                    returnValue[insideKey] = insideValue
        else:
            returnValue[key] = value

    return returnValue
```

`ExtractSegmentDetails()` is used to extract all the information from the Program Header of an ELF File.

```
from elftools.elf.elffile import ELFFile


def ExtractSegmentDetails(elffile):
    returnValue = {} # Dictionary to hold the unique attributes of all
    the segments

    # Check if any segment information exists in the file
    # If it does, collect all the information of all the attributes in
    all the segments
    if(elffile.num_segments() > 0):
        prefixDict = {} # Dictionary to hold the unique segment
        attributes for all the segment names

        # Each ELF File may have one or more number of segments
        # Loop through all the segments
        for segment in elffile.iter_segments():
            prefix = ""

          # In each segment, there can be one or more number of attributes
            # The attribute "p_type" contains the segment name
```

```
# Under each segment, the attributes may be different from
the other segments

for attribute in segment.header:

    # The segment name is stored in the attribute "p_type"

    # So, we prefix the segment name to all the other
    attributes to uniquely identify each attribute for all
    the segments

    if(attribute == 'p_type'):

        ctr = 0

        prefix = segment.header[attribute]

      # Here we check if 2 or more segments have the same name

        # If there are 2 or more segments with the same name,

        # then each of the segments is uniquely identified by
        adding a running counter to the end of the segment
        name

        while True:

            if prefix in prefixDict:

                ctr += 1

                prefix = (segment.header[attribute] + "-" +
                str(ctr))

            else:

                break

        prefixDict[prefix] = 1 # Keep a note of the segments
        processed so far

    else:

      # Create a key as the "&lt;segment name&gt;-&lt;attribute name&gt;"

        # And add it to the unique list of attributes

        key = prefix + "-" + attribute
```

```
                returnValue[key] = segment.header[attribute]


    return returnValue
```

`ExtractSectionDetails()` extracts all the information from all sections in an ELF File.

```
from elftools.elf.elffile import ELFFile


def ExtractSectionDetails(elffile):

    returnValue = {}


    # ELF Files with malware contain Section Names which have been tampered.

    # If such a Section Name is found, then we store the tampered
    Section Name as a feature.

    # To be able to store these in unique attributes, we set a counter
    across the file.

    malwareSectionNameCounter = 0


    # Check if any section information exists in the file

    # If it does, collect all the information of all the attributes in
    all the sections

    if(elffile.num_sections() > 0):

        # Iterate through all the sections and gather the attributes.

        for section in elffile.iter_sections():

            # Every section has a name.

            # Section Name has to be a valid ASCII string.

            # If the Section Name contains non-ASCII characters, then
            the file has been tampered.

            if all((ord(char) > 32 and ord(char) < 128) for char in
            section.name):
```

```
        sectionName = section.name
    else:
        # In case the Section Name contains non-ASCII
        characters, we store the Section Name as a feature in
        our data set
        malwareSectionNameCounter = malwareSectionNameCounter +
        1
        sectionName = MALWARE_SECTION_NAME_PREFIX +
        str(malwareSectionNameCounter)
        returnValue[sectionName] = section.name

    # Attributes of all the sections may have the same name.
    # So, section name will be prefixed to the attribute name to
    form the key for the dictionary.
    sectionName = sectionName.lstrip('.') # Remove leading dot
    ('.') from the section name
    sectionName = sectionName.lstrip('_') # Remove leading
    underscores ('_') from the section name
    sectionName = sectionName.replace('.', '-') # Remove all the
    dots ('.') and replace with a dash ('-')
    sectionName = sectionName.strip()

    if len(sectionName) == 0:
        sectionName = EMPTY_SECTION_NAME_SUBSTITUTE

    # Every section has a header.
    # Iterate through all the attributes in the header of the
    section.
    # The attributes of the section header are prefixed by the
    section name to form the attribute name.
    for key, value in section.header.items():
```

```
            attributeName = sectionName + "-" + key

            returnValue[attributeName] = value


    return returnValue
```

The last function in this series **isELFFile()**, which is used to check if a file is a valid ELF File.

```
from elftools.elf.elffile import ELFFile


def isELFFile(file):

    with open(file, 'rb') as elffile:

        returnValue = True


        try:

            ELFFile(elffile) # The constructor of the ELFFile class checks
            whether the magic number for an ELF File exists in the
            provided file


        except:

            returnValue = False


        finally:

            elffile.close()


    return returnValue
```

Now we call the function **extractInformationFromADirectory()** to extract all the information from the six different types of ELF Files available to us. We need to call this function once for each file type. After the call to this function, we will get the number of files useful for our purpose.

```
benignFileFeatures, nValidFiles, nInvalidFiles, nFilesWithNoFileHeader,
nFilesWithNoProgramHeader, nFilesWithNoSections = \

            extractInformationFromADirectory("Data/benign_ELF/*")
```

```
print("BENIGN FILES:\nValid - %d\nInvalid - %d\nNo File Header - %d\nNo Program Header - %d\nNo Sections - %d" % \
      (nValidFiles, nInvalidFiles, nFilesWithNoFileHeader,
      nFilesWithNoProgramHeader, nFilesWithNoSections))
```

```
BENIGN FILES:
Valid - 2038
Invalid - 30
No File Header - 0
No Program Header - 0
No Sections - 10
```

We see that there are only 2,038 valid ELF Files of the benign type which can be used to create our model. The function returns a list of dictionaries of all the features extracted from an ELF File.

```
backdoorFileFeatures, nValidFiles, nInvalidFiles, nFilesWithNoFileHeader, nFilesWithNoProgramHeader, nFilesWithNoSections = \
                extractInformationFromADirectory("Data/malware_ELF/Backdoor/*")
print("BACKDOOR FILES:\nValid - %d\nInvalid - %d\nNo File Header - %d\nNo Program Header - %d\nNo Sections - %d" % \
      (nValidFiles, nInvalidFiles, nFilesWithNoFileHeader,
      nFilesWithNoProgramHeader, nFilesWithNoSections))
```

```
BACKDOOR FILES:
Valid - 589
Invalid - 36
No File Header - 0
No Program Header - 1
No Sections - 50
```

```
botnetFileFeatures, nValidFiles, nInvalidFiles, nFilesWithNoFileHeader, nFilesWithNoProgramHeader, nFilesWithNoSections = \
```

```
                extractInformationFromADirectory("Data/malware_ELF/
                Botnet/*")

print("BOTNET FILES:\nValid - %d\nInvalid - %d\nNo File Header - %d\nNo
Program Header - %d\nNo Sections - %d" % \

      (nValidFiles, nInvalidFiles, nFilesWithNoFileHeader,
      nFilesWithNoProgramHeader, nFilesWithNoSections))

BOTNET FILES:

Valid - 616

Invalid - 64

No File Header - 0

No Program Header - 0

No Sections - 33


ddosFileFeatures, nValidFiles, nInvalidFiles, nFilesWithNoFileHeader,
nFilesWithNoProgramHeader, nFilesWithNoSections = \

                extractInformationFromADirectory("Data/malware_ELF/
                Ddos/*")

print("DDOS FILES:\nValid - %d\nInvalid - %d\nNo File Header - %d\nNo
Program Header - %d\nNo Sections - %d" % \

      (nValidFiles, nInvalidFiles, nFilesWithNoFileHeader,
      nFilesWithNoProgramHeader, nFilesWithNoSections))

DDOS FILES:

Valid - 642

Invalid - 74

No File Header - 0

No Program Header - 0

No Sections - 9


trojanFileFeatures, nValidFiles, nInvalidFiles, nFilesWithNoFileHeader,
nFilesWithNoProgramHeader, nFilesWithNoSections = \
```

```
                extractInformationFromADirectory("Data/malware_ELF/
                Trojan/*")
print("TROJAN FILES:\nValid - %d\nInvalid - %d\nNo File Header - %d\nNo
Program Header - %d\nNo Sections - %d" % \
      (nValidFiles, nInvalidFiles, nFilesWithNoFileHeader,
      nFilesWithNoProgramHeader, nFilesWithNoSections))
TROJAN FILES:
Valid - 369
Invalid - 46
No File Header - 0
No Program Header - 0
No Sections - 46

virusFileFeatures, nValidFiles, nInvalidFiles, nFilesWithNoFileHeader,
nFilesWithNoProgramHeader, nFilesWithNoSections = \
                extractInformationFromADirectory("Data/malware_ELF/
                Virus/*")
print("VIRUS FILES:\nValid - %d\nInvalid - %d\nNo File Header - %d\nNo
Program Header - %d\nNo Sections - %d" % \
      (nValidFiles, nInvalidFiles, nFilesWithNoFileHeader,
      nFilesWithNoProgramHeader, nFilesWithNoSections))
VIRUS FILES:
Valid - 452
Invalid - 29
No File Header - 0
No Program Header - 0
No Sections - 58
```

At this stage, we have six lists of dictionaries. We will now determine all the unique features available in the input files provided as the training set. This is done by making a set of all the unique keys in the dictionaries. In Python, a **set** is a data structure in which there can be no duplicate entries (For example, if we try to make a set using three elements as 'a', 'b', 'a', the set will contain ('a', 'b')). So, using a set will ensure that we have only the unique features extracted from the input ELF Files. We save the unique features to the variable **featureList**.

```
featureList = set()


for i in benignFileFeatures:

    for k in i.keys():

        if type(k) == int:

            featureList.add(NUMERIC_COLUMN_IDENTIFIER + str(k))

        else:

            featureList.add(k)


for i in backdoorFileFeatures:

    for k in i.keys():

        if type(k) == int:

            featureList.add(NUMERIC_COLUMN_IDENTIFIER + str(k))

        else:

            featureList.add(k)


for i in botnetFileFeatures:

    for k in i.keys():

        if type(k) == int:

            featureList.add(NUMERIC_COLUMN_IDENTIFIER + str(k))

        else:

            featureList.add(k)


for i in ddosFileFeatures:
```

```
    for k in i.keys():
        if type(k) == int:
            featureList.add(NUMERIC_COLUMN_IDENTIFIER + str(k))
        else:
            featureList.add(k)

for i in trojanFileFeatures:
    for k in i.keys():
        if type(k) == int:
            featureList.add(NUMERIC_COLUMN_IDENTIFIER + str(k))
        else:
            featureList.add(k)

for i in virusFileFeatures:
    for k in i.keys():
        if type(k) == int:
            featureList.add(NUMERIC_COLUMN_IDENTIFIER + str(k))
        else:
            featureList.add(k)
import pickle

pickle.dump(featureList, open("./FeatureList", 'wb'))
```

At the end of this step, we used the **pickle** library to save the variable **featureList** to a file. This is so we can load this object from the file instead of computing it again. You would be aware that all ELF Files are stored on the disk, and disk Input/Output (I/O) always has higher latency than reading from memory. So, having saved the **featureList** to a file, we can read just one file and get the list of all features instead of reading all the input ELF files.

Now we write a function to read all the features of the different file types stored as a list of dictionaries and create a data frame containing all the data needed to create the model. The function **fillDataInDataFrame()** takes a list of dictionaries as input and outputs a data frame. We must call this function six times for our six different file types.

```
import pandas as pd


def fillDataInDataFrame(featureDictionary, p_featureList, fileType):

    # Create an Dummy variable to hold a DataFrame object

    df = None


    for record in featureDictionary:

        # Create an empty Dictionary

        oneRecord = {}


        # Initialize all the columns

        for colName in p_featureList:

            oneRecord[colName] = pd.to_numeric(0, downcast = 'integer')


        # Loop through all the features in a record

        for k in record.keys():

            # Extract the column name from the record

            if type(k) == int:

                extractedColumnName = NUMERIC_COLUMN_IDENTIFIER + str(k)

            else:

                extractedColumnName = k


            # Check if the column name exists in the feature list

            if extractedColumnName in p_featureList:
```

```
            # Extract the value for the key and store in the Dictionary

            if ((type(record[k]) == int) | (type(record[k]) == float)):

                oneRecord[extractedColumnName] = pd.to_
                numeric(record[k], downcast = 'integer')

             else:

                oneRecord[extractedColumnName] = record[k]

        # Add column to mark Dependent Column as per the provided File Type

        oneRecord[FILE_TYPE_COLUMN_NAME] = pd.to_numeric(fileType,
        downcast = 'integer')


        # Add the Record to the Data Frame

        if df is None:

            df = pd.DataFrame([oneRecord], columns = oneRecord.keys())

        else:

            df = pd.concat([df, pd.DataFrame([oneRecord], columns =
            oneRecord.keys())],

                               ignore_index = True)


    return df
```

Now, we will call the function **fillDataInDataFrame()** for the six different file types.

```
benignFileDF = fillDataInDataFrame(benignFileFeatures, featureList,
BENIGN_FILE)

backdoorFileDF = fillDataInDataFrame(backdoorFileFeatures, featureList,
BACKDOOR_FILE)

botnetFileDF = fillDataInDataFrame(botnetFileFeatures, featureList,
BOTNET_FILE)

ddosFileDF = fillDataInDataFrame(ddosFileFeatures, featureList, DDOS_
FILE)
```

```
trojanFileDF = fillDataInDataFrame(trojanFileFeatures, featureList,
TROJAN_FILE)
virusFileDF = fillDataInDataFrame(virusFileFeatures, featureList, VIRUS_
FILE)
```

So now we have six data frames containing the data required for modeling. However, we need one data frame to contain all the data for modeling. We will concatenate these six data frames into a single data frame.

```
import pandas as pd


df = pd.concat([benignFileDF,
                backdoorFileDF,
                botnetFileDF,
                ddosFileDF,
                trojanFileDF,
                virusFileDF], ignore_index=True)
df[FILE_TYPE_COLUMN_NAME] = pd.to_numeric(df[FILE_TYPE_COLUMN_NAME],
                                          downcast = 'integer')
```

So now we have a data frame named **df** containing labeled data, which can be processed further to create the model's dataset.

Preparing the data for creating the model

Before we proceed further, we need to remove all the **NULL characters** (character 0) from the data in the data frame **df**. This is because when our following code reads this data, it will stop reading it further if it encounters a **NULL character**.

```
# Remove NULL character from all the Strings
for col in df.columns:
    if df[col].dtypes == 'object':
        df[col].replace(chr(0), '', inplace = True)
```

At this stage, let us check how many data points we have for the six file types.

```
df[FILE_TYPE_COLUMN_NAME].value_counts()
```

```
0    2038
3     642
2     616
1     589
5     452
4     369
Name: FileType, dtype: int64
df.shape
(4706, 2540)
```

Note that we have 4,706 data points, each containing 2,540 features. However, we see that the number of data points for each file type is quite varied. So, this is an unbalanced dataset. Later, we must balance this dataset to develop a better model. We cannot balance the dataset at this point as the dataset contains both numeric and non-numeric data. Before balancing the dataset, we need all the data to be numeric.

When you try this program, you will realize that the program so far, to execute to this point, will take a reasonable amount of time. So that we do not have to spend this time every time, we can save the dataset to a **Comma Separated Values (CSV)** File. Once we do that, next time, we can start our effort for creating the model by loading this CSV File into a data frame. We can read a CSV File and create a data frame from the file's contents by using the function **`read_csv()`** from the **pandas** library.

```
df.to_csv('./ELFDataSet.csv')
```

We discussed that the dataset's contents can be numeric and non-numeric. We can use the numeric contents of the dataset to create the model. However, before we can use the non-numeric contents to create the model, we need to find a way to convert these non-numeric contents to numeric contents.

To achieve this, we will separate the numeric and non-numeric contents. Then we will form a single string for each data point to contain all the non-numeric values for that data point. We will use the TF-IDF Vectorizer on these strings to create the TF-IDF vectors. TF-IDF vectors will only contain numbers. Once we have the TF-IDF vectors, we will concatenate these vectors for each data point to the numeric data for the data points. This way, we will have a set of features for each data point which will only contain numeric data.

The following code separates the numeric and non-numeric features:

```
import numpy as np


dfNumeric = df.select_dtypes(include = [np.number])

dfNonNumeric = df.select_dtypes(exclude = [np.number])

print(dfNumeric.shape)

print(dfNonNumeric.shape)

(4706, 2274)

(4706, 266)
```

Note that we have 2,274 numeric and 266 non-numeric features.

We will treat the non-numeric features further to form a single string for each data point.

```
dfNonNumeric['ConcatenatedString'] = ""

for i in range(len(dfNonNumeric)):

    oneStr = ""

    for col in dfNonNumeric.columns:

        if type(dfNonNumeric[col][i]) == type("abc"):

            oneStr = oneStr + " " + dfNonNumeric[col][i]


    dfNonNumeric.loc[i, 'ConcatenatedString'] = oneStr


dfNonNumeric['ConcatenatedString'].head()

0      SHT_PROGBITS SHT_GNU_versym ELFCLASS64 SHT_PR...

1      SHT_PROGBITS SHT_PROGBITS SHT_NOBITS SHT_PROG...

2      SHT_PROGBITS SHT_GNU_versym ELFCLASS64 SHT_PR...

3      SHT_PROGBITS SHT_GNU_versym ELFCLASS64 SHT_PR...

4      SHT_PROGBITS SHT_GNU_versym ELFCLASS64 SHT_PR...

Name: ConcatenatedString, dtype: object
```

Note that we have created the column named **ConcatenatedString**. We will use the data in this column to create TF-IDF vectors.

The following code forms TF-IDF vectors:

```
from sklearn.feature_extraction.text import TfidfVectorizer


tfidfconverter = TfidfVectorizer(max_features = 90000, ngram_range = (1,1))

arrNonNumericTFIDF = tfidfconverter.fit_transform(dfNonNumeric.
ConcatenatedString).toarray()

dfNonNumericTFIDF = pd.DataFrame(arrNonNumericTFIDF,

                                 columns = tfidfconverter.get_feature_
                                 names())

print(dfNonNumericTFIDF.shape)

(4706, 53)
```

Note that we now have 53 more features.

The following code concatenates the features containing numeric data and the TF-IDF vectors:

```
import pandas as pd


dfForModel = pd.concat([dfNumeric, dfNonNumericTFIDF], axis = 1)

import pickle


print(dfForModel.shape)

pickle.dump(dfForModel, open(“./XColumns”, ‘wb’))

(4706, 2327)
```

Note that we now have 4,706 data points, each containing 2,327 features. The dataset is stored in the variable **dfForModel**.

The data frame **dfForModel** contains only numeric data. We can use this data frame to balance the data. The following code creates a balanced dataset:

```
import imblearn as ib
```

```
XTransform = dfForModel.drop([FILE_TYPE_COLUMN_NAME], axis = 1)
yTransform = dfForModel[FILE_TYPE_COLUMN_NAME]

# Transform the dataset
oversample = ib.over_sampling.SMOTE(random_state = 42)
XTrain, yTrain = oversample.fit_resample(XTransform, yTransform)
print(XTrain.shape)
print(yTrain.value_counts())
(12228, 2326)
0    2038
1    2038
2    2038
3    2038
4    2038
5    2038
Name: FileType, dtype: int64
```

Note that, we now have 2,038 data points for each file type.

Building Random Forest model

Having prepared the data, we can now create the model. The following code creates the Random Forest model.

```
From sklearn.ensemble import RandomForestClassifier
import datetime
import pickle

print('Start Time: %s' % datetime.datetime.now())

# Create the Random Forest Model
modelRF = RandomForestClassifier(n_estimators = 1000,
```

```
                                    criterion = "entropy",
                                    oob_score = True)

modelRF.fit(Xtrain, yTrain)
pickle.dump(modelRF, open("./RFModelELFMalwareDetection", 'wb'))

print('End Time: %s' % datetime.datetime.now())
Start Time: 2023-03-08 23:28:26.552642
End Time: 2023-03-08 23:29:26.652041
```

Note that the model is saved to the file after creating the model. This is an essential step when we need to create an application to make predictions using the model. Typically, we will create a web service that will load this model from this file and call the method(s) to make predictions for the input data provided to the web service. The web service could be called by any client application which will send the input data. In such a case, the input data would be one or more ELF file(s) to be tested for whether it contains malware.

Now that the model has been built, we will check the metrics of the model on the training dataset.

```
Import matplotlib.pyplot as plt
import seaborn as sns
from sklearn import metrics

y_pred = modelRF.predict(Xtrain)

cm = metrics.confusion_matrix(yTrain, y_pred)

ax = plt.subplot()
sns.heatmap(cm, annot = True, fmt = 'g', ax = ax);

# labels, title and ticks
ax.set_xlabel('Predicted labels');
```

```
ax.set_ylabel('True labels');

ax.set_title('Confusion Matrix');

ax.xaxis.set_ticklabels(['Benign', 'Backdoor', 'Botnet', 'DDOS',
'Trojan', 'Virus']);

ax.yaxis.set_ticklabels(['Benign', 'Backdoor', 'Botnet', 'DDOS',
'Trojan', 'Virus']);


print("\n\n\nAccuracy of the Model:", metrics.accuracy_score(yTrain, y_
pred))

print("\n\nClassification Report\n")

print(metrics.classification_report(yTrain, y_pred))
```

```
Accuracy of the Model: 0.9868334968923782


Classification Report

              precision    recall  f1-score   support

           0       1.00      1.00      1.00      2038
           1       0.98      1.00      0.99      2038
           2       1.00      0.98      0.99      2038
           3       1.00      1.00      1.00      2038
           4       0.96      0.99      0.97      2038
           5       0.99      0.96      0.98      2038

    accuracy                           0.99     12228
   macro avg       0.99      0.99      0.99     12228
weighted avg       0.99      0.99      0.99     12228
```

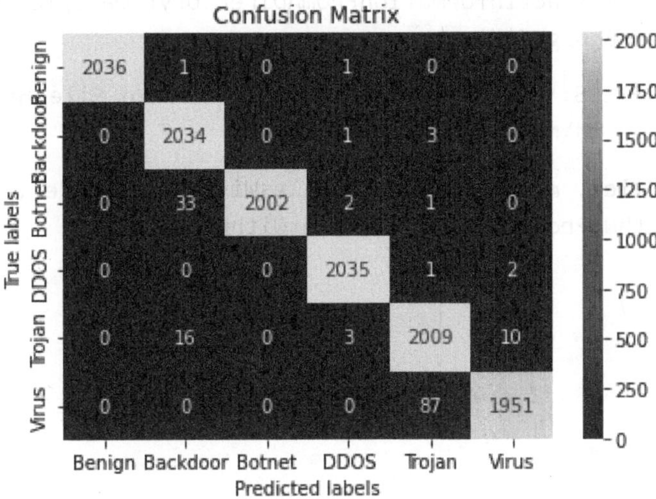

***Figure 7.4**: Confusion Matrix of the test of the model on the Training dataset*

Note that the model performs at 98.68% accuracy on the Training dataset.

Testing the model

We have the model now. We can test the model on the Test dataset that we kept aside. Note that the Test dataset is as good as the live data as the model has never seen any ELF Files in the Test dataset while the model was being created. The only difference with live data is that the Test dataset is labeled as we know whether these files contain malware or not and, if these files contain malware, what is the nature of the malware.

Before subjecting these ELF Files in the test dataset to the model, we must preprocess the data in these files.

The following steps perform all the required preprocessing and then apply the model to make predictions.

Step 1: Read all the features from the ELF files.

We have discussed that the function **`extractInformationFromADirectory()`** extracts all the information from all ELF Files in a directory. We will call this function to extract all the features of the ELF Files in the Test dataset.

```
benignTestFileFeatures,nValidFiles,nInvalidFiles,nFilesWithNoFileHeader,
nFilesWithNoProgramHeader, nFilesWithNoSections = \
```

```
                extractInformationFromADirectory("Data/TestData/
                Benign/*")

print("BENIGN FILES:\nValid - %d\nInvalid - %d\nNo File Header - %d\nNo
Program Header - %d\nNo Sections - %d" % \

      (nValidFiles, nInvalidFiles, nFilesWithNoFileHeader,
      nFilesWithNoProgramHeader, nFilesWithNoSections))

BENIGN FILES:

Valid - 222

Invalid - 10

No File Header - 0

No Program Header - 0

No Sections - 5


backdoorTestFileFeatures, nValidFiles, nInvalidFiles,
nFilesWithNoFileHeader, nFilesWithNoProgramHeader, nFilesWithNoSections
= \

                extractInformationFromADirectory("Data/TestData/
                Backdoor/*")

print("BACKDOOR FILES:\nValid - %d\nInvalid - %d\nNo File Header - %d\nNo
Program Header - %d\nNo Sections - %d" % \

      (nValidFiles, nInvalidFiles, nFilesWithNoFileHeader,
      nFilesWithNoProgramHeader, nFilesWithNoSections))

BACKDOOR FILES:

Valid - 62

Invalid - 2

No File Header - 0

No Program Header - 0

No Sections - 4
```

```
botnetTestFileFeatures,nValidFiles,nInvalidFiles,nFilesWithNoFileHeader,
nFilesWithNoProgramHeader, nFilesWithNoSections = \
                extractInformationFromADirectory("Data/TestData/
                Botnet/*")
print("BOTNET FILES:\nValid - %d\nInvalid - %d\nNo File Header - %d\nNo
Program Header - %d\nNo Sections - %d" % \
      (nValidFiles, nInvalidFiles, nFilesWithNoFileHeader,
      nFilesWithNoProgramHeader, nFilesWithNoSections))
BOTNET FILES:
Valid - 61
Invalid - 6
No File Header - 0
No Program Header - 0
No Sections - 2

ddosTestFileFeatures, nValidFiles, nInvalidFiles, nFilesWithNoFileHeader,
nFilesWithNoProgramHeader, nFilesWithNoSections = \
                extractInformationFromADirectory("Data/TestData/Ddos/*")
print("DDOS FILES:\nValid - %d\nInvalid - %d\nNo File Header - %d\nNo
Program Header - %d\nNo Sections - %d" % \
      (nValidFiles, nInvalidFiles, nFilesWithNoFileHeader,
      nFilesWithNoProgramHeader, nFilesWithNoSections))
DDOS FILES:
Valid - 71
Invalid - 3
No File Header - 0
No Program Header - 0
No Sections - 0
```

```
trojanTestFileFeatures,nValidFiles,nInvalidFiles,nFilesWithNoFileHeader,
nFilesWithNoProgramHeader, nFilesWithNoSections = \
                extractInformationFromADirectory("Data/TestData/
                Trojan/*")
print("TROJAN FILES:\nValid - %d\nInvalid - %d\nNo File Header - %d\nNo
Program Header - %d\nNo Sections - %d" % \
      (nValidFiles, nInvalidFiles, nFilesWithNoFileHeader,
      nFilesWithNoProgramHeader, nFilesWithNoSections))
TROJAN FILES:
Valid - 40
Invalid - 3
No File Header - 0
No Program Header - 0
No Sections - 4

virusTestFileFeatures,nValidFiles,nInvalidFiles,nFilesWithNoFileHeader,
nFilesWithNoProgramHeader, nFilesWithNoSections = \
                extractInformationFromADirectory("Data/TestData/
                Virus/*")
print("VIRUS FILES:\nValid - %d\nInvalid - %d\nNo File Header - %d\nNo
Program Header - %d\nNo Sections - %d" % \
      (nValidFiles, nInvalidFiles, nFilesWithNoFileHeader,
      nFilesWithNoProgramHeader, nFilesWithNoSections))
VIRUS FILES:
Valid - 48
Invalid - 4
No File Header - 0
No Program Header - 0
No Sections - 4
```

Step 2: Form a data frame of extracted features.

We will call the function **`fillDataInDataFrame()`** for each type of file to create a data frame of features for that type.

```
benignTestFileDF = fillDataInDataFrame(benignTestFileFeatures, featureList,
BENIGN_FILE)

backdoorTestFileDF = fillDataInDataFrame(backdoorTestFileFeatures,
featureList, BACKDOOR_FILE)

botnetTestFileDF = fillDataInDataFrame(botnetTestFileFeatures, featureList,
BOTNET_FILE)

ddosTestFileDF = fillDataInDataFrame(ddosTestFileFeatures, featureList,
DDOS_FILE)

trojanTestFileDF = fillDataInDataFrame(trojanTestFileFeatures, featureList,
TROJAN_FILE)

virusTestFileDF = fillDataInDataFrame(virusTestFileFeatures, featureList,
VIRUS_FILE)
```

Next, we will concatenate these six data frames to form a single data frame. This is optional, and the contents of each of the six data frames can be tested individually. However, you will realize that the coding effort will increase if this strategy is chosen.

```
import pandas as pd


dfTest = pd.concat([benignTestFileDF,

                    backdoorTestFileDF,

                    botnetTestFileDF,

                    ddosTestFileDF,

                    trojanTestFileDF,

                    virusTestFileDF], ignore_index = True)

dfTest[FILE_TYPE_COLUMN_NAME] = pd.to_numeric(dfTest[FILE_TYPE_COLUMN_
NAME],

                                              downcast = 'integer')
```

So now we have all the extracted features from all the ELF Files in the Test dataset in the data frame **dfTest**.

Step 3: Remove the NULL characters in the dataset.

We must remove the **`NULL character`** from the data in the data frame **`dfTest`**. Otherwise, the following programs may not read all the data in the data frame **`dfTest`**.

```
# Remove NULL character from all the String

for col in dfTest.columns:

    if dfTest[col].dtypes == 'object':

        dfTest[col].replace(chr(0), '', inplace = True)
```

Step 4: Separate the numeric data and the non-numeric data.

We need to separate the non-numeric data in the dataset and convert that to numeric data using the TF-IDF Vectorizer.

```
import numpy as np


dfTestNumeric = dfTest.select_dtypes(include = [np.number])

dfTestNonNumeric = dfTest.select_dtypes(exclude = [np.number])

print(dfTestNumeric.shape)

print(dfTestNonNumeric.shape)

(504, 2416)

(504, 124)
```

We have numeric data in the data frame **`dfTestNumeric`** and non-numeric data in the data frame **`dfTestNonNumeric`**.

Step 5: From the numeric data, drop all the columns that are not present in the Training Dataset

The ELF Files in the Test dataset may contain features not present in the ELF Files in Training dataset. Since we have created the model on the Training dataset, we cannot have such features in the Test dataset. We need to drop all the features from the Test dataset which are not present in the Training dataset.

```
columnsInModel = XTrain.columns

columnsToDrop = []

for col in dfTestNumeric.columns:
```

```
    if col not in set(columnsInModel):
        columnsToDrop.append(col)
dfTestNumeric.drop(columnsToDrop, axis = 1, inplace = True)
dfTestNumeric.shape
(504, 2273)
```

Step 6: Create the TF-IDF vectors for the non-numeric data.

We will convert the non-numeric data to numeric data using the TF-IDF Vectorizer. Note that we have created the TF-IDF Vectorizer on the Training dataset. We need to transform the Test data using the same TF-IDF Vectorizer.

Before we can apply the TF-IDF Vectorizer, we need to form a single string out of all the non-numeric data for each data point.

```
dfTestNonNumeric['ConcatenatedString'] = ""
for i in range(len(dfTestNonNumeric)):
    oneStr = ""
    for col in dfTestNonNumeric.columns:
        if type(dfTestNonNumeric[col][i]) == type("abc"):
            oneStr = oneStr + " " + dfTestNonNumeric[col][i]

    dfTestNonNumeric.loc[i, 'ConcatenatedString'] = oneStr

dfTestNonNumeric['ConcatenatedString'].head()
0     SHT_PROGBITS SHT_GNU_versym ELFCLASS64 SHT_PR...
1     SHT_PROGBITS SHT_GNU_versym ELFCLASS64 SHT_PR...
2     SHT_PROGBITS SHT_GNU_versym ELFCLASS64 SHT_PR...
3     SHT_PROGBITS SHT_GNU_versym ELFCLASS64 SHT_PR...
4     SHT_PROGBITS SHT_GNU_versym SHT_PROGBITS ELFC...
Name: ConcatenatedString, dtype: object
```

Now we can apply the TF-IDF Vectorizer on the column **ConcatenatedString** data frame **dfTestNonNumeric**.

```
arrTestNonNumericTFIDF = tfidfconverter.transform(dfTestNonNumeric.
ConcatenatedString).toarray()

dfTestNonNumericTFIDF = pd.DataFrame(arrTestNonNumericTFIDF, columns =
tfidfconverter.get_feature_names())

print(dfTestNonNumericTFIDF.shape)

(504, 53)
```

Step 7: Create a single data frame concatenating the numeric data and the TF-IDF vectors.

We now concatenate the data frame to contain the numeric features of the Test dataset and the TF-IDF vectors formed from the non-numeric features.

```
import pandas as pd


XTest = pd.concat([dfTestNumeric, dfTestNonNumericTFIDF], axis = 1)

print(XTest.shape)

yTest = dfTest[FILE_TYPE_COLUMN_NAME]

(504, 2326)
```

Step 8: Make the predictions.

Now that we have the data in the form that can be applied to the model, we can make the predictions.

```
import matplotlib.pyplot as plt

import seaborn as sns

from sklearn import metrics


y_pred = modelRF.predict(XTest)


cm = metrics.confusion_matrix(yTest, y_pred)


ax= plt.subplot()

sns.heatmap(cm, annot = True, fmt = 'g', ax = ax);
```

```
# labels, title and ticks

ax.set_xlabel('Predicted labels');

ax.set_ylabel('True labels');

ax.set_title('Confusion Matrix');

ax.xaxis.set_ticklabels(['Benign', 'Backdoor', 'Botnet', 'DDOS',
'Trojan', 'Virus']);

ax.yaxis.set_ticklabels(['Benign', 'Backdoor', 'Botnet', 'DDOS',
'Trojan', 'Virus']);


print("\n\n\nAccuracy of the Model:", metrics.accuracy_score(yTest, y_
pred))

print("\n\nClassification Report\n")

print(metrics.classification_report(yTest, y_pred))
```

```
Accuracy of the Model: 0.8630952380952381


Classification Report

              precision    recall  f1-score   support

           0       0.99      0.99      0.99       222
           1       0.83      0.73      0.78        62
           2       0.80      0.70      0.75        61
           3       0.82      0.87      0.84        71
           4       0.58      0.75      0.65        40
           5       0.77      0.75      0.76        48

    accuracy                           0.86       504
```

```
   macro avg       0.80      0.80      0.79       504
weighted avg       0.87      0.86      0.86       504
```

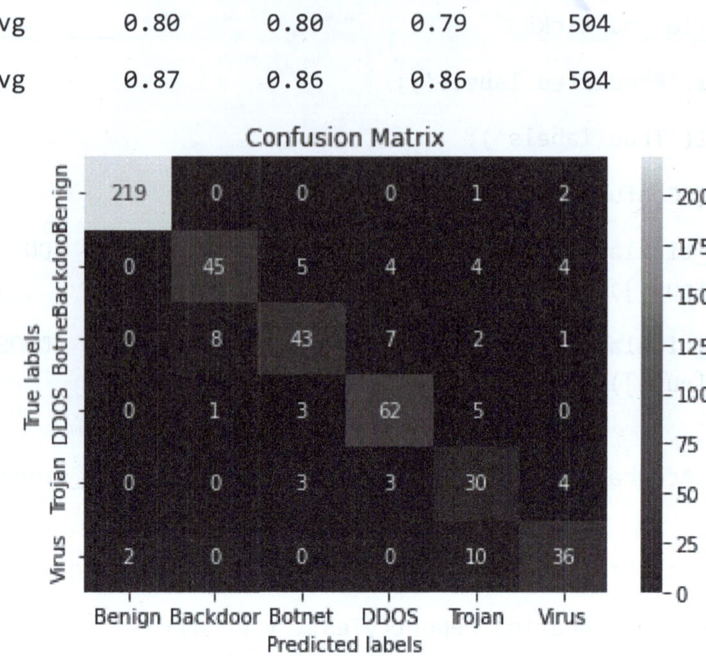

Figure 7.5: Confusion Matrix of the test of the model on the Test dataset

We get an accuracy of 86.30% on the Test dataset. The dataset to train the model is small, so this performance is excellent. As an exercise, train the Training dataset using other algorithms like the Naïve Bayes algorithm, K-Nearest algorithm, Logistic Regression algorithm, Decision Tree algorithm, Voting Ensemble Model, and Bagging Ensemble Model. Then check which models provide the best metrics on the Test dataset. **Link to Notebook: https://drive.google.com/file/d/1jgeKTBmlEFrmac4Lapw8YE_GOM3M_2bk/view?usp=share_link**

Conclusion

Random Forest algorithm is a very powerful algorithm mainly because the models built using this algorithm generalize very well and thus generally make accurate predictions on the live data. Models built using the Random Forest algorithm generally do not overfit, mainly because the component models used in the Random Forest algorithm get to train on only a tiny part of the complete data used for training.

In the next chapter, we will discuss Boosting Ensemble Models.

Points to remember

- The Random Forest algorithm is a particular case of the Bagging Ensemble Model.
- The original dataset is split horizontally and vertically in the Random Forest algorithm.
- The key to splitting the original dataset in the Random Forest algorithm is that the data distribution in each subset should be nearly the same as in the original dataset.
- The Random Forest algorithm uses the Decision Tree algorithm to train the model for each subset of the original dataset.

Chapter 8
Boosting Algorithm

The last algorithm we discuss in this book is the Boosting algorithm. In *Chapter 6, Ensemble Models,* these algorithms were called Boosting ensemble models. In Boosting ensemble models, we train on the entire original dataset in iterations using the same algorithm. The main difference is that in each iteration, we try to minimize the mistakes in predictions made in the previous iteration.

Figure 8.1

Structure

In this chapter, we will discuss the following topics:

- The AdaBoost algorithm
    - o Walkthrough of the AdaBoost algorithm
    - o AdaBoost algorithm for multi-class classification
- AdaBoost algorithm implementation in Scikit-Learn
- Recognizing traffic signs
    - o About the data
    - o Building and testing the model

Objectives

After reading this chapter, you will clearly understand the Boosting algorithm. Further, this chapter details how to capture information from image files. And this chapter discusses the mechanisms for making data from images useful for machine learning before it can be modeled.

AdaBoost algorithm

Boosting algorithms are also called Sequential ensemble models. This is because, in the Boosting algorithm, we take the complete dataset and train a model on that data. While any algorithm can be used to train a model on the dataset, generally, we use Decision Tree algorithm to train the models. Before we train the model, we assign equal weight to each data point so that each data point gets equal importance in creating the model. After training the model on the complete dataset, we discover the mistakes in predictions made by the model. On figuring out the mistakes made by the model, we assign weights to the data points such that the data points where the mistake was made in making the prediction get higher weights. This action of giving more weight to the data points where errors were made in making predictions is called **boosting**.

Having boosted the data points where mistakes were made, we trained another model using the same algorithm in creating the first model. We then make predictions from the new model. We, once again, find out the mistakes made by the new model, and boost the data points where mistakes were made to create a fresh model. We will repeat this process until we have the least errors in the predictions from the last model we train.

At the end of this exercise, we will have several models. As we generally use the Decision Tree algorithm to train these models, we will have several decision trees at the end of the exercise. When we are presented with a new data point to make a prediction, we will subject the data point to all the decision trees we trained and get a prediction from each decision tree. Then, we will consider the decision of most of the decision trees. However, we will assign a weight for every decision of each decision tree.

Adaptive Boosting (AdaBoost) is a robust boosting algorithm. This algorithm was formulated by *Yoav Freund* and *Robert Schapire* in 1995.

Let us walk through an example to understand the AdaBoost algorithm.

Walkthrough of the AdaBoost algorithm

We will use an example dataset for the walkthrough, as provided in *Table 8.1*:

x	y
0	0
1	0
2	0
3	1
4	1
5	1
6	0
7	0
8	1
9	1

***Table 8.1**: The raw data*

The data in *Table 8.1* shows that the dependent variable y has two values, 0 and 1. So, the data has been classified into two classes, 0 and 1.

The first step in building the model using AdaBoost algorithm is assigning weight to each data point. As this is the first iteration in our sequence, we give equal weights to each data point, that is, the weight for each data point will be $^1/_n$, where n is the number of data points. As we have 10 data points, each will be assigned a weight of $^1/_{10} = 0.1$, as shown in *Table 8.2*:

x	y	Weight
0	0	0.1
1	0	0.1
2	0	0.1
3	1	0.1
4	1	0.1
5	1	0.1
6	0	0.1
7	0	0.1
8	1	0.1
9	1	0.1

***Table 8.2**: Weights assigned to each data point.*

Now, we will create a Decision tree on this dataset. The Decision trees we will form will have a depth of 1, that is, the decision trees will only have one decision node, the root node. We will be creating Decision trees in each iteration of the AdaBoost algorithm. In AdaBoost terminology, these decision trees are called **Decision stumps**.

From *Chapter 5, Decision Tree Algorithm,* go through the mechanism for forming a decision tree using the Gini index. I will provide the final calculations here. After the calculations, we get the table, as shown in *Figure 8.2*:

Decision Points	mLeft	mRight	P(0|Left)		P(1|Left)		P(0|Right)		P(1|Right)		Gini(Left)	Gini(Right)	Loss
0.50	1	9	1/1	1.00000	0/1	-	4/9	0.44444	5/9	0.55556	-	0.49383	0.44444
1.00	2	8	2/2	1.00000	0/2	-	3/8	0.37500	5/8	0.62500	-	0.46875	0.37500
1.50	2	8	2/2	1.00000	0/2	-	3/8	0.37500	5/8	0.62500	-	0.46875	0.37500
2.00	3	7	3/3	1.00000	0/3	-	2/7	0.28571	5/7	0.71429	-	0.40816	0.28571
2.50	3	7	3/3	1.00000	0/3	-	2/7	0.28571	5/7	0.71429	-	0.40816	0.28571
3.00	4	6	3/4	0.75000	1/4	0.25000	2/6	0.33333	4/6	0.66667	0.37500	0.44444	0.41667
3.50	4	6	3/4	0.75000	1/4	0.25000	2/6	0.33333	4/6	0.66667	0.37500	0.44444	0.41667
4.00	5	5	3/5	0.60000	2/5	0.40000	2/5	0.40000	3/5	0.60000	0.48000	0.48000	0.48000
4.50	5	5	3/5	0.60000	2/5	0.40000	2/5	0.40000	3/5	0.60000	0.48000	0.48000	0.48000
5.00	6	4	3/6	0.50000	3/6	0.50000	2/4	0.50000	2/4	0.50000	0.50000	0.50000	0.50000
5.50	6	4	3/6	0.50000	3/6	0.50000	2/4	0.50000	2/4	0.50000	0.50000	0.50000	0.50000
6.00	7	3	4/7	0.57143	3/7	0.42857	1/3	0.33333	2/3	0.66667	0.48980	0.44444	0.47619
6.50	7	3	4/7	0.57143	3/7	0.42857	1/3	0.33333	2/3	0.66667	0.48980	0.44444	0.47619
7.00	8	2	5/8	0.62500	3/8	0.37500	0/2	-	2/2	1.00000	0.46875	-	0.37500
7.50	8	2	5/8	0.62500	3/8	0.37500	0/2	-	2/2	1.00000	0.46875	-	0.37500
8.00	9	1	5/9	0.55556	4/9	0.44444	0/1	-	1/1	1.00000	0.49383	-	0.44444
8.50	9	1	5/9	0.55556	4/9	0.44444	0/1	-	1/1	1.00000	0.49383	-	0.44444

***Figure 8.2**: Calculations for Decision Stump based on data in Table 8.1*

Figure 8.2 shows that the loss is the least for decision points x <= 2 and x <= 2.5. So, we select the root node as x <= 2.5.

Now, we see that for all the data points where x <= 2.5, y is always 0. So, we will consider that if x <= 2.5, y = 0, else y = 1. So, our decision stump is shown in *Figure 8.3*:

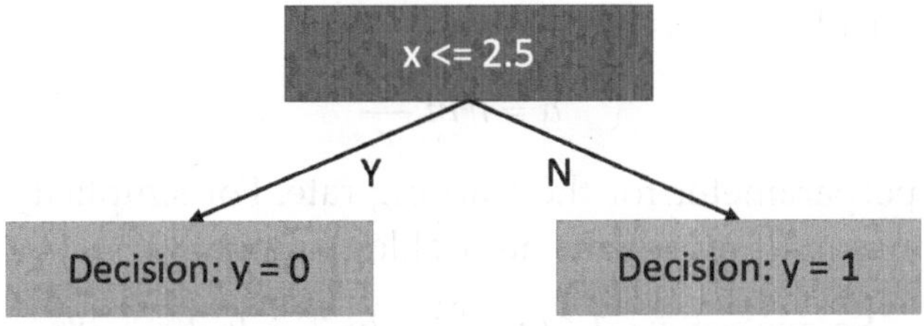

***Figure 8.3**: Decision Stump for the first tree*

Now that we have formed the decision stump let us make predictions using this decision stump on the data in *Table 8.1*, as shown in *Table 8.3*:

x	y	Weight	$\overline{y_1}$
0	0	0.1	0
1	0	0.1	0
2	0	0.1	0
3	1	0.1	1
4	1	0.1	1
5	1	0.1	1
6	0	0.1	1
7	0	0.1	1
8	1	0.1	1
9	1	01	1

***Table 8.3**: Predictions using the decision stump as shown in Figure 8.6. The predictions are in the column $\overline{y_1}$.*

We see that the predictions where x = 6 and x = 7 made using the decision tree in *Figure 8.3* on the dataset in *Table 8.1* are incorrect.

When some predictions are wrong in an iteration using the AdaBoost algorithm, we add the weights of the data points where the wrong predictions have been made. This will give a figure for the prediction error, which we will refer to as the **r**.

Table 8.3 shows that **r = 0.1 + 0.1 = 0.2.**

When we have the value for error, we can calculate the value of **α**, which will be the weight of the estimator (that is, the model we created using the decision stump).

We will boost the weights of the data points where a wrong prediction is made by a factor of **α**. We will also reduce the weights of the data points where the correct predictions were made by a factor of **α**.

The formula for calculating α is as follows:

$$\alpha = \eta \, ln \frac{1-r}{r}$$

Here η is the hyperparameter for the learning rate. For simplicity, we will assume that we have set η as 1. (lt represents natural log or loge).

$$\text{So, we get } \alpha = 1 * ln \frac{1-0.2}{0.2} = ln \frac{0.8}{0.2} = ln\ 4 = 1.386$$

Using α, we will calculate the new weights for all the data points. We calculate the new weights for the data points where wrong predictions have been made.

$$newWeightwrongPrediction = oldWeightwrongPrediction * e\alpha$$

If α is positive, the new weight will be greater than the old weight. As we apply this formula to the data points where wrong predictions have been made, these data points will get boosted.

Alongside this, we will reduce the weights of the data points where the correct predictions have been made using the following formula.

$$newWeightcorrectPrediction = oldWeightcorrectPrediction * e\text{-}\alpha$$

In this case, if α is positive, the new weight will be less than the old weight.

We calculate the new weights for the data points using these formulae, as shown in *Table 8.7*:

x	y	Weight	$\overline{y_1}$	New Weight
0	0	0.1	0	$0.1 * e^{-ln4} = 0.1 * 0.25 = 0.025$
1	0	0.1	0	$0.1 * e^{-ln4} = 0.1 * 0.25 = 0.025$
2	0	0.1	1	$0.1 * e^{-ln4} = 0.1 * 0.25 = 0.025$
3	1	0.1	1	$0.1 * e^{-ln4} = 0.1 * 0.25 = 0.025$
4	1	0.1	1	$0.1 * e^{-ln4} = 0.1 * 0.25 = 0.025$
5	1	0.1	1	$0.1 * e^{-ln4} = 0.1 * 0.25 = 0.025$
6	0	0.1	0	$0.1 * e^{ln4} = 0.1 * 4 = 0.4$
7	0	0.1	0	$0.1 * e^{ln4} = 0.1 * 4 = 0.4$
8	1	0.1	0	$0.1 * e^{-ln4} = 0.1 * 0.25 = 0.025$
9	1	01	1	$0.1 * e^{-ln4} = 0.1 * 0.25 = 0.025$

***Table 8.4**: New weights calculated for each data point*

If we add all the new weights, they may not add up to 1. This example differs, as all the new weights add up to 1. If all the new weights do not add up to 1, we need to normalize the new weights by dividing each weight by the sum of all the weights, as shown in *Table 8.8*. If you add all the values in the column **New Weight** in *Table 8.5*, you will get 1:

x	y	Weight	$\overline{y_1}$	New Weight	Normalized New Weights
0	0	0.1	0	0.025	0.025/1 = 0.025
1	0	0.1	0	0.025	0.025/1 = 0.025
2	0	0.1	1	0.400	0.025/1 = 0.025
3	1	0.1	1	0.025	0.025/1 = 0.025
4	1	0.1	1	0.025	0.025/1 = 0.025
5	1	0.1	1	0.025	0.025/1 = 0.025
6	0	0.1	0	0.025	0.400/1 = 0.400
7	0	0.1	0	0.025	0.400/1 = 0.400
8	1	0.1	0	0.400	0.025/1 = 0.025
9	1	01	1	0.025	0.025/1 = 0.025

***Table 8.5**: Normalized new weights*

So, we have completed the first iteration of using the AdaBoost algorithm at this stage.

> ***Note:*** We can get the value of r as 0.5 or greater than 0.5 or less than 0.5.
>
> If r = 0.5, then $\alpha = \eta \text{ loge} \frac{1-0.5}{0.5} = \eta \text{ loge} \frac{0.5}{0.5} = \eta \text{ loge } 1 = 0$. So, under this circumstance, the new weights will remain the same as the old weights, that is, e0 = 1. So, the model will not learn any further.
>
> Also, if r > 0.5, say 0.7, then $\alpha = \eta \text{ loge } \frac{1-0.7}{0.7} = \eta \text{ loge } \frac{0.3}{0.7} = \eta \text{ loge } 0.428 = -0.847$. So, when r > 0.5, α is negative; as a result, the data points with wrong predictions will get less weight instead of getting boosted. So, in this circumstance, the model cannot improve any further.
>
> Only when r < 0.5 α will be positive, and as a result, the data points with wrong predictions will get boosted.
>
> Remember that if r is close to 0.5, the estimator (or the model) is weak, as it merely makes a guess. If r is close to 0, the estimator is strong as it has a high chance of making the correct prediction. Also, if r is close to 1, the estimator is strong, as the chance it will make a wrong prediction is very high. If an estimator is likely to make a wrong decision, we can always flip its decision as our decision.

We will perform the next iteration so that the next model learns from the mistakes made in the first iteration. For proceeding to the next iteration, we need to form the dataset on which the data stump will be prepared.

The first step to forming the new dataset is to make ranges for each data point by cumulating the values of calculated normalized new weights, as shown in *Table 8.6*:

x	y	Weight	$\overline{y_1}$	New Weight	Normalized New Weights	Lower Limit	Upper Limit
0	0	0.1	0	0.025	0.025/1 = 0.025	0.000	0.025
1	0	0.1	0	0.025	0.025/1 = 0.025	0.025	0.050
2	0	0.1	1	0.400	0.025/1 = 0.025	0.050	0.075
3	1	0.1	1	0.025	0.025/1 = 0.025	0.075	0.100
4	1	0.1	1	0.025	0.025/1 = 0.025	0.100	0.125
5	1	0.1	1	0.025	0.025/1 = 0.025	0.125	0.150
6	0	0.1	0	0.025	0.400/1 = 0.400	0.150	0.550
7	0	0.1	0	0.025	0.400/1 = 0.400	0.550	0.950
8	1	0.1	0	0.400	0.025/1 = 0.025	0.950	0.975
9	1	01	1	0.025	0.025/1 = 0.025	0.975	1.000

Table 8.6**: Ranges formed from normalized weights. See the columns **Lower Limit** and **Upper Limit

To create the new dataset, we need to select the same number of data points as in the original dataset by randomly choosing the data points from the original dataset with replacements. One way to achieve this is to generate n number of random numbers between 0 and 1 (note that in our example, n = 10, n being the number of data points in the dataset). Based on the generated random numbers, we select the data points whose lower limit < random number < upper limit. Notice that the range for the data points where the wrong prediction was made is far larger for the data points where the correct prediction was made. So, the chance that the data point with the wrong predictions will be picked for the new dataset is much higher than the data points where the correct prediction was made.

Let us understand this by generating ten random numbers between 0 and 1:

```
import random


for x in range(10):

    n = random.uniform(0,1)
```

```
    print(n)
0.9724993774095615
0.8077553943105392
0.34226990825021064
0.7457845825725092
0.09602112485743897
0.253775848540571
0.7134304936851307
0.73542610690173
0.3530574686977209
0.5755371067120092
```

Now, the number 0.972 lies between 0.950 and 0.975. This corresponds to the data point where x = 8. So, we pick this data point for the new dataset. We follow the same method for the rest of the nine randomly generated numbers and get the dataset, as shown in *Table 8.7*:

Lower Limit	Upper Limit	Random Number	x	y
0.950	0.975	0.9724993774095615	8	1
0.550	0.950	0.8077553943105392	7	0
0.150	0.550	0.34226990825021064	6	0
0.550	0.950	0.7457845825725092	7	0
0.075	0.100	0.09602112485743897	3	1
0.150	0.550	0.253775848540571	6	0
0.550	0.950	0.7134304936851307	7	0
0.550	0.950	0.73542610690173	7	0
0.150	0.550	0.3530574686977209	6	0
0.550	0.950	0.5755371067120092	7	0

***Table 8.7**: Dataset formed for the second iteration.*

Notice that the dataset formed, as shown in *Table 8.7*, majorly contains the data points where a wrong prediction was made in the first iteration. For our convenience, let us sort these data points in *Table 8.7* in the ascending order of the value of x. We get the dataset as shown in *Table 8.8*:

x	y
3	1
6	0
6	0
6	0
7	0
7	0
7	0
7	0
7	0
8	1

Table 8.8: *Dataset as formed in Table 8.7 sorted by the value of x*

We need to assign weights for each data point. Here, we again give equal weights to each data point, as shown in *Table 8.9*:

x	y	Weight
3	1	0.1
6	0	0.1
6	0	0.1
6	0	0.1
7	0	0.1
7	0	0.1
7	0	0.1
7	0	0.1
7	0	0.1
8	1	0.1

Table 8.9: *Dataset as formed in Table 8.7 sorted by the value of x*

Now, we form the decision stump on this dataset. The calculations are shown in *Figure 8.4*:

Decision Points	mLeft	mRight	P(0|Left)		P(1|Left)		P(0|Right)		P(1|Right)		Gini(Left)	Gini(Right)	Loss
3.50	1	9	0/1	-	1/1	1.00000	8/9	0.88889	1/9	0.11111	-	0.19753	0.17778
4.00	1	9	0/1	-	1/1	1.00000	8/9	0.88889	1/9	0.11111	-	0.19753	0.17778
4.50	1	9	0/1	-	1/1	1.00000	8/9	0.88889	1/9	0.11111	-	0.19753	0.17778
5.00	1	9	0/1	-	1/1	1.00000	8/9	0.88889	1/9	0.11111	-	0.19753	0.17778
5.50	1	9	0/1	-	1/1	1.00000	8/9	0.88889	1/9	0.11111	-	0.19753	0.17778
6.00	4	6	3/4	0.75000	1/4	0.25000	5/6	0.83333	1/6	0.16667	0.37500	0.27778	0.31667
6.50	4	6	4/7	0.75000	1/4	0.25000	5/6	0.83333	1/6	0.16667	0.37500	0.27778	0.31667
7.00	9	1	8/9	0.88889	1/9	0.11111	0/1	-	1/1	1.00000	0.19753	-	0.17778
7.50	9	1	8/9	0.88889	1/9	0.11111	0/1	-	1/1	1.00000	0.19753	-	0.17778

***Figure 8.4**: Calculations for Decision Stump based on data in Table 8.8*

We select x <= 5.50 as the decision point. So, we get the decision stump, as shown in *Figure 8.5*:

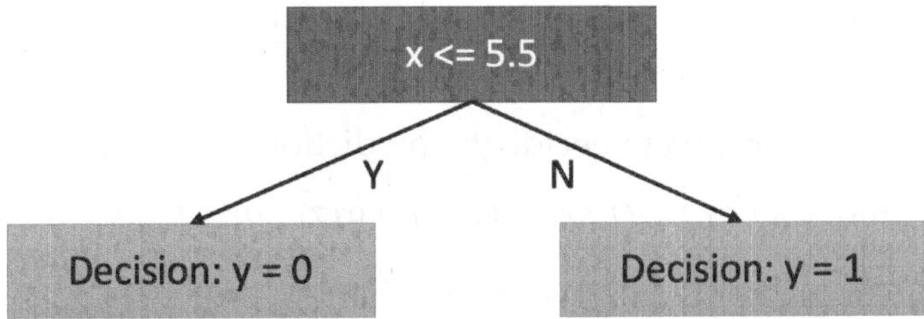

***Figure 8.5**: Decision Stump for the second tree*

Now that we have formed the decision stump, let us make predictions using this decision stump on the data in *Table 8.8*, as shown in *Table 8.10*:

x	y	Weight	$\overline{y_2}$
3	1	0.1	0
6	0	0.1	1
6	0	0.1	1
6	0	0.1	1
7	0	0.1	1
7	0	0.1	1
7	0	0.1	1
7	0	0.1	1
7	0	0.1	1
8	1	01	1

***Table 8.10**: Predictions using decision stump as shown in Figure 8.4. The predictions are in the column*

We see that the predictions where x = 3, x = 6, and x = 7 made using the decision stump in *Figure 8.5* on the dataset in *Table 8.8* are incorrect. So, we get **r = 0.9**. Now, we can calculate the value for α as

$$\alpha = 1 * ln\,\frac{1-0.9}{0.9} = ln\,\frac{0.1}{0.9} = ln\,\frac{1}{9} = ln\,0.11 = \text{-}2.917.$$

We will stop the iterations here. So, now we have the following:

α_1 = 1.386. α_1 is the weight in the final decision for the model from the first iteration.

α_2 = -2.917. α_2 is the weight in the final decision for the model from the second iteration.

We will use this model created using the AdaBoost algorithm to make predictions. Suppose that our new data point has x = 4.5. Then, according to the first decision stump (*Figure 8.3*), y = 1 (we will refer to this as p_1), and according to the second decision stump (*Figure 8.5*), y = 0 (we will refer to this as p_2).

We use the following formula to decide the prediction for the data point x = 4.5.

$$\overline{y} = \alpha 1 * p1 + \alpha 2 * p2 = (1.386 * 1) + ((\text{-}2.917) * 0) = 1.386 + 0 = 1.386$$

As the value of $\overline{y}$ is greater than 1, we decide that y = 1 for x = 4.5.

We test the model with one more new data point. Suppose that our new data point has x = 1.5. Then, according to the first decision stump (*Figure 8.3*), y = 0 (we will refer to this as p_1), and according to the second decision stump (*Figure 8.5*), y = 0 (we will refer to this as p_2).

We use the following formula to decide the prediction for the data point x = 1.5.

$$\overline{y} = \alpha 1 * p1 + \alpha 2 * p2 = (1.386 * 0) + ((\text{-}2.917) * 0) = 0 + 0 = 0$$

So, we decide that y = 0 for x = 1.5.

We will make many decision stumps when we create a model using the AdaBoost algorithm. Let us say that we create n decision stumps. Then, we will have an α for each decision stump. Let us call the α for k^{th} decision stump as α_k. Also, let us call the prediction from the kth decision stump for a new data point p_k. Then,

$$\overline{y} = \sum_{k=1}^{n} (\alpha_k * p_k).$$

> ***Note:*** Notice that while making predictions, the term (αk * pk) becomes ZERO when considering the two classes in a binary classification scenario as 0 and 1. We have used this to illustrate and keep it consistent with the other classification problems discussed in the book. However, in actual implementations of the AdaBoost algorithm, for binary classification scenarios, we will consider the two classes to be 1 and -1. In this case, when the prediction from the model is greater than 0, we will conclude that the prediction is for class 1. When the prediction from the model is less than 0, we will conclude that the prediction is for class -1.

AdaBoost algorithm for multi-class classification

AdaBoost algorithm can be used for multi-class classification. **Stagewise Modeling using a Multiclass Exponential Loss (SAMME)** is a variation of the AdaBoost algorithm used for multi-class classification. The Scikit-Learn package uses the SAMME algorithm to implement the AdaBoost algorithm.

Scikit-Learn provides two algorithms, SAMME and SAMME.R (R stands for real). SAMME is used for discrete classification, that is, its output is 0, 1, 2, and so on. SAMME.R is used for multi-class classification, and its output is probabilities of the different classes.

SAMME.R normally converges faster than SAMME.

Other variants of the AdaBoost algorithm include Real AdaBoost, Gentle AdaBoost, Modest AdaBoost, Parameterized AdaBoost, Margin-Pruning Boost, and Penalized AdaBoost.

As we have discussed, when the dataset is balanced, the accuracy of the Classification algorithm can be higher. This is true for the AdaBoost algorithm as well. Read the paper *The improved AdaBoost algorithms for imbalanced data classification*[1] for more details.

> ***Note:*** **The** AdaBoost algorithm does not require the data to be scaled because the splitting of the decision stumps is based on values.

1 https://www.sciencedirect.com/science/article/abs/pii/S0020025521002875

AdaBoost Algorithm implementation in Scikit-Learn

In the Scikit-Learn package, AdaBoost algorithm implementation is available in the library **sklearn.ensemble.AdaBoostClassifier**. The details of the essential parameters of AdaBoostClassifier are as follows:

- **`estimator`**: This parameter is used to set the algorithm that will be used to create all the models for each iteration. By default, this parameter is set to DecisionTreeClassifier (that is, using the Decision Tree algorithm for solving classification problems). Setting this parameter to DecisionTreeClassifier creates Decision Trees of depth, one at each iteration of the AdaBoost algorithm implementation. As we have discussed, these decision trees are called Decision Stumps.
- **`n_estimators`**: This parameter decides the maximum number of iterations created during the learning process. In other words, if the estimator is DecisionTreeClassifier, this parameter decides the number of decision stumps created to build the model. By default, this parameter is set to 50. However, it must be noted that no further iterations are undertaken once the model learns everything from the data (that is, the model does not make any errors in predictions).
- **`learning_rate`**: This parameter sets the value for η used in calculating α. Recall that α is the weight of the estimator when the prediction from the model built using the AdaBoost algorithm is made. The default value for learning_rate is 1.
- **`algorithm`**: By default, the Scikit-Learn implementation of the AdaBoost algorithm uses the SAMME.R algorithm. This parameter can also be set to SAMME. Recall that the SAMME algorithm makes discrete decisions, while SAMME.R provides probabilities of classes as floating-point numbers.

Note: **The** AdaBoost algorithm was initially created for solving classification problems. However, the AdaBoost algorithm can also be used for solving regression problems. In the Scikit-Learn package, AdaBoost algorithm implementation for solving regression problems is available in the library sklearn.ensemble.AdaBoostRegressor.

However, for solving regression problems using Boosting Models, it is better to use the Gradient Boosting algorithm. Two powerful and popular implementations of the Gradient Boosting algorithm are XGBoost and CATBoost. Again, note that XGBoost and CATBoost algorithms can also be used for solving classification problems.

Recognizing traffic signs

We will apply the AdaBoost algorithm to recognize traffic signs. Recognizing traffic signs is an **Image classification** problem. Traffic sign recognition is a challenging, real-world problem relevant to AI-based transportation systems. Traffic signs show a wide range of variations between classes in terms of color, shape, and the presence of pictograms or text. However, subsets of classes (For example, speed limit signs) are very similar. Further, the classifier needs to be robust against significant variations in visual appearances due to changes in illumination, partial occlusions, rotations, weather conditions, and so on. Using a comprehensive traffic sign detection dataset; here we will perform classification of traffic signs, train and evaluate the classification model created using AdaBoost algorithm.

Recognize the fact that Image Classification is best done using Neural Networks. **Convolutional Neural Networks (CNN)** works exceptionally best for image and video classification problems. However, we use AdaBoost here to demonstrate how the AdaBoost algorithm can be used.

About the data

The data for this exercise is from the **German Traffic Sign Detection Benchmark (GTSDB)**.[2] This archive contains the training set used during the IJCNN 2013 competition.

The German traffic sign detection benchmark is a single-image detection. It was introduced at the IEEE International Joint Conference on Neural Networks, 2013.

The main archive - **FullIJCNN2013.zip** - includes the images (1360 x 800 pixels) in PPM format. This file must be unzipped before the data can be used to create the model. There are 900 image files in this dataset.

A file in CSV format, named gt.txt, contains the details of the coordinates in the images where a traffic sign can be found and an associated label stating the class of the traffic sign. The text file contains lines for each traffic sign in the dataset of the form:

```
ImgNo.ppm;leftCol;topRow;rightCol;bottomRow;ClassID
```

The first field refers to the image file in which the traffic sign is located. The contents of a few image files are provided in *Figure 8.5*:

2 https://benchmark.ini.rub.de/gtsdb_dataset.html

Figure 8.6: Images of a few image files

Fields 2 to 5 describe that image's **region of interest** (**ROI**). So, in each image file, the rectangle formed between the points (leftCol, topRow) and (rightCol, bottomRow) contains the traffic sign. This portion from each image needs to be extracted for traffic sign recognition. Note that one image may have more than one traffic sign.

The ClassID is an integer number representing the kind of traffic sign. The mapping is as follows:

ClassID	Description
0	Speed limit 20 (prohibitory)
1	Speed limit 30 (prohibitory)
2	Speed limit 50 (prohibitory)
3	Speed limit 60 (prohibitory)
4	Speed limit 70 (prohibitory)
5	Speed limit 80 (prohibitory)
6	Restriction ends 80 (other)
7	Speed limit 100 (prohibitory)
8	Speed limit 120 (prohibitory)
9	No overtaking (prohibitory)
10	No overtaking (trucks) (prohibitory)
11	Priority at next intersection (danger)
12	Priority road (other)

ClassID	Description
13	Give way (other)
14	Stop (other)
15	No traffic both ways (prohibitory)
16	No trucks (prohibitory)
17	No entry (other)
18	Danger (danger)
19	Bend left (danger)
20	Bend right (danger)
21	Bend (danger)
22	Uneven road (danger)
23	Slippery road (danger)
24	Road narrows (danger)
25	Construction (danger)
26	Traffic signal (danger)
27	Pedestrian crossing (danger)
28	School crossing (danger)
29	Cycles crossing (danger)
30	Snow (danger)
31	Animals (danger)
32	Restriction ends (other)
33	Go right (mandatory)
34	Go left (mandatory)
35	Go straight (mandatory)
36	Go right or straight (mandatory)
37	Go left or straight (mandatory)
38	Keep right (mandatory)
39	Keep left (mandatory)
40	Roundabout (mandatory)
41	Restriction ends (overtaking) (other)
42	Restriction ends (overtaking (trucks)) (other)

***Table 8.11**: Description of the classes of the different traffic signs in the dataset*

As you will notice, the traffic signs have been classified into 43 classes. In the description, see that in the **Description** column in *Table 8.11*, the text is provided within brackets for each ClassID. These texts, like mandatory, danger, and so on., group the classes into super classes. So, if one would like to reduce the number of classes for the classification problem, one can form classes from these super classes.

The dataset used for this exercise can be found at:

https://sid.erda.dk/public/archives/ff17dc924eba88d5d01a807357d6614c/FullIJCNN2013.zip.

Building and testing the model

The first step is to obtain the dataset from the website where the dataset is hosted:

```
!wget -qq https://sid.erda.dk/public/archives/
ff17dc924eba88d5d01a807357d6614c/FullIJCNN2013.zip

!unzip -qq FullIJCNN2013.zip
```

The preceding shell commands download the dataset as a ZIP file and unzip the ZIP file.

Among the files extracted, we will read the file name **gt.txt** to extract all the metadata for this dataset:

```
import pandas as pd


dfLabels = pd.read_csv('./FullIJCNN2013/gt.txt', sep = ";", header =
None,

                      names = ['FileName',

                               'TopLeft',

                               'TopRight',

                               'BottomLeft',

                               'BottomRight',

                               'Label'])

print("Shape:", dfLabels.shape)

print(dfLabels.head())

Shape: (1213, 6)
```

	FileName	TopLeft	TopRight	BottomLeft	BottomRight	Label
0	00000.ppm	774	411	815	446	11
1	00001.ppm	983	388	1024	432	40
2	00001.ppm	386	494	442	552	38
3	00001.ppm	973	335	1031	390	13
4	00002.ppm	892	476	1006	592	39

Note that the dataset provides 1,213 images of traffic signs in the 900 image files. As mentioned earlier, one image file may contain more than one traffic sign.

Using the metadata, we will extract the images of the traffic signs and create a data frame containing all the information about the traffic signs using the following code. Notice that an image file can be opened using the **open()** method of the Image library. Similarly, an opened image file can be cropped using the **crop()** method, and the images can be resized using the **resize()** method.

```
import numpy as np

import os, glob

from PIL import Image

from tqdm import tqdm


RESIZE_X = 30

RESIZE_Y = 30

CHANNELS = 3


COLUMN_IDENTIFIER = 'id'

COLUMN_LABEL = 'Label'

COLUMN_FILENAME = 'FileName'

COLUMN_FILEPATH = 'FilePath'


def extractNeededPartsOfTheImage(filePath,
                                 topLeft,
```

```
                                            topRight,
                                            bottomLeft,
                                            bottomRight):
  # Read the Image
  image = Image.open(filePath)

  # Crop the portion of the image which has a signal in it
  cropped = image.crop((topLeft,
                               topRight,
                               bottomLeft,
                               bottomRight))

  # Resize the image
  imageResized = cropped.resize((RESIZE_X, RESIZE_Y))

  return imageResized

def createImageDataFrame():
  # Declare a data frame to hold all the data to use for modeling
  df = pd.DataFrame(columns = [COLUMN_FILEPATH, COLUMN_FILENAME, COLUMN_
  LABEL])
  for i in range(RESIZE_X * RESIZE_Y * CHANNELS):
    df[COLUMN_IDENTIFIER + str(i)] = None

  for filePath in tqdm(glob.glob('./FullIJCNN2013/*ppm')):
    # Get the coordinates for the file
    fileName = filePath.split("/")[-1]
    fileDetails = dfLabels.loc[dfLabels['FileName'] == fileName]
```

```
# Extract all the sections of the image which has traffic signals
for i in range(len(fileDetails)):
  imageResized = extractNeededPartsOfTheImage(filePath,
                                              fileDetails.TopLeft.
                                              tolist()[i],
                                              fileDetails.TopRight.
                                              tolist()[i],
                                              fileDetails.BottomLeft.
                                              tolist()[i],
                                              fileDetails.
                                              BottomRight.tolist()
                                              [i]
                                              )

  # Convert the image to a numpy array
  data = np.asarray(imageResized)

  # Flatten the image data to a 1-D numpy array
  data1DArray = np.ndarray.flatten(data)

  # Store the image data in the data frame
  dictTemp = {}
  for j in range(len(data1DArray)):
    dictTemp[COLUMN_IDENTIFIER + str(j)] = data1DArray[j]

  dictTemp[COLUMN_FILENAME] = fileName
  dictTemp[COLUMN_FILEPATH] = filePath
  dictTemp[COLUMN_LABEL] = fileDetails.Label.tolist()[i]
  dfTemp = pd.DataFrame([dictTemp])
```

```
        df = pd.concat([df, dfTemp]).reset_index(drop = True)

    return df

df = createImageDataFrame()
print("Shape:", df.shape)
print(df.head())
df.to_csv('./ImageData.csv', index = False)
100%|██████████| 900/900 [05:05<00:00,  2.94it/s]
Shape: (1213, 2703)
                     FilePath   FileName Label   id0  id1  id2   id3  id4
                     id5  \
0  ./FullIJCNN2013/00497.ppm  00497.ppm    38     9    9   11     9    9
11
1  ./FullIJCNN2013/00159.ppm  00159.ppm    39   111   76   69    90   70
59
2  ./FullIJCNN2013/00159.ppm  00159.ppm    39  -109  113  123  -109  116
122
3  ./FullIJCNN2013/00159.ppm  00159.ppm    38    36   45   48    25   31
34
4  ./FullIJCNN2013/00159.ppm  00159.ppm    38    65   56   34    62   54
33

   id6  ... id2690 id2691 id2692 id2693 id2694 id2695 id2696 id2697
id2698  \
0    9  ...     22     15     19     21     15     17     19     15     18
1   79  ...     38     49     43     37     43     40     34     46     43
2 -108  ...     45     37     48     31     34     39     31     29     31
3   21  ...     79     49     49     65     56     61     74     68     81
4   62  ...     37     62     51     36     56     46     34     53     44
```

```
  id2699
0     19
1     37
2     28
3     99
4     32

[5 rows x 2703 columns]
```

Note that for each image, we have 2,702 features (1 column out of the 2,703 columns being developed for the label).

Now let us visualize the images. First, we will randomly pick any data point and see the traffic sign in that image. Notice that we can use the method **imshow()** from the matplotlib library to display an image.

```
from skimage.io import imread, imshow
import matplotlib.pyplot as plt
%matplotlib inline

dfTemp = df.drop([COLUMN_FILEPATH, COLUMN_FILENAME, COLUMN_LABEL],
                 axis = 1, inplace = False)
columns = dfTemp.columns

def getImage(rowNumber):
  image1DArray = np.empty([RESIZE_X * RESIZE_Y * CHANNELS])

  for column in columns:
    columnNumber = int(column.replace(COLUMN_IDENTIFIER, ''))
    image1DArray[columnNumber] = int(dfTemp.iloc[rowNumber][column])
```

```
    imageArray = image1DArray.reshape(RESIZE_X, RESIZE_Y, CHANNELS)
    imageArray /= 255
    imageArray = np.clip(imageArray, 0, 1)

    return imageArray

imageToDisplay = getImage(701)
plt.imshow(imageToDisplay, interpolation = 'nearest')
plt.show()
```

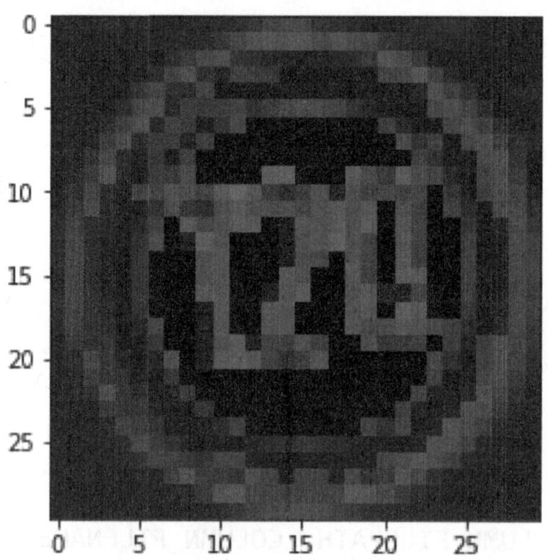

***Figure 8.7**: Image of a data point picked at random*

Now, let us see one image of each class of the traffic signs available in the dataset:

```
from mpl_toolkits.axes_grid1 import ImageGrid
import math

NUM_COLUMNS = 8

# Get the unique Labels
uniqueLabels = df[COLUMN_LABEL].unique().tolist()
```

```
displayImageList = [None] * len(uniqueLabels)
imageTitleList = [None] * len(uniqueLabels)

fig = plt.figure(figsize=(20, 15))
grid = ImageGrid(fig, 111,
                 nrows_ncols=(math.ceil(len(uniqueLabels) / NUM_
                 COLUMNS), NUM_COLUMNS),
                 axes_pad=0.1,  # pad between axes in inch.
                 )

imageNumber = 0
for i in tqdm(range(len(df))):
  labelForFile = df.loc[i][COLUMN_LABEL]
  if labelForFile in uniqueLabels:
    imageTitleList[imageNumber] = labelForFile
    displayImageList[imageNumber] = getImage(i)
    uniqueLabels.remove(labelForFile)
    imageNumber += 1

  if len(uniqueLabels) < 1:
    break

for ax, im in zip(grid, displayImageList):
    # Iterating over the grid returns the Axes.
    ax.imshow(im)

plt.show()
 52%|█████     | 626/1213 [00:06<00:05, 99.01it/s]
```

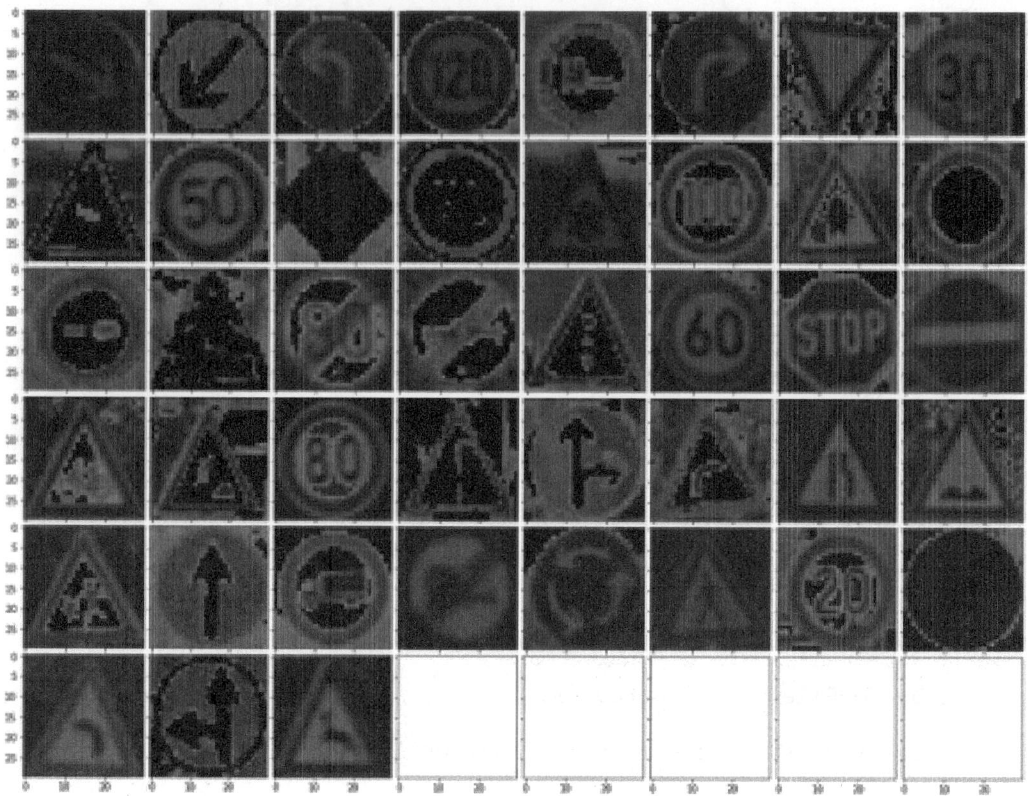

Figure 8.8: One image of each class of Traffic Signs in the dataset

Let us see the data point distribution among the different classes of traffic signs:

```
dfCounts = df[COLUMN_LABEL].value_counts().rename_axis(COLUMN_LABEL).
reset_index(name='counts')


fig = plt.figure(figsize=(20, 15))

plt.pie(dfCounts.counts, labels = dfCounts.Label, autopct='%1.2f')

plt.show()
```

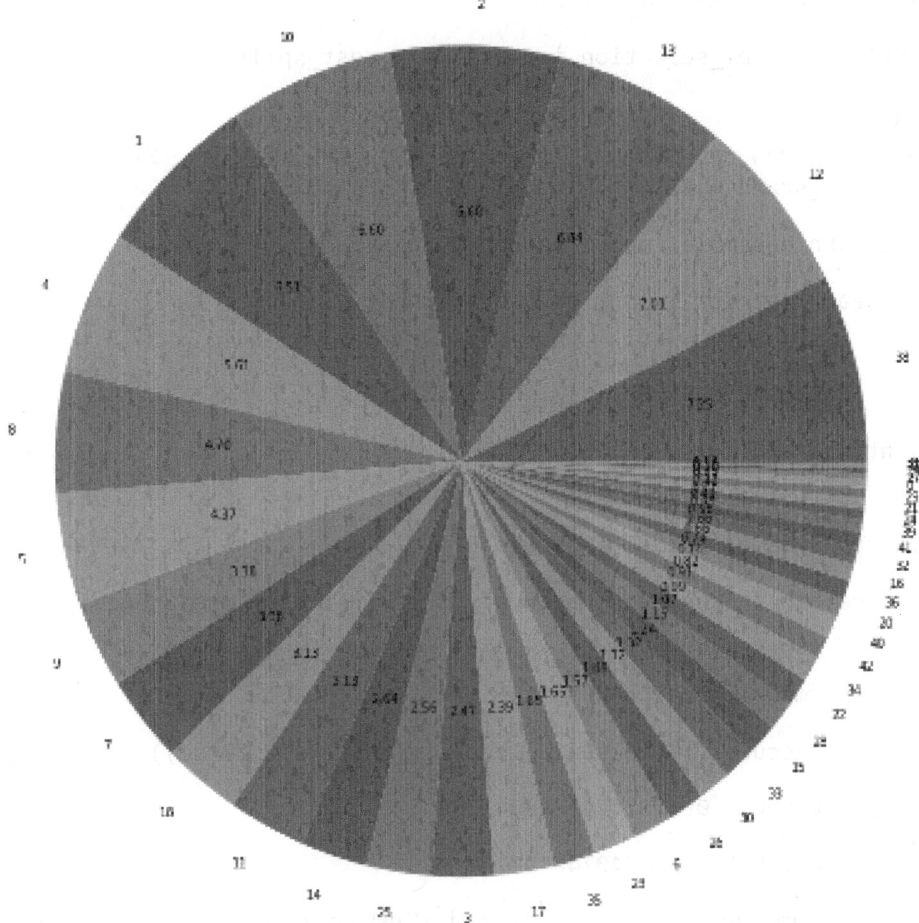

***Figure 8.9**: Distribution of data points among the different classes of Traffic Signs in the dataset*

So, the dataset is unbalanced. Nevertheless, we can use this dataset to create our Image classification model.

Now, for most image data, the pixel values are integers with values between 0 and 255. So, we will normalize the data.

```
from sklearn.preprocessing import normalize


X = normalize(dfTemp)

y = df[COLUMN_LABEL].astype('int')
```

Lastly, we train the model and test it.

```
from sklearn.model_selection import train_test_split


X_train, X_test, y_train, y_test = train_test_split(X, y, test_size =
0.2, random_state = 42)

from sklearn.ensemble import AdaBoostClassifier

from sklearn.metrics import accuracy_score


model = AdaBoostClassifier()

model.fit(X_train, y_train)


yTrainPred = model.predict(X_train)

print("Training Accuracy:", accuracy_score(y_train, yTrainPred))


yTestPred = model.predict(X_test)

print("Test Accuracy:", accuracy_score(y_test, yTestPred))

Training Accuracy: 0.10824742268041238

Test Accuracy: 0.07407407407407407
```

We get a training accuracy of 10.82% and a test accuracy of 7.4%. So, this is not a good model. As mentioned earlier, we need to use Neural Networks for Image Classification. Nevertheless, this exercise should have provided information on extracting features from images for building machine learning models.

Another question arises, how to implement the AdaBoost algorithm for classification?

For the sake of demonstration, let us train a basic neural network and see its performance. However, discussion on neural networks is beyond the scope of this book.

```
from sklearn.neural_network import MLPClassifier


model1 = MLPClassifier(activation = 'relu', random_state = 42)

model1.fit(X_train, y_train)
```

```
yTrainPred = model1.predict(X_train)

print("Training Accuracy:", accuracy_score(y_train, yTrainPred))


yTestPred = model1.predict(X_test)

print("Test Accuracy:", accuracy_score(y_test, yTestPred))

Training Accuracy: 0.9876288659793815

Test Accuracy: 0.49382716049382713
```

Notice that with a basic Neural Network, we get a test accuracy of 49.38%.

Conclusion

In this chapter, we discussed a very powerful and popular algorithm for solving classification problems: AdaBoost. The AdaBoost algorithm is a Boosting Model which works in a sequence of iterations. In each iteration, the algorithm identifies the classification errors made in the previous iteration and tries to reduce the number of errors. This process continues until the algorithm can either find that the current iteration does not make any error in classification, or the algorithm can no longer reduce the number of errors.

That is the end of this book. Refer to the annexures for details on related topics discussed in the chapters.

Happy learning!

Points to remember

- In Boosting Models, we create a sequence of models. For developing each model, we use the entire dataset initially. Also, each model is developed using the same algorithm.
- In each iteration of the sequence, the Boosting models try to eliminate the errors in the prediction made in the previous iteration.
- AdaBoost is a powerful Boosting algorithm. AdaBoost is the short form of Adaptive Boosting.
- In AdaBoost, generally, the algorithm used for training the individual models in the sequence is the Decision Tree Algorithm.

- When we create models using the AdaBoost algorithm by implementing the Decision Tree algorithm to train each model, we create decision trees of depth 1 (that is, containing only the root node and two leaf nodes). These decision trees are called Decision stumps.
- In each iteration of the AdaBoost algorithm, we find the data points where there has been an error in making a prediction and boost these data points by increasing their weights. Also, we reduce the weights of the data points where the correct prediction has been made.
- At each iteration, we calculate α, which is the individual model's weight in making the AdaBoost algorithm's final decision.

ANNEXURE 1
Jupyter Notebook

All the codes in this book have been written using Python programming. There are many platforms where Python programs can be run. In this annexure, the Jupyter Notebook is introduced. Jupyter Notebook can be used for running Python programs. Besides writing and running Python code, notes can be made using Jupyter Notebook. All the worked-out programs are provided as downloadable attachments, and this book has been created using Jupyter Notebook.

Jupyter Notebook is available free of cost. It can also be used on platforms like Google Colab.

Structure

In this annexure, we will discuss the following topics:

- Installing Jupyter notebook
- Creating a new notebook
- Adding markdowns to the notebook
- Adding code to the notebook
- Running the notebook

Installing Jupyter notebook

Instructions for installing Jupyter Notebook are available on the website.[1] While it is possible to install the Jupyter Notebook, it is better to install Jupyter Lab. The advantage of Jupyter Lab is that it allows opening more than 1 Jupyter Notebook in the same **Integrated Development Environment (IDE)**. To install Jupyter Lab, go to the shell of the machine and issue the following command.

```
pip install jupyterlab
```

Once Jupyter lab is installed, issue the following command on the shell of the machine to invoke Jupyter lab:

```
jupyter-lab
```

On invoking Jupyter Lab, one would see a web page shown in *Figure Annexure1.1*:

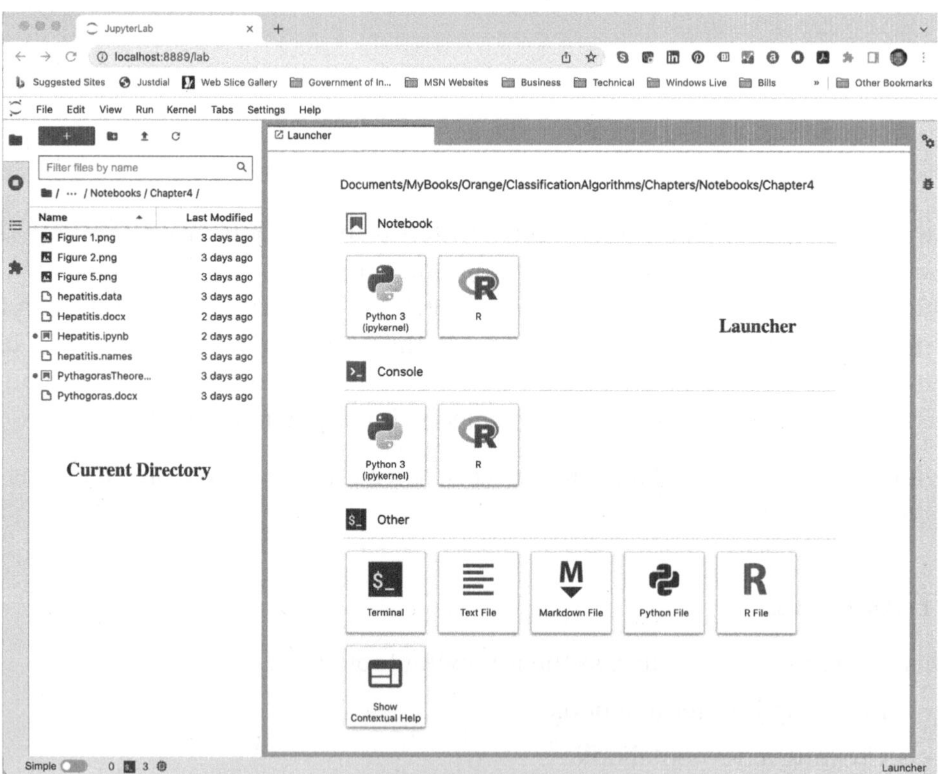

Figure Annexure1.1: Initial Screen on launching Jupyter lab

Notice that Jupyter lab opens a web page served by the local host. The initial screen has two sections. On the left-hand side, the current directory is displayed. Any file

1 https://jupyter.org/install.

from the said directory can be opened by double-clicking on the appropriate file. Also, one can change the current directory.

The Launcher on the right-hand side can open a new Notebook. Notice that Jupyter Lab can be used for creating Notebooks using Python language or R language.

> *Note:* A preferred way of installing and using Jupyter Lab and Jupyter Notebook is to install Anaconda. Anaconda provides many more tools than just the Jupyter Lab and Jupyter Notebook. While Jupyter Lab and Jupyter Notebook are available free of cost, some of the other tools require a subscription.

Creating a new notebook

Once Jupyter Lab is opened, follow these steps to create a new notebook:

1. Click the **+** button indicated by the rectangle and marked with the number **1** in *Figure Annexure1.2*.
2. After clicking the **+** button, the launcher will open on the left-hand panel. In the left-hand panel, click the **`Python`** option indicated by the rectangle and marked with the number **2** in *Figure Annexure 1.2*:

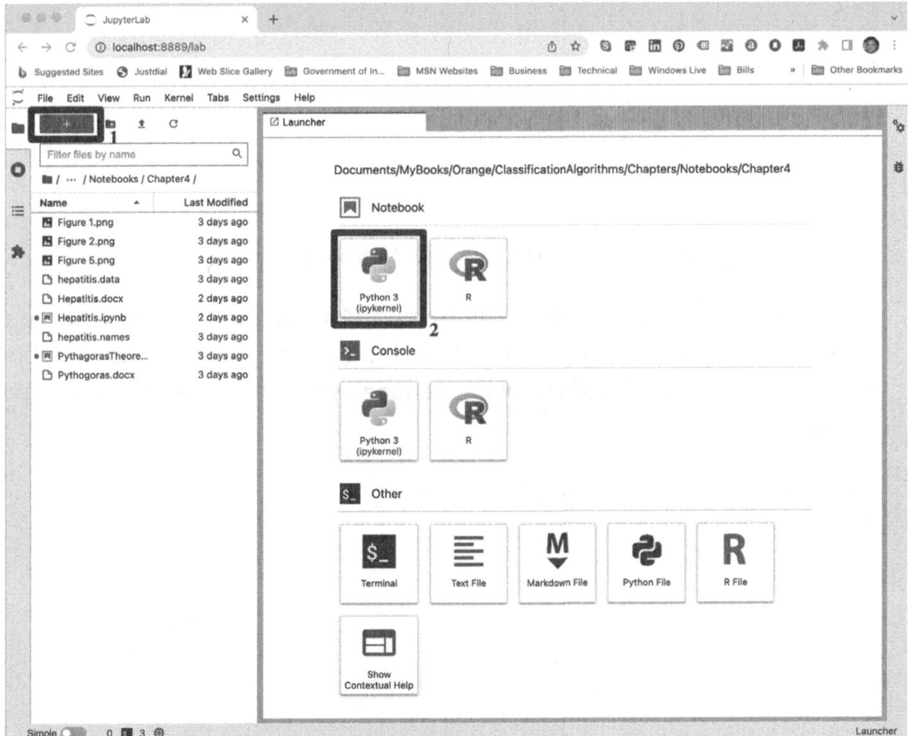

***Figure Annexure1.2**: Buttons to open a new Notebook.*

On conducting the steps stated in *Figure Annexure1.2*, the screen in *Figure Annexure1.3* is displayed:

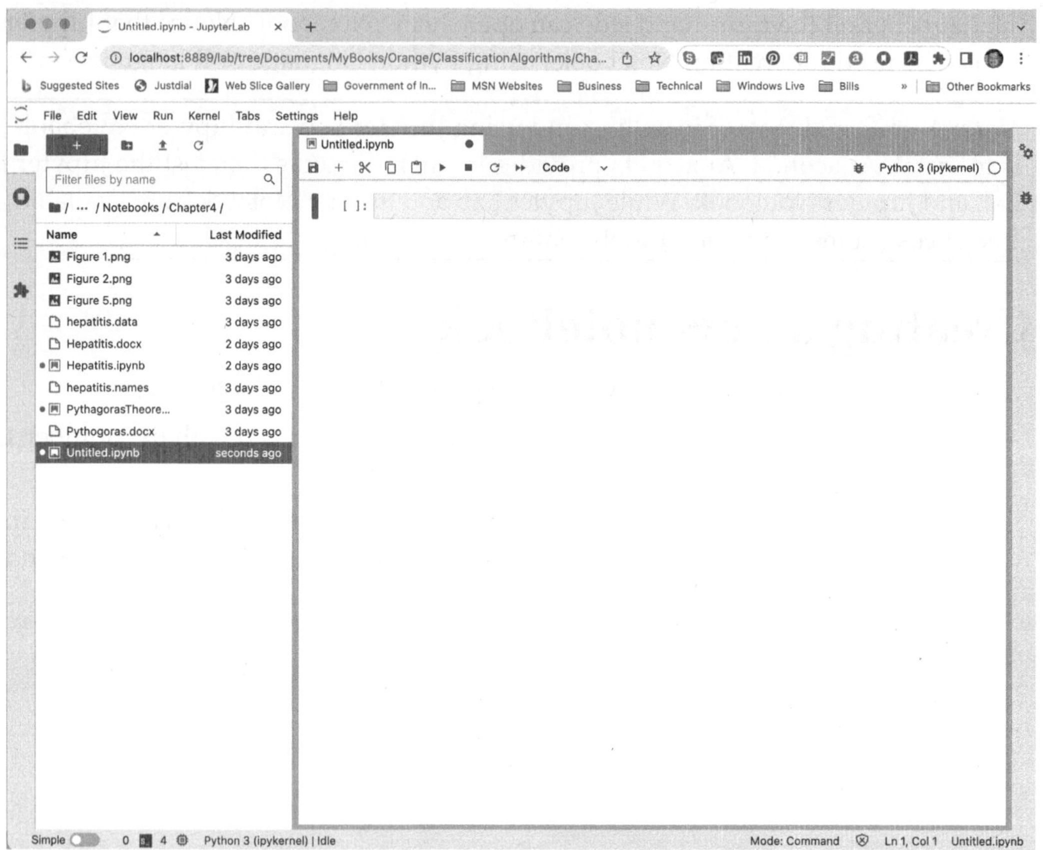

***Figure Annexure1.3**: A new Notebook is created*

3. Notice that the new Notebook is named **`Untitled.ipynb`**. The name of the Notebook can be changed by right-clicking on the name of the Notebook on the right-hand panel and choosing **`Rename`** option from the displayed pop-up menu.

Adding markdown to a notebook

The notebooks can contain code and markdowns. To add a markdown, click on the cell of the Notebook as marked by **1** in *Figure Annexure1.4*. Once the cursor is in the cell, click to select "Markdown" as indicated by **2** in *Figure Annexure1.4*:

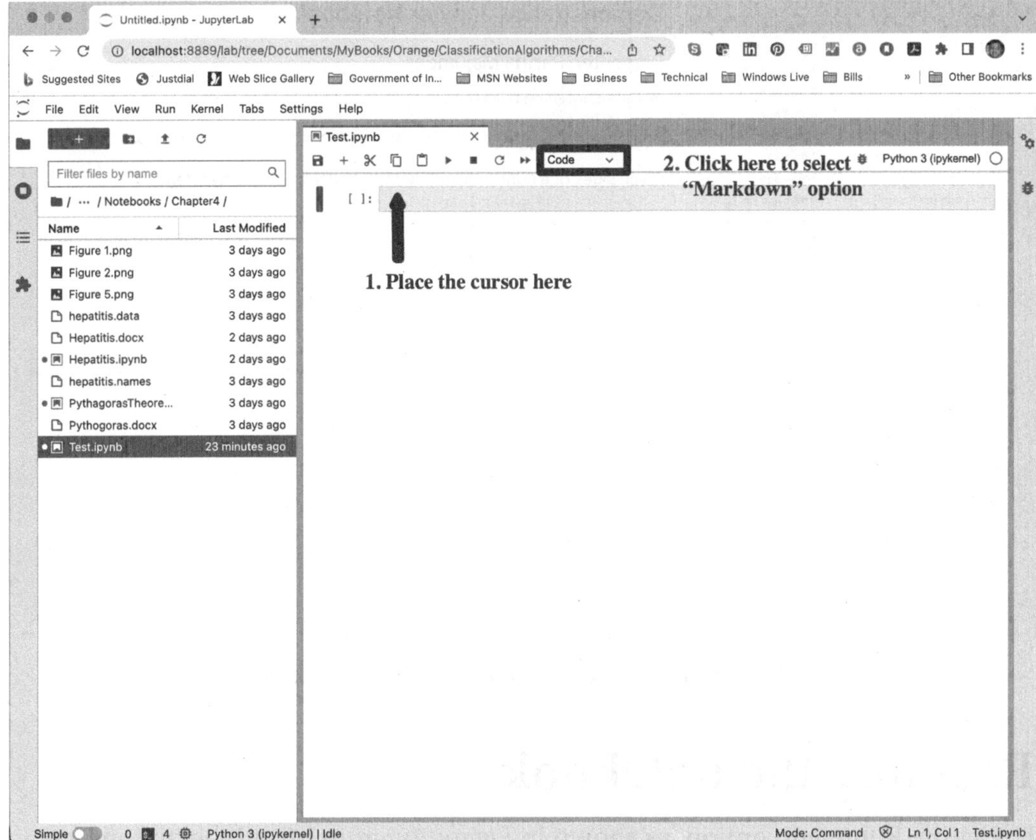

Figure Annexure1.4: *Steps for adding a Markdown*

Adding code to a notebook

The most needed feature of the notebooks is to write code and execute them. To add code, place the cursor in the cell where the code needs to be added. Ensure the cell type is `Code` as shown in *Figure Annexure1.5*:

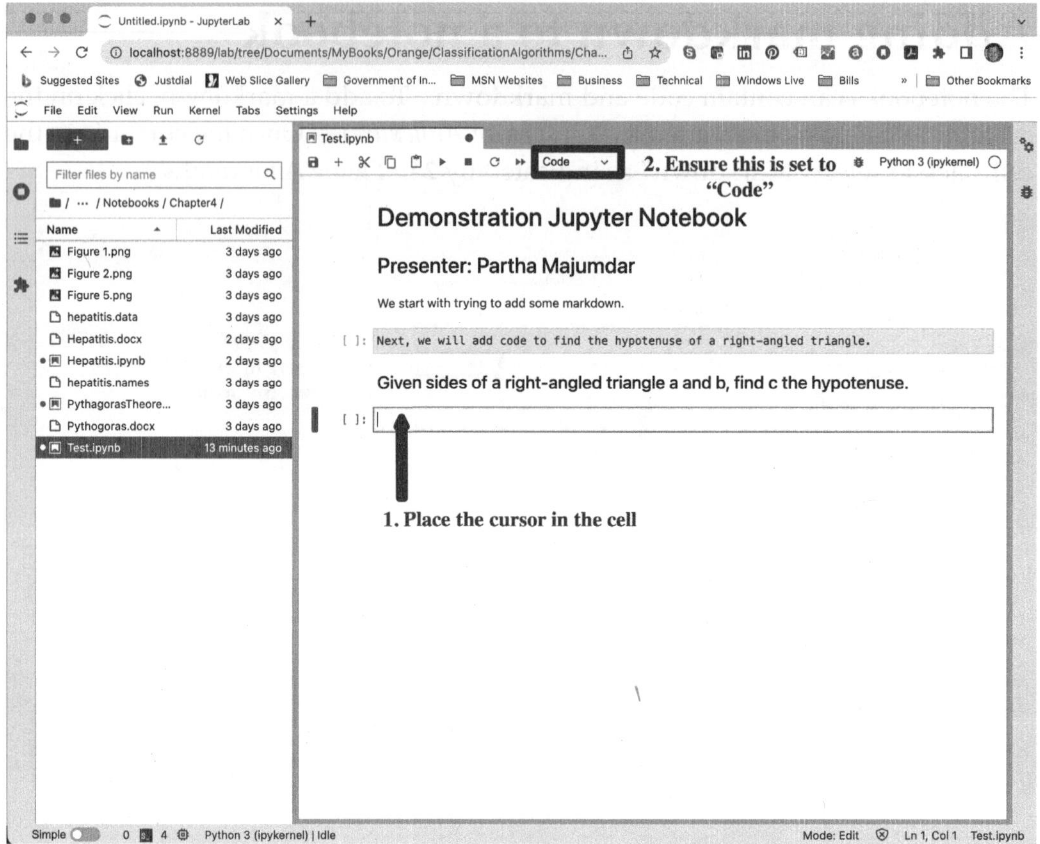

***Figure Annexure1.5**: Adding code to the notebook*

Running the notebook

Under the **Run** menu option, as shown in *Figure Annexure1.6*, all the options to run the Notebook are provided. Select the appropriate option and run the full notebook or part of the notebook.

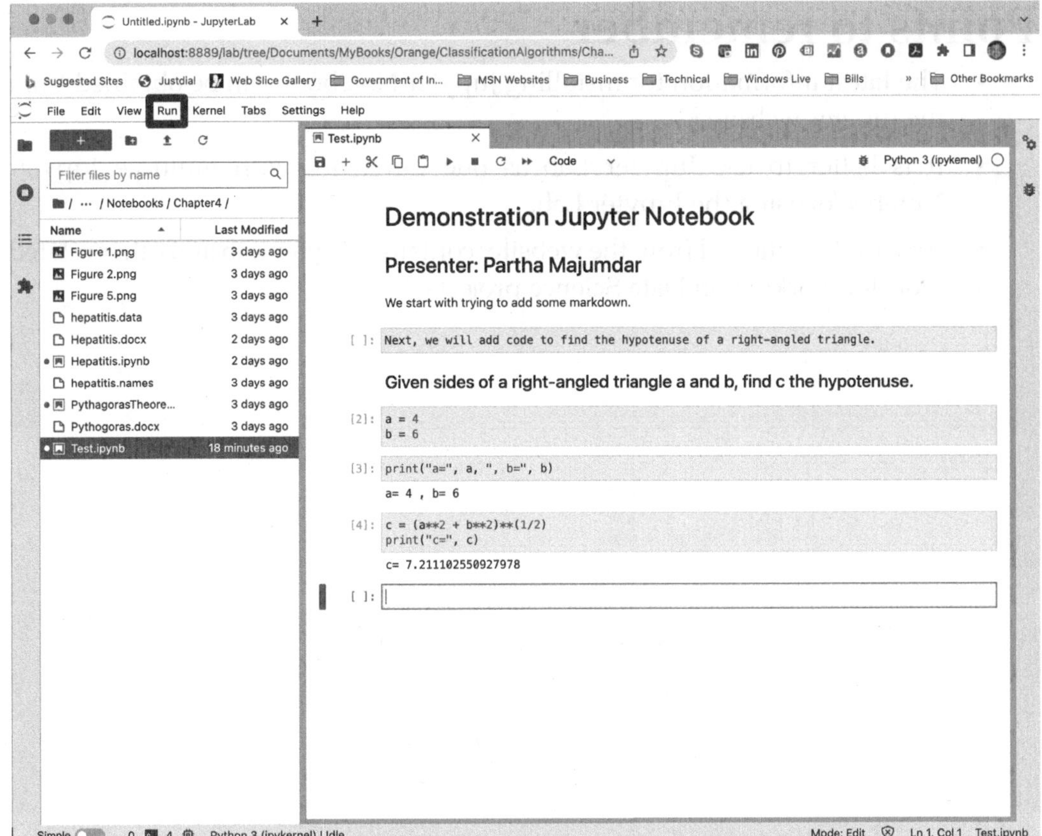

***Figure Annexure1.6**: Run the menu option marked with the rectangle*

Conclusion

It is easy to use the Jupyter notebook. This annexure discusses the essential features of the Jupyter Notebook that will be needed to use the Notebooks provided with this book. With some experience, one should take advantage of all the features of the Jupyter notebook.

Points to remember

- The latest information for installing Jupyter Notebook can be obtained from the Jupyter website.[2]
- It is better to use Jupyter Lab as one can work with multiple Jupyter Notebooks using the Jupyter Lab.
- Anaconda, obtained from the website[3] contains Jupyter Lab and other related tools for working on Data Science projects.

2 https://www.jupyter.org.
3 https://www.anaconda.org,

ANNEXURE 2
Python

All the codes in this book have been written using Python anguage. Python is a powerful and popular programming language, especially for developing Data Sciences applications. The book expects the readers to have had an exposure to Python programming. However, this annexure is a bridge in case the reader has a Python programming knowledge gap. It is assumed that the readers have experience with computer software programming and have used one or more programming languages.

This annexure introduces essential details of Python programming as it is required to understand the code in this book. Python is a vibrant language and thus requires extensive study. Basic features of Python programming have been used in this book so that the code is easily comprehensible. Readers interested in deepening Python programming are advised to search for appropriate material.

Structure

In this chapter, we will discuss the following topics:

- Data types
  - o Sequence data types
  - o Set data types

    - Boolean data types
- Operators
    - Arithmetic operators
    - Assignment operators
    - Comparison operators
    - Logical operators
- Statements
    - Condition statements
    - Loop statements
- Functions
- Using libraries in Python

Data types

Python is a dynamic programming language. Unlike languages like C, C++, or Java, there is no need to declare the data type of variables in Python. Python interpreter assigns a data type to a variable when it is declared. Let us understand this through some examples.

Everything in Python is an object. Every object in Python has three components: an identifier, a value, and a type. Suppose we declare a variable named **a** and assign it a value of **4**. Then, **a** is the identifier, and **4** is the value. Python provides the **`type()`** function to find the variable's type. Check the following code:

```
a = 4
```

Here, we have declared the variable **a** and assigned it a value of **4**.

We need to provide the variable's identifier to see variable **a**'s value.

```
type(a)
```

```
int
```

Here, we see the type of the variable **a** using the **`type()`** function. Notice that Python has created **a**, a variable of the type of integer.

Let us take another example.

```
b = 4.0
```

```
b
```

```
4.0
type(b)
float
```

Notice that we have declared **b** as a variable of the floating-point number type and assigned a value of 4.

Lastly, let us see how to declare a string-type variable.

```
c = "I am a String"
c
'I am a String'
type(c)
str
```

Sequence data types

Python provides data types that can hold sequences. These are the **Tuple**, **List**, and **Range** data types.

Tuple data types

Tuples can hold a sequence of zero or more elements of a sequence. Tuple holds immutable data. This means that the data in a Tuple cannot be changed once it is declared. To declare a Tuple, the first brackets or () are required. See the following example to understand this:

```
t = (1, 2, 3)
t
(1, 2, 3)
type(t)
tuple
```

To access the elements of a Tuple, use the syntax shown in the following code:

```
t[0]
1
```

Notice that indexing starts with 0 in Python. In other words, the index of the first element is 0.

List data types

Lists can hold a sequence of zero or more elements of a sequence. The third brackets, square brackets, or [] are required to declare a List. See the following example to understand this:

```
l = [1, 2, 3]
```

```
l
```

```
[1, 2, 3]
```

```
type(l)
```

```
list
```

We can add elements to a List using the **append()** method:

```
l.append(4)
```

```
l
```

```
[1, 2, 3, 4]
```

We can add a List to a List using the **extend()** method:

```
l.extend([5, 6, 7])
```

```
l
```

```
[1, 2, 3, 4, 5, 6, 7]
```

The way to access elements of a List is like how we access elements of a Tuple. This will apply to most data types in Python. In the following code, we access more than one list element:

```
l[1:4]
```

```
[2, 3, 4]
```

In the preceding code, we access the elements at position 1 until the element at position 4.

To access the last element of a List, we can provide the position as -1:

```
l[-1]
```

```
7
```

Try l[-2]. Also, type l[-3:-1]. You can do these operations with a Tuple as well.

To find the number of elements in a List, we can use the **len()** function:

```
len(l)

7
```

Range data types

The **range()** function is heavily used in Python programming, especially when creating loops. The **range()** function returns a sequence starting with 0 (by default) and incremented by 1 (by default). The sequence stops at a specified number supplied to the **range()** function. Let us understand this through some examples:

```
r = range(10)

r

range(0, 10)
```

The preceding code creates a sequence of 10 numbers, starting at 0 and incrementing by 1. So, **r** will return 0, 1, 2, 3, 4, 5, 6, 7, 8, 9.

The syntax for the **range()** function is **range(<start value>, <end value>, step value>)**. Let us understand this through the following example:

```
r1 = range(10, 100, 5)

for x in r1:

    print(x, end = " ")

10 15 20 25 30 35 40 45 50 55 60 65 70 75 80 85 90 95
```

Set data types

Sets can hold a sequence of zero or more elements. However, each element of a Set needs to be unique. In other words, there can be no duplicate elements in a Set. A handy feature of a Set is that when we need to get a set of unique values from a List of values, we can convert the List to a Set.

The second brackets or curly braces or {} is required to declare a Set. See the following example to understand this:

```
s = {1, 2, 3}
```

```
s
```

```
{1, 2, 3}
```

```
type(s)
```

```
set
```

We can use the **add()** method to add an element to a Set:

```
s.add(4)
```

```
s
```

```
{1, 2, 3, 4}
```

However, if we try to add an element already existing in a Set, no change happens.

```
s.add(2)
```

```
s
```

```
{1, 2, 3, 4}
```

Mapping data types

Python provides a data type called a dictionary, which stores mappings. Dictionaries in Python hold key-value pairs. Let us understand this through an example in the following code:

```
d = {10: "Ram", 20: "Shyam", 30: "Jadu", 40: "Madhu"}
```

```
d
```

```
{10: 'Ram', 20: 'Shyam', 30: 'Jadu', 40: 'Madhu'}
```

Notice that the dictionary **d** contains four elements, each of which is a key-value pair.

To access the values of a dictionary, we need to pass the key as shown in the following code:

```
d[20]
```

```
'Shyam'
```

To see all the keys in a dictionary, we can use the **keys()** method:

```
d.keys()
```

```
dict_keys([10, 20, 30, 40])
```

To see all the values in a dictionary, we can use the **`values()`** method:

```
d.values()
```

```
dict_values(['Ram', 'Shyam', 'Jadu', 'Madhu'])
```

Boolean data types

Python provides for a Boolean data type. The Boolean variables can take two values, **True** and **False**. Notice the case of the values of the Boolean variable.

Operators

The types of operators provided by Python which are of interest in the context of this book are as follows:

- Arithmetic operators
- Assignment operators
- Comparison operators
- Logical operators

Other types of operators Python provides are Bitwise operators, Identity operators, and Membership operators.

Arithmetic operators

Table Annexure 2.1 lists the arithmetic operators provided by Python:

Operator	Description	Examples		
+	Addition	2 + 3 = 5	10 + 7 = 17	10.5 + 1.4 = 11.9
-	Subtraction	5 - 2 = 3	12 – 5 = 7	11.2 – 12.1 = -0.9
*	Multiplication	2 * 3 = 6	9 * 12 = 108	2.3 * 1.2 = 2.76
/	Division	6 / 3 = 2	9 / 2 = 4.5	9.6 / 2 = 4.8
//	Floor Division	10 // 3 = 3	5 // 2 = 2	9.8 // 3.3 = 2.0
%	Modulus	10 % 3 = 1	15 % 3 = 0	9.88 % 2.2 = 1.08
**	Power	3 ** 2 = 9	2 ** 3 = 8	4 ** (1/2) = 2

***Table Annexure 2.1**: Arithmetic Operators in Python*

Assignment operators

Table Annexure 2.2 lists the assignment operators provided by Python:

Operator	Description	Examples
=	Assign	a = 2
+=	Add and assign	a += 2 (a = a + 2)
-=	Subtract and assign	a -= 2 (a = a - 2)
*=	Multiply and assign	a *= 2 (a = a * 2)
/=	Divide and assign	a /= 2 (a = a / 2)
%=	Find Modulus and assign	a %= 2 (a = a % 2)
**=	Find Power and assign	a **= 2 (a = a **2)

Table Annexure 2.2: *Assignment Operators in Python*

Comparison operators

Table Annexure 2.3 lists the comparison operators provided by Python:

Operator	Description	Examples
==	Is Equal to	**2 == 2** is True
!=	Is Not Equal to	**3 != 2** is True
>	Greater Than	**3 > 2** is True
>=	Greater Than or Equal to	**3 >= 2** is True
<	Less Than	**2 < 3** is True
<=	Less Than or Equal to	**2 <= 3** is True

Table Annexure 2.3: *Comparison Operators in Python*

Logical operators

Table Annexure 2.4 lists the logical operators provided by Python:

Operator	Description	Examples
and	Logical AND	**(2 == 2) and (3 == 3)** is True
or	Logical OR	**(2 == 2) or (3 == 2)** is True
not	Logical NOT	**not (3 < 2)** is True

Table Annexure 2.4: *Logical Operators in Python*

Statements

Any instruction written in Python which can be interpreted and executed by Python Interpreter is called a statement. So, when we write as is shown in the following code, we have written a statement in Python:

```
a = 4
```

Here, we have declared the variable **a** and assigned it a value of **4**.

When we write multiple statements, it is called a block of statements. The following code shows a block of statements.

```
l = [1, 2, 3]

l.append(4)

l.extend([5, 6, 7])
```

Condition statements

Python provides for condition statements through the **if…elif…else** construct. The syntax for the **If** statement in Python is as follows:

```
if <condition>:

   Block to Python code

elif <condition>:

   Block to Python code

else:

   Block to Python code
```

As Python has no delimiters, indentations are extremely important in Python.

Let us understand through an example:

```
a = 20

b = 30


if a > b:

    print("a is greater")
```

```
elif b > a:
    print("b is greater")
else:
    print("Both are the same")
b is greater
```

Loop statements

Python provides the **while** construct and the **for** construct for creating loops.

while Loop statement

Let us understand the **while** loop construct through an example of printing all even numbers from 0 to 20. The following code achieves this objective:

```
ctr = 0
while ctr <= 20:
    print(ctr, end = " ")
    ctr += 2
0 2 4 6 8 10 12 14 16 18 20
```

for Loop statement

Let us start our discussion on **for** loops in Python with the same example of printing the even numbers between 0 and 20:

```
for ctr in range(0, 21, 2):
    print(ctr, end = " ")
0 2 4 6 8 10 12 14 16 18 20
```

Notice the differences with the **while** loop implementation.

Functions

Python supports functions just like any other programming language. All functions are declared with the **def** statement. We understand this through an example of printing ten even numbers given a number to start from:

```
def print10EvenNumbers(startingNumber):
    # Check if starting number is even
    if (startingNumber % 2) != 0:
        startingNumber += 1

    # Generate 10 even numbers starting with the Starting Number
    ctr = 0
    while ctr < 10:
        print(startingNumber + (ctr * 2), end = " ")
        ctr += 1
    print("\n")

print10EvenNumbers(33)
print10EvenNumbers(60)
34 36 38 40 42 44 46 48 50 52

60 62 64 66 68 70 72 74 76 78
```

Using libraries in Python

A Python library can be available to a program using the **`import`** statement. Suppose we want to find the factorial of a number and know that the **`factorial()`** function is available in the Python math library. We can import the math library and use the **`factorial()`** function from the math library, as shown in the following code:

```
import math
math.factorial(10)
3628800
```

The **`import math`** statement imports the complete math library. However, this may not always be desirable. We only need the **`factorial()`** function and not any other functions in the math library. So, we can use the **`from`** statement in these circumstances:

```
from math import factorial
factorial(10)
3628800
```

Conclusion

Python was designed to be a language for learning programming. So, the constructs of Python have been kept extremely easy. Due to this characteristic of the Python language, Python is the preferred programming language of the Scientific community, as the people here, are all domain experts and get their programming needs completed with the least effort. If one analyses the contributors to the various Python libraries, one will find people, including Physicians, Microphysicists, Mathematicians, Civil Engineers, and Mechanical Engineers, contributing to the libraries, rather than Computer Scientists or Computer Engineers.

Python is also an extremely powerful language and is nowadays heavily used in developing enterprise-class software. The best feature of Python is that there exist many libraries in Python for almost all domains. More and more libraries in Python are getting added regularly.

Points to remember

- Python provides integers, floating-point numbers, strings, and Boolean data types.
- Python provides sequence-type data types through Tuples, Lists, and Ranges.
- Python provides set type data type and dictionary type data type.
- Python provides Arithmetic Operators, Assignment Operators, Comparison Operators, and Logical Operators.
- Python has support for conditional statements and loop statements.
- Python supports functions.
- Python libraries can be made available using the import statement.

Join our book's Discord space

Join the book's Discord Workspace for Latest updates, Offers, Tech happenings around the world, New Release and Sessions with the Authors:

https://discord.bpbonline.com

ANNEXURE 3

Singular Value Decomposition

Data in any form used in Machine Learning is expressed as a Matrix. Various operations, like matrix addition, matrix subtraction, Hadamard multiplication, etc., are performed on these matrices to create the mathematical model for machine learning. As we deal with thousands and millions of data points in tens and hundreds of features, the matrix operations must be optimized. So, we need to use Linear Algebra to make these operations feasible on the computers on which we build the machine learning models.

One of the needs for matrix operation simplification is to reduce the matrix size without much loss of information from the original matrix. The **Singular Value Decomposition** (**SVD**) of a matrix is a technique for reducing the dimensions of a matrix while retaining the core information in the matrix.

In this chapter, we understand SVD through the example of Image Compression.

Structure

In this chapter, we will discuss the following topics:

- Matrix decomposition using SVD
- Image compression using SVD

- o Compressing black and white images
- o Compressing color images

Matrix decomposition using SVD

Let A be an m x n matrix with rank r. Then there exists an m x n matrix Σ for which the diagonal entries in D are the first r singular values of A, $\sigma_1 \geq \sigma_2 \geq \cdots \geq \sigma_r > 0$ and there exists an m x m orthogonal matrix U and an n x n orthogonal matrix V such that:

$$A = U \Sigma V^T$$

Any factorization $A = U\Sigma V^T$, with U and V orthogonal, Σ as $\mathbf{\Sigma} = \begin{bmatrix} D & 0 \\ 0 & 0 \end{bmatrix}$ and positive diagonal entries in D, is called a **singular value decomposition** (**SVD**) of A. U and V matrices are not uniquely determined by A, but the diagonal entries of Σ are necessarily the singular values of A. The columns of U in such a decomposition are called **left singular vectors** of A, and the columns of V are called **right singular vectors** of A.

> ***Note:*** A Square Matrix for which the Inverse of the Matrix does not exist is called a Singular Matrix. The Determinant of a Singular Matrix is always 0.
>
> Suppose A and B are two matrices of dimensions n * n. If AB = I = BA, then A and B are non-Singular Matrix. Here, I is the Identity Matrix, that is, a Matrix which has all 1s in the diagonal elements and 0s in all non-diagonal elements.

Let us understand this through an example.

Let us consider matrix A as defined below.

$$A = \begin{bmatrix} 1 & 0 & -1 \\ 1 & -1 & 1 \end{bmatrix}$$

We can see that A is a 2 * 3 matrix, i.e., A has two rows and three columns. Using SVD, we will decompose A into three matrices U, Σ, and V such that $A = U\Sigma VT$ and Σ is of the form $\begin{bmatrix} D & 0 \\ 0 & 0 \end{bmatrix}$, where D is a diagonal matrix with all positive elements.

First, we need to find the singular values σ_i. As A is not a square matrix, we find the eigenvalues of A^TA, where A^T is the transpose of matrix A.

$$B = A^TA = \begin{bmatrix} 1 & 1 \\ 0 & -1 \\ -1 & 1 \end{bmatrix} \begin{bmatrix} 1 & 0 & -1 \\ 1 & -1 & 1 \end{bmatrix} = \begin{bmatrix} 2 & -1 & 0 \\ -1 & 1 & -1 \\ 0 & -1 & 2 \end{bmatrix}$$

To find the eigenvalues of the matrix B, we need to find a scaler λ such that determinant $(B - \lambda I) = 0$, where I is an identity matrix. Determinant $(B - \lambda I)$ is written as $|B - \lambda I|$.

$$B - \lambda I = \begin{bmatrix} 2 & -1 & 0 \\ -1 & 1 & -1 \\ 0 & -1 & 2 \end{bmatrix} - (\lambda \begin{bmatrix} 1 & 0 & 0 \\ 0 & 1 & 0 \\ 0 & 0 & 1 \end{bmatrix}) = \begin{bmatrix} 2-\lambda & -1 & 0 \\ -1 & 1-\lambda & -1 \\ 0 & -1 & 2-\lambda \end{bmatrix}$$

$$|B - \lambda I| = -\lambda^3 + 5\lambda^2 - 6\lambda = 0 \qquad \text{--- eq1}$$

If we solve the equation eq1, we will get three values for λ. These three values are the eigenvalues of the matrix B or A^TA.

$$\lambda = 0, 2, 3$$

Now we need to find the eigenvectors of matrix B or A^TA. We need to find a vector X such that BX = eigenvalue for finding the eigenvectors. So, we get:

$$\begin{bmatrix} 2 & -1 & 0 \\ -1 & 1 & -1 \\ 0 & -1 & 2 \end{bmatrix} X = \begin{bmatrix} 2 & -1 & 0 \\ -1 & 1 & -1 \\ 0 & -1 & 2 \end{bmatrix} \begin{bmatrix} x_1 \\ x_2 \\ x_3 \end{bmatrix} = 0 \quad \text{--- eq2}$$

$$\begin{bmatrix} 2 & -1 & 0 \\ -1 & 1 & -1 \\ 0 & -1 & 2 \end{bmatrix} X = \begin{bmatrix} 2 & -1 & 0 \\ -1 & 1 & -1 \\ 0 & -1 & 2 \end{bmatrix} \begin{bmatrix} x_1 \\ x_2 \\ x_3 \end{bmatrix} = 2 \quad \text{--- eq3}$$

$$\begin{bmatrix} 2 & -1 & 0 \\ -1 & 1 & -1 \\ 0 & -1 & 2 \end{bmatrix} X = \begin{bmatrix} 2 & -1 & 0 \\ -1 & 1 & -1 \\ 0 & -1 & 2 \end{bmatrix} \begin{bmatrix} x_1 \\ x_2 \\ x_3 \end{bmatrix} = 3 \quad \text{--- eq4}$$

Solving the above three equations, we get the 3 eigenvectors as follows. Let us solve the equation eq2.

$$2x_1 - x_2 + 0 = 0$$

$$-x_1 + x_2 - x_3 = 0$$

$$0 - x_2 + 2x_3 = 0$$

So, we have a system of 3 equations in 3 variables. Solving, we get $x_1 = 1, x_2 = 2, x_3 = 1$. So, the eigenvector is $\begin{bmatrix} 1 \\ 2 \\ 1 \end{bmatrix}$

Similarly, we can find the other two eigenvectors as $\begin{bmatrix} -1 \\ 0 \\ 1 \end{bmatrix}$ and $\begin{bmatrix} 1 \\ -1 \\ 1 \end{bmatrix}$.

To find the matrix V, we take the eigenvectors and divide each eigenvector element by the eigenvector's norm. The norm of an eigenvector is the square root of the sum of all the elements. So, the norm of the eigenvector $\begin{bmatrix} 1 \\ 2 \\ 1 \end{bmatrix}$ is $\sqrt{1^2 + 2^2 + 1^2} = \sqrt{6}$.

Similarly, the norm of $\begin{bmatrix} -1 \\ 0 \\ 1 \end{bmatrix} = \sqrt{2}$ and the norm of $\begin{bmatrix} 1 \\ -1 \\ 1 \end{bmatrix} = \sqrt{3}$.

We need to order the eigenvectors in the same order as the eigenvalues. So, we get

$$V = \begin{bmatrix} 1/\sqrt{3} & -1/\sqrt{2} & 1/\sqrt{6} \\ -1/\sqrt{3} & 0 & 2/\sqrt{6} \\ 1/\sqrt{3} & 1/\sqrt{2} & 1/\sqrt{6} \end{bmatrix}$$

To get the matrix Σ, arrange the eigenvalues in descending order. The square roots of the eigenvalues are the singular values of the matrix A^TA. So, create the matrix Σ as follows. Here, $\sigma 1 = \sqrt{3}, \sigma 2 = \sqrt{2}, \sigma 3 = 0$.

$$\Sigma = \begin{bmatrix} \sqrt{3} & 0 & 0 \\ 0 & \sqrt{2} & 0 \\ 0 & 0 & 0 \end{bmatrix}$$

We remove the last row from Σ so that Σ is non-singular. So, we get as follows:

$$\Sigma = \begin{bmatrix} \sqrt{3} & 0 & 0 \\ 0 & \sqrt{2} & 0 \end{bmatrix}$$

If we represent $D = \begin{bmatrix} \sqrt{3} & 0 \\ 0 & \sqrt{2} \end{bmatrix}$, then we get $\Sigma = [D \quad 0]$.

We need to determine the matrix U to complete the Singular Value Decomposition. When the rank of the matrix A is r, then to construct U, we take the first r columns of U such that they are the normalized vectors Av_1, Av_2, …, and AV_r. Here, v_1, v_2, …, and v_r are the columns of the matrix V.

In our example, the rank of $A = min\{2, 3\} = 2$. So, we need to find u_1 and u_2, where u_1 and u_2 are the columns of the matrix U. So, we get

$$ui = \frac{1}{\|Av_i\|} Av_i$$

Now, $\|Av_i\| = \sqrt{\lambda_i}$. So, we get

$$ui = \frac{1}{\sqrt{\lambda_i}} Av_i$$

So, we get

$$u1 = \begin{bmatrix} 1 & 0 & -1 \\ 1 & -1 & 1 \end{bmatrix} \begin{bmatrix} 1/\sqrt{3} \\ -1/\sqrt{3} \\ 1/\sqrt{3} \end{bmatrix} / \sqrt{3} = \begin{bmatrix} 0 \\ 1 \end{bmatrix}$$

$$u2 = \begin{bmatrix} 1 & 0 & -1 \\ 1 & -1 & 1 \end{bmatrix} \begin{bmatrix} -1/\sqrt{2} \\ 0 \\ 1/\sqrt{2} \end{bmatrix} / \sqrt{2} = \begin{bmatrix} -1 \\ 0 \end{bmatrix}$$

So, we get

$$U = \begin{bmatrix} 0 & -1 \\ 1 & 0 \end{bmatrix}$$

Let us verify if $A = U\Sigma V^T$

$$U\Sigma V^T = \begin{bmatrix} 0 & -1 \\ 1 & 0 \end{bmatrix} \begin{bmatrix} \sqrt{3} & 0 & 0 \\ 0 & \sqrt{2} & 0 \end{bmatrix} \begin{bmatrix} 1/\sqrt{3} & -1/\sqrt{3} & 1/\sqrt{3} \\ -1/\sqrt{2} & 0 & 1/\sqrt{2} \\ 1/\sqrt{6} & 2/\sqrt{6} & 1/\sqrt{6} \end{bmatrix} =$$

$$\begin{bmatrix} 0 & -\sqrt{2} & 0 \\ \sqrt{3} & 0 & 0 \end{bmatrix} \begin{bmatrix} 1/\sqrt{3} & -1/\sqrt{3} & 1/\sqrt{3} \\ -1/\sqrt{2} & 0 & 1/\sqrt{2} \\ 1/\sqrt{6} & 2/\sqrt{6} & 1/\sqrt{6} \end{bmatrix} = \begin{bmatrix} 1 & 0 & -1 \\ 1 & -1 & 1 \end{bmatrix} = A$$

Now, let us reduce the dimensions of matrix A. If $A = UDVT$, we would have reduced the dimension by 1. Let us check this out:

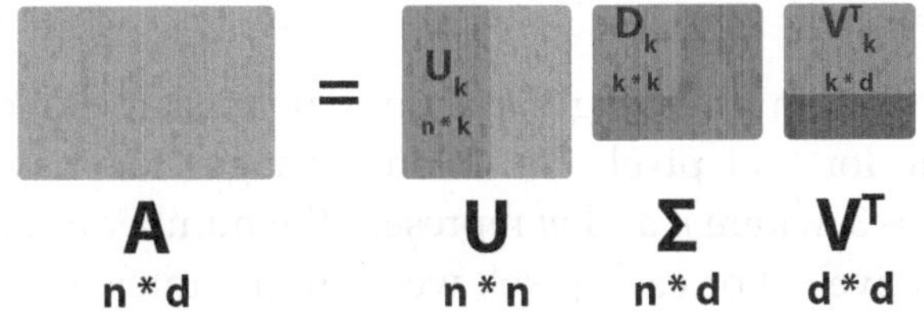

Figure Annexure 3.1: Singular Value Decomposition (SVD)

Now, we know that D is a 2 * 2 matrix. So, we keep two columns in U and 2 rows in V. We get:

$$U_2DV_2^T = \begin{bmatrix} 0 & -1 \\ 1 & 0 \end{bmatrix} \begin{bmatrix} \sqrt{3} & 0 \\ 0 & \sqrt{2} \end{bmatrix} \begin{bmatrix} 1/\sqrt{3} & -1/\sqrt{3} & 1/\sqrt{3} \\ -1/\sqrt{2} & 0 & 1/\sqrt{2} \end{bmatrix} =$$

$$\begin{bmatrix} 0 & -\sqrt{2} \\ \sqrt{3} & 0 \end{bmatrix} \begin{bmatrix} 1/\sqrt{3} & -1/\sqrt{3} & 1/\sqrt{3} \\ -1/\sqrt{2} & 0 & 1/\sqrt{2} \end{bmatrix} = \begin{bmatrix} 1 & 0 & -1 \\ 1 & -1 & 1 \end{bmatrix} = A$$

Image compression using SVD

Let A be n * m matrix. Let k be a natural number, where $k \leq$ rank $(A) \leq min\{n, m\}$.

> ***Note:*** The Rank of a Matrix is a number that is equal to the maximum number of linearly independent rows (or columns) in the Matrix.
>
> A row (or column) of a matrix is linearly independent if the row (or column) cannot be expressed as a linear combination of any of the other rows (or columns) of the matrix.

Using the SVD-decomposition of A, if $A = UDV^T$, we keep the first k values in D and set the following singular values to zero. Let us denote the resulting diagonal matrix by D_k. It is easy to see that we only need to keep the first k columns of U and the first k rows of V since their other columns would be multiplied by zeros, as shown in *Figure A3.1*. To sum up, the matrix $A_k = U_k D_k V_k^T$ is the closest matrix to A having rank k, where U_k and V_k consist of the first k columns and rows of U and V, respectively.

If A is a large matrix, n, m are large, and k is relatively small, then the information we need to store to approximate the information content stored in A is much smaller. That is, we can reduce the storage space significantly and still store almost the same information that the original matrix has.

Here we will see how a **low-rank approximation** of a matrix provides a solution to compress an image.

Images are represented in a rectangular array where each element corresponds to the grayscale value for that pixel. For colored images, we have a 3-dimensional array of size $n \times m \times 3$, where n and m represent the number of pixels vertically and horizontally, respectively. For each pixel, we store the intensity for red, green, and blue colors.

We will repeat the low-rank approximation procedure above on a larger matrix; that is, we create the low-rank approximation of a matrix that represents an image for each color separately. The resulting 3-dimensional array will be a good approximation of the original image.

Different values of k result in different compression qualities; the higher the k is, the closer the compressed image is to the original, but increasing k means larger matrices.

Compressing black and white images

We first discuss how to compress black and white images.

The image used for this demonstration can be found at this **link**.

First, we load the image.

```
import numpy as np

from PIL import Image


# Read image and store it as array

imageArray = np.array(Image.open('./TempleBW.jpeg'))

imageArray.shape

(4032, 3024)
```

So, 4032 * 3024 pixels are in this image.

We see that this is a 2-dimensional series of bytes. If we study the bytes, we will find that each contains a number between 0 and 255.

```
imageArray[:20]

array([[227, 227, 226, ..., 190, 190, 190],

       [226, 226, 228, ..., 192, 193, 193],

       [224, 226, 227, ..., 193, 195, 196],

       ...,

       [227, 226, 224, ..., 190, 190, 190],

       [228, 227, 225, ..., 192, 191, 191],

       [230, 229, 227, ..., 191, 190, 191]], dtype=uint8)
```

Each data point is an intensity value. First, let us normalize the intensity values. We will divide each data point by 255 so that each data point is a number between 0 and 1.

```
image = imageArray / 255
```

Let us plot the image.

```
import matplotlib.pyplot as plt
```

```
%matplotlib inline

# Display image
fig = plt.figure(figsize = (12, 10))
a = fig.add_subplot(1, 1, 1)
plt.tick_params(bottom = False, left = False, labelbottom = False,
labelleft = False)

imgplot = plt.imshow(image, cmap = 'gray')

plt.show()
```

***Figure Annexure 3.2**: Original Black & White image*

Let us check the space required to store the image:

```
originalBytes = image.nbytes

print("Space needed to store this image is", originalBytes/1024/1024,
'MB')
```

```
Space needed to store this image is 93.0234375 MB
```

Now, we start the process of compressing the image using the SVD method.

```
# SVD decomposition

U, D, VT = np.linalg.svd(image, full_matrices = True)

# Check for the bytes to be stored

bytesToBeStored = sum([matrix.nbytes for matrix in [U, D, VT]])

print("The matrix that we store has a total size (in bytes):",
bytesToBeStored)
```

```
The matrix that we store has a total size (in bytes): 203236992
```

We will keep only the first k values in matrix D and set the remaining to 0. Let us put $k = 1000$. 1000 is much smaller than either of the image's dimensions, which are 4032 and 3024.

```
k = 1000


# Selecting k columns from U matrix and k rows from VT matrix

U_k  = U[:, 0:k]

VT_k = VT[0:k, :]


D_k = D[0:k]

compressedBytes = sum([matrix.nbytes for matrix in [U_k, D_k, VT_k]])

print("Compressed matrix that we store now has a total size:",
compressedBytes/1024/1024, 'MB')
```

```
Compressed matrix that we store now has a total size: 53.84063720703125 MB
```

Let us see how much compression we have achieved.

```
ratio = compressedBytes / originalBytes * 100
```

```
print("The compression ratio between the original image size and the compressed image is %.2f%s" % (ratio, '%'))
```

```
The compression ratio between the original image size and the compressed image is 57.88%
```

Now let us reconstruct the compressed image.

```
imageApprox = np.dot(U_k, np.dot(np.diag(D_k), VT_k))

# Correct the pixels where intensity value is outside the range [0,1]
imageApprox[imageApprox < 0] = 0
imageApprox[imageApprox > 1] = 1
```

Now let us display our compressed image and save the compressed image.

```
import math

# Display the reconstructed image
fig = plt.figure(figsize=(math.ceil(12.0 * ratio / 100), math.ceil(10.0 * ratio / 100)))
a = fig.add_subplot(1, 1, 1)
plt.tick_params(bottom = False, left = False, labelbottom = False, labelleft = False)

imgplot = plt.imshow(imageApprox, cmap = 'gray')

plt.savefig('compressedBW.png')
plt.show()
plt.close()
```

Refer to *Figure Annexure 3.3:*

Figure Annexure 3.3: *Compressed Black & White image*

Compressing color images

Now, we walk through the process of compressing color images. The process would be the same except that we have three channels per pixel in color images - one for Red, one for Green, and one for Blue.

The image used for this demonstration can be found at this **link**.[1]

Let us load the image and visualize it.

```
imageArray = np.array(Image.open('./Temple.jpeg'))


imageArray.shape

(4032, 3024, 3)

# Normalize the intensity values in each pixel

image = imageArray / 255
```

1 https://drive.google.com/file/d/1rqGt1XnuxzBfLse0ZXeMC7RTq9EY0uG5/view

```
# Display the image

fig = plt.figure(figsize = (12, 10))

a = fig.add_subplot(1, 1, 1)

plt.tick_params(bottom = False, left = False, labelbottom = False,
labelleft = False)


imgplot = plt.imshow(image)


plt.show()
```

Figure Annexure 3.4: *Original Color image*

Let us check the space required to store the image.

```
originalBytes = image.nbytes

print("Space needed to store this image is", originalBytes / 1024 / 1024,
'MB')

Space needed to store this image is 279.0703125 MB
```

Now we start the process of compressing the image using the SVD method.

First, we break the image matrix into three matrices - one for each color channel.

```
# Break the image into three different arrays based on colors

image_red = image[:, :, 0]

image_green = image[:, :, 1]

image_blue = image[:, :, 2]
```

Then we perform SVD for each matrix. Let **`k = 1000`**.

```
U_r, D_r, VT_r = np.linalg.svd(image_red, full_matrices = True)

U_g, D_g, VT_g = np.linalg.svd(image_green, full_matrices = True)

U_b, D_b, VT_b = np.linalg.svd(image_blue, full_matrices = True)


# Check for the bytes to be stored

bytesToBeStored = sum([matrix.nbytes for matrix in [U_r, D_r, VT_r, U_g,
D_g, VT_g, U_b, D_b, VT_b]])

print("The matrices that we store have total size (in bytes):",
bytesToBeStored, 'bytes')

The matrices that we store have a total size (in bytes): 609710976 bytes

k = 1000


# Selecting k columns from U matrix and k rows from VT matrix

U_r_k  = U_r[:, 0:k]

VT_r_k = VT_r[0:k, :]

U_g_k  = U_g[:, 0:k]

VT_g_k = VT_g[0:k, :]

U_b_k  = U_b[:, 0:k]

VT_b_k = VT_b[0:k, :]


D_r_k = D_r[0:k]
```

```
D_g_k = D_g[0:k]

D_b_k = D_b[0:k]


compressedBytes = sum([matrix.nbytes for matrix in [U_r_k, D_r_k,
VT_r_k, U_g_k, D_g_k, VT_g_k, U_b_k, D_b_k, VT_b_k]])

print("Compressed matrices that we store now have total size:",
compressedBytes/1024/1024, 'MB')


ratio = compressedBytes / originalBytes * 100

print("\nThe compression ratio between the original image size and the
compressed image is %.2f%s" % (ratio, '%'))

Compressed matrices that we store now have a total size: 161.52191162109375
MB


The compression ratio between the original image size and the compressed
image is 57.88%
```

Now let us reconstruct the compressed image.

```
# Reconstruct matrices for each color

image_red_approx = np.dot(U_r_k, np.dot(np.diag(D_r_k), VT_r_k))

image_green_approx = np.dot(U_g_k, np.dot(np.diag(D_g_k), VT_g_k))

image_blue_approx = np.dot(U_b_k, np.dot(np.diag(D_b_k), VT_b_k))


# Reconstruct the original image from color matrices

imageReconstructed = np.zeros((image.shape[0], image.shape[1], 3))


imageReconstructed[:, :, 0] = image_red_approx

imageReconstructed[:, :, 1] = image_green_approx

imageReconstructed[:, :, 2] = image_blue_approx


# Correct the pixels where intensity value is outside the range [0,1]
```

```
imageReconstructed[imageReconstructed < 0] = 0

imageReconstructed[imageReconstructed > 1] = 1
```

Lastly, we display the compressed image and save it.

```
# Display the reconstructed image

fig = plt.figure(figsize=(math.ceil(12.0 * ratio / 100), math.ceil(10.0 * ratio / 100)))

a = fig.add_subplot(1, 1, 1)

plt.tick_params(bottom = False, left = False, labelbottom = False, labelleft = False)


imgplot = plt.imshow(imageReconstructed)


plt.savefig('compressed.png')

plt.show()

plt.close()
```

***Figure Annexure 3.5**: Compressed Color image*

Conclusion

In this annexure, we have seen how we can reduce the dimensions of a matrix using SVD. This method is used in many machine learning problems to reduce dimensionality. The **Principal Component Analysis (PCA)** algorithm uses this technique.

Annexure 4
Preprocessing Textual Data

When we are dealing with textual data, we receive data in documents. A document could be an article from a newspaper, a chapter of a book, a paragraph of a chapter of a book, an email, an SMS, a tweet from Twitter, a post from Facebook, etc. Each such document is called a corpus. A collection of such documents is called corpora.

Before we can analyze a corpus, it is essential to perform some preprocessing. This annexure discusses some preprocessing steps that are generally essential for any corpus. The steps discussed in this annexure are a subset of all the steps necessary for an application. Discussing all such preprocessing steps is impossible as they vary from application to application. Also, the preprocessing steps discussed in this annexure must be applied or not as per the application's needs. Lastly, one needs to decide how these preprocessing steps must be applied to the corpus per the application's needs.

Structure

In this chapter, we will discuss the following topics:

- Removing stop words
- Removing special characters
- Removing punctuations

- Removing numbers
- Removing extra white spaces
- Detecting and treating URLs in the text
- Detecting and treating email addresses in the text
- Detecting and treating hashtags and mentions in the text
- Dealing with emojis

Removing stop words

Stop Words are commonly used words in a language. In the English language, words like "I", "me", "so", "this", "that", "you", "us", etc. are termed as stop words. Generally, stop words do not add value in analyzing textual data. So, the general practice is to remove the stop words from the corpus before analyzing the data.

The list of stop words in the English Language is available in many libraries. The package **Natural Language Toolkit (nltk)** is generally used to get a list of stop words. The library nltk is available in Python and R. We will discuss how to use the nltk library to remove stop words.

Before the nltk library can be used, it must be available on the machine where it is intended. The code below installs the `nltk` library for use in Python.

```
!pip install nltk
```

This is the command to use when used from inside a Jupyter Notebook. If the `nltk` library must be installed from the shell in a Linux machine or a Mac, use the command below:

```
pip install nltk
```

The code below accepts a text as input and returns the text after removing all the stop words. The function `removeStopWords()` breaks down the text into each word in the text and analyzes whether the word is a stop word. The function joins back all the words which are not stop words in the order they appear in the text and returns the text.

```
import nltk

from   nltk.corpus import stopwords

from   nltk.tokenize import word_tokenize


# Gather the list of Stop Words
```

```
stopWordList = nltk.corpus.stopwords.words('english')


# Function to remove Stop Words

def removeStopWords(text):

    # splitting strings into tokens (list of words)

    tokens = word_tokenize(text)

    tokens = [token.strip() for token in tokens]

    # filtering out the stop words

   filtered_tokens = [token for token in tokens if token not in stopWordList]

    filtered_text = ' '.join(filtered_tokens)


    return filtered_text
```

We can test the function **removeStopWords()**.

```
removeStopWords("This is a test of Stop Word remover".lower())


'test stop word remover'
```

Removing special characters

In textual analysis, we are generally concerned about the text's words. However, there can be exceptions based on the nature of the analysis. Special characters are often removed from the text so that only words remain. We must decide at what stage we would eliminate the special characters. Special characters are parts of important text pieces, like those included in an email address, hashtags, URLs, references to persons, etc.

Removing special characters means that we need to retain only alphabets and numbers and remove all else. So, we can substitute anything which is not an alphabet or a number with an empty string. For substitution, we can use the **re** library available in Python.

```
import re


def removeSpecialCharacters(text):
```

```
    pattern = r'[^a-zA-z0-9\s]'
    return re.sub(pattern, '', text)

removeSpecialCharacters("'This'; is a #test $tring, sent: to @someone.")

'This is a test tring sent to someone'
```

Removing punctuations

This is a special case of removing special characters.

```
import string

def removePunctuations(text):
  return text.translate(str.maketrans('', '', string.punctuation))

removePunctuations("This is a test; of removal of punctuation. Does it work? Of course!!!")
'This is a test of removal of punctuation Does it work Of course'
```

Removing numbers

Many applications involve textual analysis, where numbers are optional for the analysis. For example, when making an application to detect spam SMS, we probably do not need to analyze numbers in the text. Under such circumstances, we remove the numbers from the text. The idea is to find any digits in the text and substitute them with an empty string.

```
import re

def removeNumbers(text):
    return re.sub('([0-9]+)', '', text)

removeNumbers("This text contains 66 numbers and 1654 characters.")

'This text contains  numbers and  characters.'
```

Removing extra spaces

Under most circumstances in textual analysis, a SPACE character is used as the separator between words. Having more than 1 SPACE character between words can result in errors in the analysis. So, it is best to remove extra spaces. The idea is to split the text using SPACE as the separator, and then once we have just the words, we join them back with just 1 SPACE between each word. The default separator for the **split()** function is SPACE.

```
def removeExtraWhiteSpaces(text):

    return " ".join(text.split())


removeExtraWhiteSpaces("This    is a     test of removing      extra white
spaces")


'This is a test of removing extra white spaces'
```

Detecting and treating URLs in the text

Frequently we come across text containing URLs (An URL is the Universal Resource Locator for a resource on the Internet). URLs must be included in the analysis in some applications like spam detection. There are also applications like emotion analysis; URLs are optional for the study. Even in applications where we need to analyze the URLs, we may only need to detect the presence of the URLs and not use them in the textual analysis. So, based on the requirement, we need to decide how to treat the URLs in the text.

```
import re


def identifyAndRemoveURLs(text, remove = True):

    present = re.search(r'\w+:\/{2}[\d\w-]+(\.[\d\w-]+)*(?:(?:\/
    [^\s/]*))*', text)

    if present:

        if remove:

            return re.sub(r'\w+:\/{2}[\d\w-]+(\.[\d\w-]+)*(?:(?:\/
            [^\s/]*))*', '', text), 1
```

```
        else:
            return text, 1
    else:
        return text, 0

print('Example 1:', identifyAndRemoveURLs("Click this link to register - https://www.fake.com OR this link for information - http://info.org or download this file - file://test.txt"))
print('Example 2:', identifyAndRemoveURLs('This contains no URLs'))

Example 1: ('Click this link to register -  OR this link for information -  or download this file - ', 1)
Example 2: ('This contains no URLs', 0)
```

Detecting and treating email addresses in the text

We must decide how to treat email addresses in textual analysis like URLs. In some applications, email addresses may be used as features; in others, they may not be required for analysis.

```
import re

def identifyAndRemoveEmailAddress(text, remove = True):
    present = re.search(r'[a-zA-Z0-9-_\.]+@[a-zA-Z0-9]+\.[a-z]{1,3}', text)
    if present:
        if remove:
            return re.sub(r'[a-zA-Z0-9-_\.]+@[a-zA-Z0-9]+\.[a-z]{1,3}', '', text), 1
        else:
            return text, 1
```

```
    else:

        return text, 0

import re


identifyAndRemoveEmailAddress('Immediately reply to some.one@somewhere.
com and send the filled form to leader@somewhere.com')

('Immediately reply to  and send the filled form to ', 1)
```

Detecting and treating hashtags and mentions in the text

We must decide how to treat hashtags and mentions like URLs and email addresses. Provided here is a function to remove hashtags and mentions. You may modify the function as per the requirement of the application.

```
import re


def removeHashtagsAndMentions(text):

  return re.sub('(@[A-Za-z0-9]+)|([^0-9A-Za-z \t][A-Za-z0-9]+ )|(\
  w+:\/\/\S+)', '', text)


removeHashtagsAndMentions("#MIT this is a test @Ramesh Harvard")

'this is a test  Harvard'
```

Dealing with emojis

In modern days, people use Emojis in the text quite frequently. Emojis are not only used in social media activities, but they are also frequently used in emails, SMS, WhatsApp messages, and even in articles. Information regarding Emojis is critical for some applications like Emotion Analysis. So, based on the application, it is necessary to decide whether to retain the information from Emojis in the text. If the information on Emojis needs to be retained, essential feature engineering must be conducted. In every situation, the Emojis must be removed from the text before the text can be analyzed.

To work with Emojis, the **emoji** library needs to be installed.

```
!pip install emoji
```

Once the emoji library is available, the functions of the library can be used to decide what needs to be done with the Emojis.

```
import emoji


emoji.is_emoji('👍')
```

```
True
```

Conclusion

Preprocessing textual data is an essential step in any application involving textual data. In most cases, textual data analysis falls under the **Natural Language Processing** (**NLP**) umbrella. In this annexure, we have discussed the most used text preprocessing requirements. The mechanism discussed can be applied to any other text preprocessing requirements. As mentioned in the annexure, we need to order the text preprocessing steps to get the best data for analysis.

Annexure 5
Stemming and Lamentation

In the text, many words arise from the same word. We need to include such words depending on the context in which the words are used. For example, we may use the words "seem", "seemed", "seeming", and "seemingly" in different sentences. However, all these words have the same root, "seem".

For analyzing any data, including text, it is advantageous to have fewer variables. So, instead of having different variables for the word "seem", "seemed", "seeming", and "seemingly", if we could have just one variable for the root word "seem", it can make the text analysis more precise. (This is a general case. There can be use cases where this may not apply).

Replacing a word with its root word is called Normalizing the Text or Text Normalization. Text Normalization is an essential step in Natural Language Processing. To normalize text, we use the techniques of Stemming and Lamentation.

Structure

In this chapter, we will discuss the following topics:

- Stemming
- Lamentation

Stemming

Stemming is the Text Normalization technique that truncates a part of the word from the beginning or the end of the word. The part of the word that is truncated is called the **affix**. For example, if we stem the word "seeming", we will get "seem".

Generally, stemming is a simple and effective text normalization technique. However, there are many instances where it may not give the desired result. For example, if we stem the word "seemingly", we will get "seemingli". Here, the meaning of the word, as would have been used in the sentence, would be lost with something irrelevant.

For stemming, we can use the functions available in the library **`nltk`**. nltk stands for **Natural Language Tool Kit**. One popular stemming algorithm is Porter Stemmer.

Here are some examples of stemming using Porter Stemmer. First, we need to instantiate the Porter Stemmer.

```
from nltk import stem

from nltk.stem import PorterStemmer


ps = PorterStemmer()
```

Once instantiated, we can use the instance of the Porter Stemmer for stemming words.

```
ps.stem('Seemingly')

'seemingli'

ps.stem('Seeming')

'seem'

ps.stem('caring')

'care'

ps.stem('boots')

'boot'

ps.stem('fishes')

'fish'

ps.stem('dangerous')
```

```
'danger'
ps.stem('studies')
'studi'
ps.stem('studying')
'studi'
```

Lamentation

Lamentation is the Text Normalization technique that conducts a morphological analysis of the word to find the lemma of a word. So, lamentation truncates the word based on the context in which the word is used.

Lamentation is generally preferred over Stemming. In the examples of Stemming, we see that the words "Studying" and "Studies" when stemmed, give "studi". This is not correct. This could be rectified by lamentation.

Lamentation libraries are provided in **`nltk`**. We need to install and initiate these libraries before we can use them.

```
import nltk
nltk.download('wordnet')
from nltk.stem import WordNetLemmatizer
wordnetLemmatizer = WordNetLemmatizer()
```

Once instantiated, we can use the instance of the Porter Stemmer for stemming words.

```
wordnetLemmatizer.lemmatize('studying')
'studying'
wordnetLemmatizer.lemmatize('studies')
'study'
wordnetLemmatizer.lemmatize('crying')
'cry'
wordnetLemmatizer.lemmatize('cries')
'cry'
```

```
wordnetLemmatizer.lemmatize('beautiful')

'beautiful'

wordnetLemmatizer.lemmatize('wonderful')

'wonderful'

wordnetLemmatizer.lemmatize('wonders')

'wonder'
```

Conclusion

Text Normalization is an essential step in preprocessing text for any analysis. Both Stemming and Lamentation are used for Text Normalization besides other preprocessing actions. While Stemming is simple, Lamentation is generally preferred as Lamentation tries to preserve the context of the words.

ANNEXURE 6
Vectorizers

Creating models from text is very important in Machine Learning. This is because there is so much data available as text. Data from newspapers, magazines, books, SMS, emails, and social media (like Facebook, Twitter, WhatsApp, LinkedIn, etc.) are all in text.

We know that machines can only understand numbers. However, we need the machine to create a model from text data. The machine can create models from text data only if the text data is represented as numbers. Text vectorization is the mechanism of converting text data to a number representation. This is because we devise a way to represent text as vectors, each containing only numbers.

In this annexure, we will discuss two text vectorizers. One is a **Count Vectorizer**. This is a relatively simple mechanism to represent text as numbers. Once we get the idea of a vectorizer through the discussion on count vectorizer, we will discuss a more complex vectorizer, i.e., the **TF-IDF vectorizer**. TF-IDF stands for **Term-Frequency Inverse Document Frequency**.

Structure

In this chapter, we will discuss the following topics:

- Count vectorizer
- TF-IDF vectorizer

Count vectorizer

In count vectorizer, we count the number of times a word appears in a given text.

For example, suppose we have the text - *"I went to the Ice Cream Parlor to have an Ice Cream."*. Suppose that this text was sent via SMS. Then this would be one SMS in our complete dataset of many SMS. We would call this data point a document from this full dataset. So, the dataset would contain many such documents. The entire collection of documents is called the **Corpus**.

For a comprehensive discussion, let us consider that in the initial corpus, we have another document as "Great. Did you enjoy the Ice Cream?". So, now our corpus has two documents, as shown in *Table Annexure 6.1*:

Document ID	Document
1	I went to the Ice Cream Parlor to have an Ice Cream.
2	Great. Did you enjoy the Ice Cream?

***Table Annexure 6.1**: Example Dataset*

To create the count vectorizer for the data in *Table Annexure 6.1*, we need to identify all the unique words in the dataset and count how many times each word appears in each document, as shown in *Table Annexure 6.2* (we will remove all the punctuation marks from the text before this exercise).

Word	Document 1	Document 2
I	1	0
went	1	0
To	1	0
The	1	1
Ice	2	1
cream	2	1
parlor	1	0
To	1	0

Word	Document 1	Document 2
have	1	0
An	1	0
great	0	1
Did	0	1
You	0	1
enjoy	0	1

Table Annexure 6.2*: List of Unique Words in the Dataset and their count in each Document*

Table Annexure 6.2 shows that we have the count of each word in both documents in our corpus. If we write this as a vector, it will look as shown in *Table Annexure 6.3*.

Document ID	Count vector
1	[1,1,1,1,2,2,1,1,1,1,0,0,0,0]
2	[0,0,0,1,1,1,0,0,0,0,1,1,1,1]

Table Annexure 6.3*: Count Vectors for a dataset given in Table A6.1*

Now, we can see that we have converted the text in the dataset in *Table Annexure 6.1* into an array of 14 numbers, as shown in *Table Annexure 6.3*. This data in *Table Annexure 6.3* is considered a dataset with 14 features that can be used for making machine learning models.

Count vectorizer is implemented in the Scikit-Learn package in the library **`sklearn.feature_extraction.text.CountVectorizer`**.

```
data = [['I went to the Ice Cream Parlor to have an Ice Cream.'],

        ['Great. Did you enjoy the Ice Cream?']

       ]

data

[['I went to the Ice Cream Parlor to have an Ice Cream.'],

 ['Great. Did you enjoy the Ice Cream?']]

import pandas as pd


df = pd.DataFrame(data, columns = ['text'])

df
```

```
                                             text
0  I went to the Ice Cream Parlor to have an Ice ...
1                    Great. Did you enjoy the Ice Cream?
from sklearn.feature_extraction.text import CountVectorizer

cv = CountVectorizer(stop_words = 'english')
transformed = cv.fit_transform(df.text)
transformed.todense()
matrix([[2, 0, 0, 0, 2, 1, 1],
        [1, 1, 1, 1, 1, 0, 0]])
dfTransformed = pd.DataFrame(transformed.todense(), columns = cv.get_feature_names_out())
dfTransformed
   cream  did  enjoy  great  ice  parlor  went
0      2    0      0      0    2       1     1
1      1    1      1      1    1       0     0
```

Notice that when **CountVectorizer** was initialized, we passed a parameter to remove English Stop Words. Stop Words are commonly used words in a language. For example, in English, we consider words like "I", "you", "the", "so", etc., as stop words. So, the count vectors were created after removing all the stop words.

TF-IDF vectorizer

For the data in *Table Annexure 6.1*, we understood that each text is considered a **document**. And within each document, each word is considered as a **term**.

TF-IDF provides a mechanism to identify the most relevant documents for a term. The full form of TF-IDF is **Term Frequency-Inverse Document Frequency**. So, TF-IDF is a product of 2 terms, **Term Frequency (TF)** and **Inverse Document Frequency (IDF)**.

TF measures how frequently a term appears in a document. We compute a term's TF as the number of times the term appears in a document divided by the total number of terms in the document.

$$TF = \frac{Number\ of\ times\ the\ term\ appears\ in\ the\ Document}{Total\ number\ of\ Terms\ in\ the\ Document}$$

For example, in *Table Annexure 6.1*, the first document (Document ID = 1) has 12 terms, and "Ice" appears two times in the document. So, the Term Frequency (TF) of the term "Ice" in the first document is $TFice = {}^{2}/_{12}$.

Inverse Document Frequency (IDF) measures the term's importance in the corpus. The formula for calculating IDF is as follows:

$$IDF = log(\frac{Total\ number\ of\ Documents\ in\ the\ corpus}{Number\ of\ documents\ containing\ the\ term})$$

Let us take two examples. First, let us calculate the IDF for the term "ice". The total number of documents in our corpus (as per the dataset in *Table Annexure 6.1*) is 2. The number of documents containing the term "ice" is 2. So, $IDFice = log(\frac{2}{2}) = log(1) = 0$.

Next, let us take the term "parlor". The total number of documents is 2. The number of documents containing the term "parlor" is 1. So, $IDFparlor = log(\frac{2}{1}) = log(2) = 0.3010$.

Notice that if a term appears in more documents, the IDF for that term is smaller.

The TF-IDF for a term is calculated as the product of the TF for the term and the IDF for the term. For example, $TF\text{-}IDFice = TFice * IDFice = {}^{2}/_{12} * 0 = 0$.

The TF-IDF value for a term is always a number between 0 and 1. As a result, the TF-IDF values do not need to be scaled.

TF-IDF vectorizer is implemented in the Scikit-Learn package in the library **`sklearn.feature_extraction.text.TfidfVectorizer`.**

```
data = [['I went to the Ice Cream Parlor to have an Ice Cream.'],
        ['Great. Did you enjoy the Ice Cream?']
       ]

data

[['I went to the Ice Cream Parlor to have an Ice Cream.'],
 ['Great. Did you enjoy the Ice Cream?']]

import pandas as pd


df = pd.DataFrame(data, columns = ['text'])
```

```
df

                                               text
0  I went to the Ice Cream Parlor to have an Ice ...
1                  Great. Did you enjoy the Ice Cream?

from sklearn.feature_extraction.text import TfidfVectorizer


tfidf = TfidfVectorizer(stop_words = 'english')

transformed = tfidf.fit_transform(df.text)

transformed.todense()

matrix([[0.57854077, 0.        , 0.        , 0.        , 0.57854077,
         0.40655943, 0.40655943],
        [0.35520009, 0.49922133, 0.49922133, 0.49922133, 0.35520009,
         0.        , 0.        ]])

dfTransformed = pd.DataFrame(transformed.todense(), columns = tfidf.get_
feature_names_out())

dfTransformed
```

	cream	did	enjoy	great	ice	parlor	went
0	0.578541	0.000000	0.000000	0.000000	0.578541	0.406559	0.406559
1	0.355200	0.499221	0.499221	0.499221	0.355200	0.000000	0.000000

Conclusion

As there are many applications where text modeling is performed, vectorizers are frequently used in machine learning. TF-IDF vectorizer is more prevalently used. While for simple applications, we also use count vectorizer.

We have discussed the concept and the working principles behind the vectorizers in this annexure. We saw how each word is used as a term, and the vectorization is performed. However, all the time, a word may not form a term. For example, a combination of 2 or 3 or 4 or more consecutive words may form a term when performing sentiment analysis. These combinations of 2 or more consecutive words are called **n-grams** (Single words are called 1-grams. Combination of 2 consecutive words is called 2-grams, and so on). Both count vectorizer and TF-IDF vectorizer have the facility to create vectors for n-grams.

Points to remember

- Vectorizers are used for converting text into vectors so that they can be used for creating machine learning models.
- In text processing, each data point is referred to as a document, and (at the least) each word in the documents is referred to as a term. The complete collection of all the documents is referred to as a corpus.
- Count vectorizer is a simple vectorizer where we determine the unique words in the corpus and count the number of times each word appears in each document.
- TF-IDF vectorizer is a more sophisticated vectorizer. TF-IDF is a product of **Term Frequency (TF)** and **Inverse Document Frequency (IDF)**.

Join our book's Discord space

Join the book's Discord Workspace for Latest updates, Offers, Tech happenings around the world, New Release and Sessions with the Authors:

https://discord.bpbonline.com

ANNEXURE 7
Encoders

There are many occasions where the data contains non-numeric values that are helpful in creating machine learning models. However, machine learning models can be made using numeric data only. So, we need a mechanism for converting non-numeric data to numeric data, such that the meaning behind the data is retained.

We use Encoders to convert non-numeric data into numeric data for certain kinds of data. This annexure will discuss different types of Encoders and their implementation in Scikit-Learn.

Structure

In this chapter, we will discuss the following topics:

- Data suitable for applying Encoders.
- Label Encoder
- One-Hot Encoder

Data suitable for applying Encoders

In *Annexure 6, Vectorizers,* we discussed converting text data into numeric data to build machine learning models. We may have some non-numeric data; however, they are specific values. For example, when capturing demographic data, we may have a data element to capture the marital status of an individual. The values of marital status could be possibly "Married", "Single", "Divorced", "Widow", or "Widower". Generally, we would capture the value of Marital Status as these literals make data capturing easy. If we use online forms, we may have a program that converts values such as "Married" to 0, "Single" to 1, and so on. If this is the case, we have numeric data and no concerns. However, if we have the data as "Married", "Single", and so on, we need a mechanism to convert them to numeric data.

Another example is the type of rooms in a hotel. These could have values such as "Deluxe", "Super Deluxe", "Suite", and so on. Or, if we are making a model for forming a suitable football team, we could have the data for the position where the player plays as "Center Forward", "Goalkeeper", "Midfielder", among others.

All these types of non-numeric data which convey a specific meaning are the types of data that can be converted to numeric data using Encoders.

Now, different Encoders can be suitable for the different kinds of data we discussed. Let us discuss the different types of Encoders.

Label Encoder

In Label Encoders, we find all the unique values for a field, and we assign a numeric code for each value. For example, suppose we have a field in our data called Marital Status. Now, we figure that the unique values of the field of Marital Status are "Married", "Single", "Divorced", "Widow", and "Widower". So, we have five values for the field of Marital Status. What we could do, is we could assign a value of 0 for "Married", 1 for "Single", 2 for "Divorced", 3 for "Widow", and "4 for "Widower". By doing this, we can distinctly distinguish which records are for married people, single people, and so on. Moreover, if we are given a value for Marital Status as a numeric code, we can convert it to its label equivalent. For example, under this scheme, if we are told that the Marital Status is 2, we know that the record is for a divorced person.

When we have data for a particular field where the different values do not relate, we can use the Label Encoder. For example, for the values of the field Marital Status, there is no relationship between the values "Married", "Single", "Divorced", "Widow", and "Widower". In this situation, we only need to assign a unique numeric code for each distinct value. In what order we assign these numeric codes to the different distinct values does not matter.

Each of the distinct values in a field is called a label. Hence, when we codify the labels into numeric codes, we call the process Label Encoding. The Encoder which conducts Label Encoding is called the Label Encoder.

Label Encoder is implemented in the Scikit-Learn package in the library **`sklearn.preprocessing.LabelEncoder`**. Let us understand the use of the library using an example. Suppose we have the following data:

Employee ID	Name	Designation	Marital Status	No. of Kids
E001	Partha	Director	Married	2
E002	Deepshree	Manager	Married	2
E003	Riya	Programmer	Single	0
E004	Ranoo	Programmer	Single	0
E005	Ujwala	Programmer	Widow	1
E006	Anita	Manager	Married	1
E007	Nomita	Programmer	Divorcee	2
E008	Anil	Programmer	Widower	0
E009	Amarendra	Programmer	Married	1
E010	Anuj	Manager	Married	2

Table Annexure 7.1: *Sample Data*

We first define the data as:

```
data = [['E001','Partha','Director','Married',2],
        ['E002','Deepshree','Manager','Married',2],
        ['E003','Riya','Programmer','Single',0],
        ['E004','Ranoo','Programmer','Single',0],
        ['E005','Ujwala','Programmer','Widow',1],
        ['E006','Anita','Manager','Married',1],
        ['E007','Nomita','Programmer','Divorcee',2],
        ['E008','Anil','Programmer','Widower',0],
        ['E009','Amarendra','Programmer','Married',1],
        ['E010','Anuj','Manager','Married',2]
```

```
    ]


data
[['E001', 'Partha', 'Director', 'Married', 2],
 ['E002', 'Deepshree', 'Manager', 'Married', 2],
 ['E003', 'Riya', 'Programmer', 'Single', 0],
 ['E004', 'Ranoo', 'Programmer', 'Single', 0],
 ['E005', 'Ujwala', 'Programmer', 'Widow', 1],
 ['E006', 'Anita', 'Manager', 'Married', 1],
 ['E007', 'Nomita', 'Programmer', 'Divorcee', 2],
 ['E008', 'Anil', 'Programmer', 'Widower', 0],
 ['E009', 'Amarendra', 'Programmer', 'Married', 1],
 ['E010', 'Anuj', 'Manager', 'Married', 2]]
```

We then create a data frame for this data, as shown:

```
import pandas as pd

df = pd.DataFrame(data, columns = ['EmployeeID',
                                   'Name',
                                   'Designation',
                                   'MaritalStatus',
                                   'NumberOfChildren'
                                  ]
                 )

df
  EmployeeID      Name Designation MaritalStatus  NumberOfChildren
0       E001    Partha    Director       Married                 2
```

```
1       E002  Deepshree     Manager       Married          2
2       E003       Riya  Programmer        Single          0
3       E004      Ranoo  Programmer        Single          0
4       E005     Ujwala  Programmer         Widow          1
5       E006      Anita     Manager       Married          1
6       E007     Nomita  Programmer      Divorcee          2
7       E008       Anil  Programmer       Widower          0
8       E009  Amarendra  Programmer       Married          1
9       E010       Anuj     Manager       Married          2
```

We now apply Label Encoder to the column MaritalStatus:

```
from sklearn.preprocessing import LabelEncoder

leMaritalStatus = LabelEncoder()
df['EncodedMaritalStatus'] = leMaritalStatus.fit_transform(df.
MaritalStatus)
df[['EmployeeID', 'Name', 'MaritalStatus', 'EncodedMaritalStatus']]
```

	EmployeeID	Name	MaritalStatus	EncodedMaritalStatus
0	E001	Partha	Married	1
1	E002	Deepshree	Married	1
2	E003	Riya	Single	2
3	E004	Ranoo	Single	2
4	E005	Ujwala	Widow	3
5	E006	Anita	Married	1
6	E007	Nomita	Divorcee	0
7	E008	Anil	Widower	4
8	E009	Amarendra	Married	1
9	E010	Anuj	Married	1

Note that the column **EncodedMaritalStatus** contains numeric data equivalent to the labels in the column MaritalStatus.

One-Hot Encoder

You would have noticed that when we used the Label Encoder, it assigned values of 0 to "Divorcee", 1 to "Married", 2 to "Single" and so on. These values of 0, 1, 2, and so on., can matter when a model is made as two would have a higher value than 0 & 1 and a lower value to 3, 4, 5, and so on. There are occasions when this can matter in making a model or while interpreting a model.

One way to overcome this problem is to use One-Hot Encoding. In One-Hot Encoding, we create a vector for every data point where only one position has a value of 1 and all the other positions have a value of 0. The value one is assigned to the position in the vector so that it represents the value we want to encode.

Let us understand this through an example. Consider the data in ***Table Annexure 7.1***. We have a column called "Designation". In the column "Designation", we have three unique values – "Director", "Manager", and "Programmer". When we use One-Hot Encoding in this column, "Designation", we will create a vector with three elements (as we have three unique values). In the vector of 3 elements we will create, the first element will represent the value "Director", the second element will represent the value "Manager" and the third element will represent the value "Programmer". Suppose the vector has the value [1, 0, 0]. In that case, it means "Director. If the vector contains the value [0, 1, 0], then it represents "Manager". And if the vector has the value [0, 0, 1], then it represents "Programmer".

In the Scikit-Learn, the library **sklearn.preprocessing.OneHotEncoder** has the implementation for One-Hot Encoding. Let us examine its working.

We have the data frame as follows:

```
import pandas as pd


df = pd.DataFrame(data, columns = ['EmployeeID',

                                   'Name',

                                   'Designation',

                                   'MaritalStatus',

                                   'NumberOfChildren'
```

```
                                ]
                )
```

```
df
  EmployeeID       Name Designation MaritalStatus  NumberOfChildren
0       E001     Partha    Director       Married                 2
1       E002  Deepshree     Manager       Married                 2
2       E003       Riya  Programmer        Single                 0
3       E004      Ranoo  Programmer        Single                 0
4       E005     Ujwala  Programmer         Widow                 1
5       E006      Anita     Manager       Married                 1
6       E007     Nomita  Programmer      Divorcee                 2
7       E008       Anil  Programmer       Widower                 0
8       E009  Amarendra  Programmer       Married                 1
9       E010       Anuj     Manager       Married                 2
```

We will apply One-Hot Encoding in the column "Designation":

```
from sklearn.preprocessing import OneHotEncoder

oheDesignation = OneHotEncoder()
transformed = oheDesignation.fit_transform(df[['Designation']]).todense()
dfTemp = pd.DataFrame(transformed, columns = oheDesignation.get_feature_
names_out())
print(dfTemp)
   Designation_Director  Designation_Manager  Designation_Programmer
0                   1.0                  0.0                     0.0
1                   0.0                  1.0                     0.0
2                   0.0                  0.0                     1.0
3                   0.0                  0.0                     1.0
```

```
4                 0.0               0.0                   1.0
5                 0.0               1.0                   0.0
6                 0.0               0.0                   1.0
7                 0.0               0.0                   1.0
8                 0.0               0.0                   1.0
9                 0.0               1.0                   0.0
```

Notice that three columns are created for the three values in the "Designation" column. We will get as follows if we add these columns to our original data frame:

```
df = pd.concat([df, dfTemp], axis = 1)

df[['Name', 'Designation', 'Designation_Director', 'Designation_Manager', 'Designation_Programmer']]

        Name Designation  Designation_Director  Designation_Manager  \
0     Partha    Director                   1.0                  0.0
1  Deepshree     Manager                   0.0                  1.0
2       Riya  Programmer                   0.0                  0.0
3      Ranoo  Programmer                   0.0                  0.0
4     Ujwala  Programmer                   0.0                  0.0
5      Anita     Manager                   0.0                  1.0
6     Nomita  Programmer                   0.0                  0.0
7       Anil  Programmer                   0.0                  0.0
8  Amarendra  Programmer                   0.0                  0.0
9       Anuj     Manager                   0.0                  1.0

   Designation_Programmer
0                     0.0
1                     0.0
2                     1.0
3                     1.0
```

```
4                       1.0
5                       0.0
6                       1.0
7                       1.0
8                       1.0
9                       0.0
```

Notice that for each value of "Designation", there is a 1 for the column for the designation value, and the remaining values are 0.

If we use One-Hot Encoding, we will get additional features for the dataset. The extra features will equal the unique values for a column on which we apply a One-Hot Ending. For example, we had three unique for "Designation". So, we got three additional features.

Conclusion

Encoders are essential for converting non-numeric data into numeric values. This step is necessary, as we can create machine learning models only with numeric data. We discussed two Encoders: Label Encoder and On-Hot Encoder. These two are the Encoders we generally use.

Other Encoders include Target Encoder, Frequency/Count Encoder, Binary Encoder, and so on. However, these are rarely used.

Points to remember

- When a column has a fixed number of unique values which are non-numeric, we use the Label Encoder to convert these non-numeric values to numeric values.
- Label Encoder in Scikit-Learn assigns unique values to the unique labels starting from 0.
- If the difference in values the Encoder provides, is a concern for modeling, then we use One-Hot Encoder.
- One-Hot Encoder creates a vector containing the same number of elements as the number of unique values in the column to be encoded.
    - The elements in the created vector can only have 0 and 1.
    - The element in the created vector is one of the elements associated with the value to be represented, and all the other values in the vector are 0.

ANNEXURE 8
Entropy

In *Chapter 5, Decision Tree Algorithm,* we discussed creating decision trees using the Gini index. There is another way to create decision trees using **Entropy** and **Information Gain**. In this annexure, we will discuss how we can create decision trees using the concepts of entropy and information gain. So that this discussion is relatable to the discussion in *Chapter 5, Decision Tree Algorithm,* we will use the same example dataset in this annexure as we used in *Chapter 5, Decision Tree Algorithm.*

Structure

In this chapter, we will discuss the following topics:

- Entropy
- Information gain
- Forming Decision Tree using Entropy
- Using Scikit-Learn to build Decision Tree using Entropy

Entropy

The concept of Entropy has been taken from Physics. Like in Physics, Entropy is a measure of randomness in an environment. When discussing data, here, Entropy refers to the amount of randomness available in the data. Entropy can take a value between 0 and 1. If the Entropy value for a dataset is 1, it implies that the dataset is entirely random. If the Entropy value for a dataset is 0, it means that the dataset is pure.

The formula used to calculate Entropy is as follows.

$$Entropy = -\sum_{i=1}^{n}(p_i \, log_2(p_i)$$

Here, i refers to the number of unique classes in the datasets and varies from 1 to n, meaning that the dataset has n classes. p_i is the probability of the availability of class i in the dataset.

To understand this, suppose a dataset has two classes, 0 and 1. Suppose this dataset has three elements of class 0 and 7 of class 1. Then, the probability of availability of class 0 in this dataset is given as $p_0 = {}^3/_{10} = 0.3$. And the probability of availability of class 1 in this dataset is given as $p_1 = {}^7/_{10} = 0.7$. So, under this circumstance, the value of Entropy is calculated as shown below:

$$Entropy = -((0.3 * log_2(0.3)) + (0.7 * log_2(0.7))) = -((0.3 * (-1.737)) + (0.7 * (-0.515))$$

$$= -((-0.521) + (-0.360)) = -(-0.881) = 0.881$$

Note: Probability is always a value between 0 and 1. Now, $log_2(1) = 0$. So, $log_2(x)$ where $0 < x < 1$ is always a negative quantity.

As the term $(p_i * log_2(p_i))$ will always return a negative value, we calculate Entropy as the negative value of the sum of all $(p_i * log_2(p_i))$ terms. This way we will get a positive value for Entropy between 0 and 1.

Also, note that $log_2(0)$ is infinity. So, we will consider $(0 * log_2(0)) = 0$ as by convention $(y * log_2(y))$ tends to 0 as y tends to 0.

If the dataset has an equal number of elements for all classes, like the dataset has five elements of class 0 and 5 elements of class 1, then Entropy is shown below. So, $p_0 = {}^5/_{10} = 0.5$ and $p_1 = {}^5/_{10} = 0.5$.

$$Entropy = -((0.5 * log_2(0.5)) + (0.5 * log_2(0.5))) = -((0.5 * (-1.0)) + (0.5 * (-1.0))$$

$$= -((-0.5) + (-0.5)) = -(-1.0) = 1$$

Also, note that if a dataset has elements of only one class, like a dataset with ten elements of class 0 and 0 elements of class 1, then Entropy is shown below. So, $p_0 = {}^{10}/_{10} = 1$ and $p_1 = {}^{0}/_{10} = 0$.

$$Entropy = -((1 * log_2(1)) + (0 * log_2(0))) = -((1 * 0) + (0) = -(0 + 0) = 0$$

Information gain

Recall that in a decision tree, we will have one root node. Under the root node, we will have two or more nodes (these nodes may be all leaf nodes, all decision nodes, or a mix of leaf nodes and decision nodes). We may have a similar structure under each decision node.

Consider the decision tree in *Figure A8.1*. Here, node A is the Root Node. Node B is a Decision Node. And nodes C, D, and E are Leaf nodes. In *Figure Annexure 8.1*, node A is the parent of node B, and node B is the child of node A.

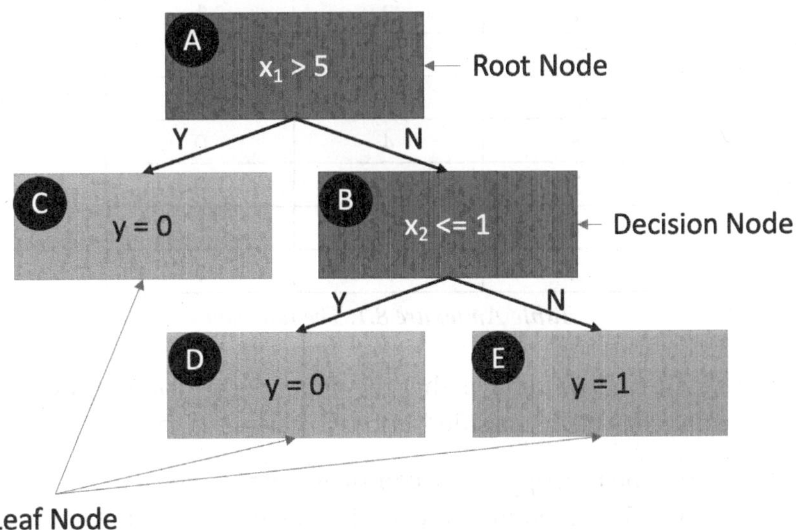

***Figure Annexure 8.1**: Example Decision Tree for illustration*

We calculate the Information Gain of a Child node.

The Information Gain of a node is given as follows:

$$Information\ Gain = Entropyparent - Entropychild$$

Suppose that the Entropy of node A is 0.9 and the Entropy of node B is 0.3. Then, the Information Gain at node B would be (0.9 – 0.3 =) 0.6.

In *Chapter 5, Decision Tree Algorithm,* we have seen that we try many values where we could split the decision tree. Using the Gini index, we consider the split at the value where the Loss is the minimum. Using Entropy, we will split the decision tree at the maximum value of the Information Gain.

Forming Decision Tree using Entropy

We have a dataset of 10 records with two independent variables and one dependent variable. Let the independent variables be x_1 and x_2. Let the dependent variable be **y**. Refer to the following table:

x_1	x_2	y
1	4	0
7	6	0
1	6	0
1	2	1
5	2	1
7	2	1
5	4	0
2	4	0
1	7	1
2	7	1

Table Annexure 8.1: *The raw data*

The data in *Table Appendix 8.1* shows that the dependent variable y has two values – 0 and 1. So, the data has been classified into two classes – 0 and 1.

First, let us compute the Entropy of the complete dataset. We see that we have 5 data points for class 0 and 5 data points for class 1. So, we get as follows.

$$p_0 = \frac{5}{10} = 0.5 \text{ and } p_1 = \frac{5}{10} = 0.5$$

Using these values of p_0 and p_1, we can calculate the Entropy for the complete dataset as follows:

$$Entropy = -\ ((0.5 * log_2\,(0.5)) + (0.5 * log_2\,(0.5))) = -\ ((0.5 * (-1.0)) + (0.5 * (-1.0))$$

$$= -\ ((-0.5) + (-0.5)) = -\ (-1.0) = 1$$

As the Entropy for the complete dataset is the Entropy of the Root Node, we will write as follows.

$$Entropy_{root} = 1$$

To make the decision tree, we need to try various points for the features x_1 and x_2 where we can split the decision. So, we compute the possible values of x_1 and x_2 where there could be a split. We will understand this concept using the data we have in Table A8.1.

To compute the different x_1, we consider the range from the minimum value of x_1 to the maximum value of x_1. Then, we take points at equal intervals in this range. The minimum(x_1) = 1 and maximum(x_1) = 7. To avoid edge conditions, we will consider the upper limit of the range as the *maximum*(x_1) + *1*. So, the range for x_1 is 1 to 8. We will consider intervals of 0.5 in our range. So, the values of x_1 that we will try to use for splitting the decision are as follows.

1.00, 1.50, 2.00, 2.50, 3.00, 3.50, 4.00, 4.50, 5.00, 5.50, 6.00, 6.50, 7.00, 7.50

Similarly, we consider the points of the variable x_2 for splitting the decision. The minimum(x_2) = 2 and maximum(x_2) = 7. So, the range for x_2 is 2 to 8. The values of x_2 that we will try to use for splitting the decision are as follows.

2.00, 2.50, 3.00, 3.50, 4.00, 4.50, 5.00, 5.50, 6.00, 6.50, 7.00, 7.50

The points we will consider for splitting the decision tree are called **thresholds**.

Let us compute the Entropy for the threshold x_1 = 1.00. So, we split the dataset for x_1 <= 1.00, then the dataset on the left-hand side of the split and the dataset on the right-hand side of the split would look as shown in *Table Annexure 8.2:*

$x_1 \leq 1.00$			$x_1 > 1.00$		
x1	x2	y	x1	x2	y
1	4	0	2	4	0
1	6	0	2	7	1
1	2	1	5	2	1
1	7	1	5	4	0
			7	2	1
			7	6	0

***Table Annexure 8.2**: The left and right dataset at split point $x_1 \leq 1.00$*

From *Table Annexure 8.2*, we get that the number of data points on the left-hand side of the split is 4, and the number of data points on the right-hand side of the split is 6. We compute the Entropy for the dataset on the left-hand side of the split and the dataset on the right-hand side.

We get as follows for computing the Entropy for the dataset on the left-hand side of the split.

$$p_0 = \frac{2}{4} = 0.5 \text{ and } p_1 = \frac{2}{4} = 0.5$$

Using these values of p_0 and p_1, we can calculate the Entropy for the dataset on the left-hand side of the split as follows.

$$Entropyleft = -((0.5 * log_2(0.5)) + (0.5 * log_2(0.5))) = -((0.5 * (-1.0)) + (0.5 * (-1.0))$$

$$= -((-0.5) + (-0.5)) = -(-1.0) = 1$$

Similarly, we calculate the Entropy of the dataset on the right-hand side of the split as follows.

$$p_0 = \frac{3}{6} = 0.5 \text{ and } p_1 = \frac{3}{6} = 0.5$$

$$Entropyright = -((0.5 * log_2(0.5)) + (0.5 * log_2(0.5))) = -((0.5 * (-1.0)) + (0.5 * (-1.0))$$

$$= -((-0.5) + (-0.5)) = -(-1.0) = 1$$

Having computed the Entropy at the left-hand and right-hand sides of the split, we calculate the weighted average of the Entropy at this decision node. Note that on the left-hand side of the split, we have 4 data points, and on the right-hand side of the split, we have 6 data points. So, we get as follows:

$$Entropyx{=}1.0 = (\frac{4}{10} * 1.0) + (\frac{6}{10} * 1.0) = 0.4 + 0.6 = 1.0$$

Now that we have the values for $Entropy_{Root}$ and $Entropy_{x=1.0}$, we can calculate the **Information Gain (IG)** at the split point x = 1.0 as follows.

$$IGx{=}1.0 = EntropyRoot - Entropyx{=}1.0 = 1.0 - 1.0 = 0$$

Using this mechanism, we can compute the Information Gain at all the split points we want to test, as shown in *Figure Annexure 8.2:*

Variable	Decision Points	Left	Right	P(0|Left)		P(1|Left)		P(0|Right)		P(1|Right)		Entropy(Left)	Entropy(Right)	Entropy(node)	Information Gain
x1	1.00	4	6	2/4	0.50000	2/4	0.50000	3/6	0.50000	3/6	0.50000	1.00000	1.00000	1.00000	-
x1	1.50	4	6	2/4	0.50000	2/4	0.50000	3/6	0.50000	3/6	0.50000	1.00000	1.00000	1.00000	-
x1	2.00	6	4	3/6	0.50000	3/6	0.50000	2/4	0.50000	2/4	0.50000	1.00000	1.00000	1.00000	-
x1	2.50	6	4	3/6	0.50000	3/6	0.50000	2/4	0.50000	2/4	0.50000	1.00000	1.00000	1.00000	-
x1	3.00	6	4	3/6	0.50000	3/6	0.50000	2/4	0.50000	2/4	0.50000	1.00000	1.00000	1.00000	-
x1	3.50	6	4	3/6	0.50000	3/6	0.50000	2/4	0.50000	2/4	0.50000	1.00000	1.00000	1.00000	-
x1	4.00	6	4	3/6	0.50000	3/6	0.50000	2/4	0.50000	2/4	0.50000	1.00000	1.00000	1.00000	-
x1	4.50	6	4	3/6	0.50000	3/6	0.50000	2/4	0.50000	2/4	0.50000	1.00000	1.00000	1.00000	-
x1	5.00	8	2	4/8	0.50000	4/8	0.50000	1/2	0.50000	1/2	0.50000	1.00000	1.00000	1.00000	-
x1	5.50	8	2	4/8	0.50000	4/8	0.50000	1/2	0.50000	1/2	0.50000	1.00000	1.00000	1.00000	-
x1	6.00	8	2	4/8	0.50000	4/8	0.50000	1/2	0.50000	1/2	0.50000	1.00000	1.00000	1.00000	-
x1	6.50	8	2	4/8	0.50000	4/8	0.50000	1/2	0.50000	1/2	0.50000	1.00000	1.00000	1.00000	-
x1	7.00	10	0	5/10	0.50000	5/10	0.50000	0/0	-	0/0	-	1.00000	-	1.00000	-
x1	7.50	10	0	5/10	0.50000	5/10	0.50000	0/0	-	0/0	-	1.00000	-	1.00000	-
x2	2.00	3	7	0/3	-	3/3	1.00000	5/7	0.71429	2/7	0.28571	-	0.86312	0.60418	0.39582
x2	2.50	3	7	0/3	-	3/3	1.00000	5/7	0.71429	2/7	0.28571	-	0.86312	0.60418	0.39582
x2	3.00	3	7	0/3	-	3/3	1.00000	5/7	0.71429	2/7	0.28571	-	0.86312	0.60418	0.39582
x2	3.50	3	7	0/3	-	3/3	1.00000	5/7	0.71429	2/7	0.28571	-	0.86312	0.60418	0.39582
x2	4.00	6	4	3/6	0.50000	3/6	0.50000	2/4	0.50000	2/4	0.50000	1.00000	1.00000	1.00000	-
x2	4.50	6	4	3/6	0.50000	3/6	0.50000	2/4	0.50000	2/4	0.50000	1.00000	1.00000	1.00000	-
x2	5.00	6	4	3/6	0.50000	3/6	0.50000	2/4	0.50000	2/4	0.50000	1.00000	1.00000	1.00000	-
x2	5.50	6	4	3/6	0.50000	3/6	0.50000	2/4	0.50000	2/4	0.50000	1.00000	1.00000	1.00000	-
x2	6.00	8	2	5/8	0.62500	3/8	0.37500	0/2	-	2/2	1.00000	0.95443	-	0.76355	0.23645
x2	6.50	8	2	5/8	0.62500	3/8	0.37500	0/2	-	2/2	1.00000	0.95443	-	0.76355	0.23645
x2	7.00	10	0	5/10	0.50000	5/10	0.50000	0/0	-	0/0	-	1.00000	-	1.00000	-
x2	7.50	10	0	5/10	0.50000	5/10	0.50000	0/0	-	0/0	-	1.00000	-	1.00000	-

***Figure Annexure 8.2**: Calculation for Information Gain to determine the first split of the decision tree.*

The maximum Information Gain is obtained at the split points $x_2 = 2.00$, $x_2 = 2.50$, $x_2 = 3.00$, and $x_2 = 3.50$. So, we can make any of these 4 points to make the first split. As a convention, we will make the split at the largest value of the variable. So, we will make our first split at $x_2 = 3.50$.

Our decision tree will look as shown in *Figure Annexure 8.3:*

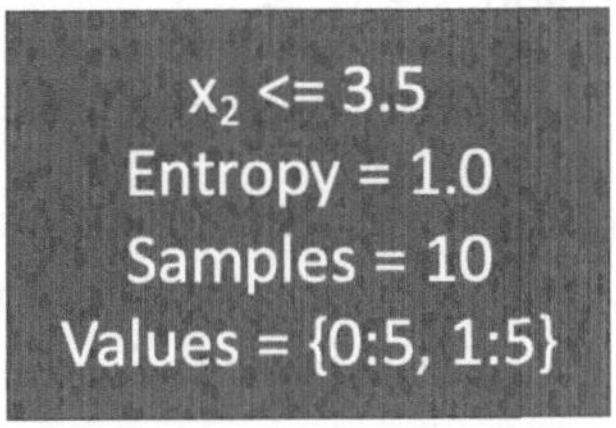

X_2 <= 3.5
Entropy = 1.0
Samples = 10
Values = {0:5, 1:5}

***Figure Annexure 8.3**: Root Node of the decision tree*

The dataset at the split $x_2 = 3.5$ looks as shown in *Table 5.6:*

$x_2 \leq 3.50$			$x_2 > 3.50$		
x1	x2	y	x1	x2	y
1	2	1	1	4	0
5	2	1	1	6	0
7	2	1	1	7	1
			2	4	0

$x_2 \leq 3.50$			$x_2 > 3.50$		
x1	x2	y	x1	x2	y
			2	7	1
			5	4	0
			7	6	0

***Table Annexure** 8.3: Dataset split at the split point $x_2 < 3.5$*

We notice that on the left-hand side, the value of y for all the data points is 1. So, we have a leaf node here, and the decision is y = 1.

So, our decision tree looks as shown in *Figure Annexure 8.4:*

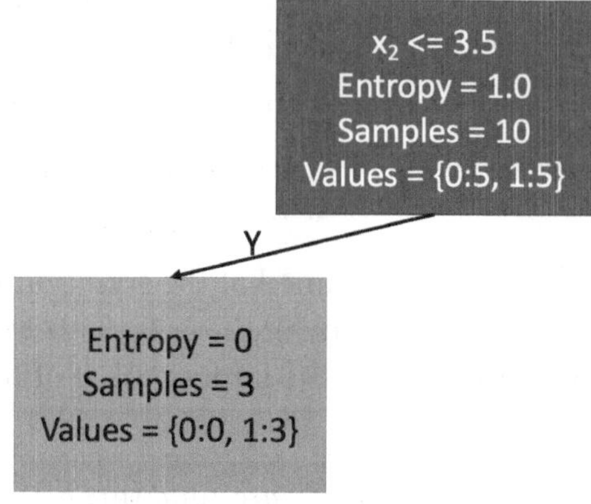

Figure Annexure 8.4: Updated Decision Tree with a Leaf Node (shown in orange color)

Now, let us consider the dataset on the right-hand side of the root node, as shown in *Figure Annexure 8.4*. In other words, we consider only the data points (as shown in *Table Annexure 5.1*) where $x_2 > 3.5$. We have the dataset as shown in *Table Annexure 8.4:*

x1	x2	y
1	4	0
7	6	0
1	6	0
5	4	0
2	4	0
1	7	1
2	7	1

***Table Annexure** 8.4: The data points in the dataset (Table Appendix 8.1) where $x_2 > 3.50$*

Let us calculate the Entropy for the data points shown in Table A8.4. We get as follows.

$$p_0 = \frac{5}{7} = 0.714 \; and \; p_1 = \frac{2}{7} = 0.286$$

Using these values of p_0 and p_1, we can calculate the Entropy for the dataset on the right-hand side of the split at $x_2 = 3.5$ as follows. We will call this $\text{Entropy}_{\text{parent}}$ as this will be the parent node for the next set of data points we will try to split.

$$Entropyparent = - ((0.714 * log_2 (0.714)) + (0.286 * log_2 (0.286)))$$

$$= - ((0.714 * (-0.485)) + (0.286 * (-1.807))$$

$$= - ((-0.347) + (-0.516)) = - (-0.863) = 0.863$$

As the Entropy of the dataset in *Table Annexure 8.4* is not 0, the dataset is impure, and thus we need to split this dataset to try to find decision points or leaf nodes. So, we must calculate the Information Gain for all the thresholds. As the range of values of x_1 and x_2 have changed, we must reestablish the thresholds. Using the same logic of using the minimum and maximum values of the features to establish the threshold, we get the threshold value to consider for x_1 as follows.

1.00, 1.50, 2.00, 2.50, 3.00, 3.50, 4.00, 4.50, 5.00, 5.50, 6.00, 6.50

And the threshold values to consider for x_2 are as follows.

4.00, 4.50, 5.00, 5.50, 6.00, 6.50

Shown in *Figure Annexure 8.5* is the calculation for Information Gain for the dataset in *Table Annexure 8.4:*

														Entropy(Parent)	0.86300
Variable	Decision Points	Left	Right	P(0|Left)		P(1|Left)		P(0|Right)		P(1|Right)		Entropy(Left)	Entropy(Right)	Entropy(node)	Information Gain
x1	1.00	3	4	2/3	0.66667	1/3	0.33333	3/4	0.75000	1/4	0.25000	0.91830	0.81128	0.85714	0.00586
x1	1.50	3	4	2/3	0.66667	1/3	0.33333	3/4	0.75000	1/4	0.25000	0.91830	0.81128	0.85714	0.00586
x1	2.00	5	2	3/5	0.60000	2/5	0.40000	0/2	-	2/2	1.00000	0.97095	-	0.69354	0.16946
x1	2.50	5	2	3/5	0.60000	2/5	0.40000	0/2	-	2/2	1.00000	0.97095	-	0.69354	0.16946
x1	3.00	5	2	3/5	0.60000	2/5	0.40000	0/2	-	2/2	1.00000	0.97095	-	0.69354	0.16946
x1	3.50	5	2	3/5	0.60000	2/5	0.40000	0/2	-	2/2	1.00000	0.97095	-	0.69354	0.16946
x1	4.00	5	2	3/5	0.60000	2/5	0.40000	0/2	-	2/2	1.00000	0.97095	-	0.69354	0.16946
x1	4.50	5	2	3/5	0.60000	2/5	0.40000	0/2	-	2/2	1.00000	0.97095	-	0.69354	0.16946
x1	5.00	6	1	4/6	0.66667	2/6	0.33333	1/1	1.00000	0/1	-	0.91830	-	0.78711	0.07589
x1	5.50	6	1	4/6	0.66667	2/6	0.33333	1/1	1.00000	0/1	-	0.91830	-	0.78711	0.07589
x1	6.00	6	1	4/6	0.66667	2/6	0.33333	1/1	1.00000	0/1	-	0.91830	-	0.78711	0.07589
x1	6.50	6	1	4/6	0.66667	2/6	0.33333	1/1	1.00000	0/1	-	0.91830	-	0.78711	0.07589
x2	4.00	3	4	3/3	1.00000	0/3	-	2/4	0.50000	2/4	0.50000	-	1.00000	0.57143	0.29157
x2	4.50	3	4	3/3	1.00000	0/3	-	2/4	0.50000	2/4	0.50000	-	1.00000	0.57143	0.29157
x2	5.00	3	4	3/3	1.00000	0/3	-	2/4	0.50000	2/4	0.50000	-	1.00000	0.57143	0.29157
x2	5.50	3	4	3/3	1.00000	0/3	-	2/4	0.50000	2/4	0.50000	-	1.00000	0.57143	0.29157
x2	6.00	5	2	5/5	1.00000	0/5	-	0/2	-	2/2	1.00000	-	-	-	0.86300
x2	6.50	3	4	5/5	1.00000	0/5	-	0/2	-	2/2	1.00000	-	-	-	0.86300

Figure Annexure 8.5*: Calculation of Information Gain for the dataset in Table A8.4*

Figure Annexure 8.5 shows that the maximum Information Gain is for the split points $x_2 = 6.0$ and $x_2 = 6.5$. As is our strategy to take the maximum value of the variable, we will split the decision tree as $x_2 = 6.5$.

So, our decision tree looks as shown in *Figure Annexure 8.6:*

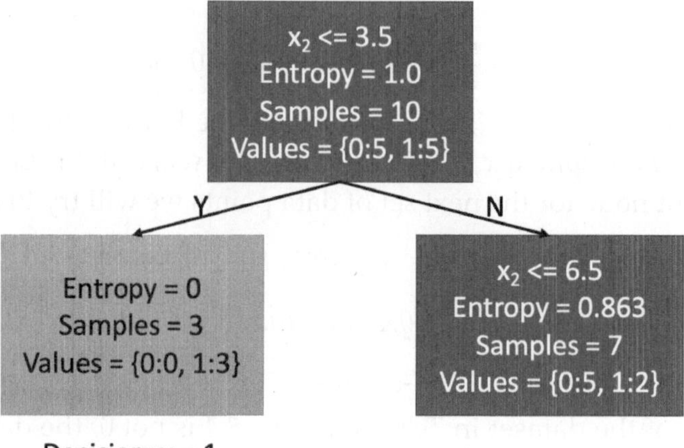

***Figure Annexure 8.6**: Decision Tree after the second split*

As we have done before, we will split the dataset, as shown in *Table Annexure 8.4,* based on the new decision node we created, as shown in *Figure Annexure 8.6,* that is, based on $x_2 <= 6.5$. Based on this, the dataset on the left-hand side is shown in *Table Annexure 8.5,* and the dataset on the right-hand side is shown in *Table Annexure 8.6:*

x1	x2	y
1	4	0
7	6	0
1	6	0
5	4	0
2	4	0

***Table Annexure 8.5**: The data points in the dataset (as shown in Table A8.4) where $x_2 \leq 6.50$*

From *Table Annexure 8.5,* we see that for all the data points, the value of y is 0. So, we have a leaf node with the decision y = 0.

x1	x2	y
1	7	1
2	7	1

***Table Annexure 8.6**: The data points in the dataset (as shown in Table A8.4) where $x_2 > 6.50$*

From *Table Annexure 8.6,* we see that for all the data points, the value of y is 1. So, we have a leaf node with the decision y = 1.

So, our final decision tree looks as shown in *Figure Annexure 8.7:*

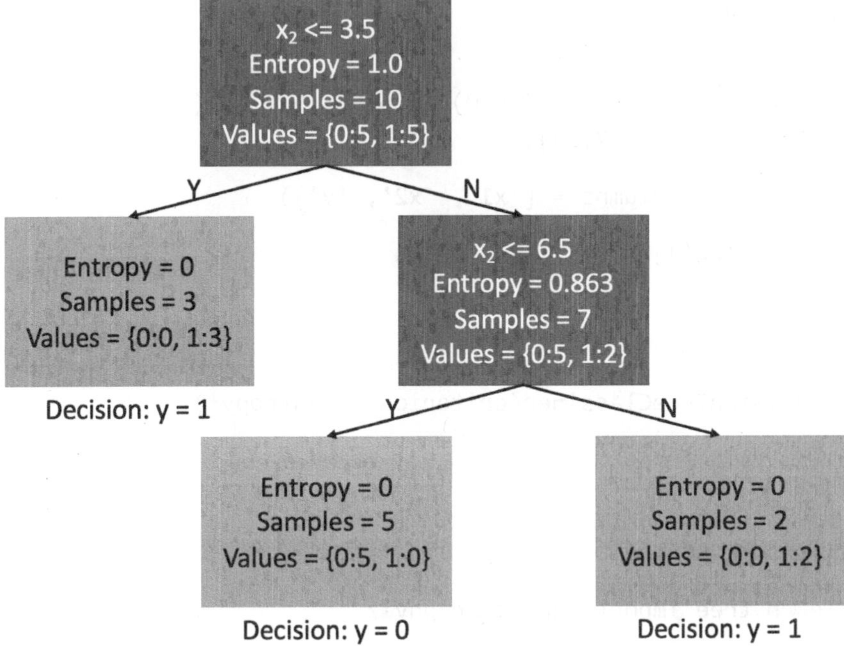

Figure Annexure 8.7: *Final decision tree for the dataset in Table A8.1.*

Using Scikit-Learn to build Decision Tree using Entropy

Using the Scikit-Learn library, it is easy to build decision trees without going through many calculations. The code sample is provided below. Notice that the decision tree created by Scikit-Learn is the same as the one created manually.

```
import warnings

warnings.filterwarnings('ignore')


!pip install pydot

!pip install pydotplus

!pip install graphviz
```

```
!conda install -y graphviz


from sklearn.tree import DecisionTreeClassifier

import pandas as pd


df = pd.DataFrame([(1,4,0),(7,6,0),(1,6,0),(1,2,1),(5,2,1),(7,2,1), (5,4
,0),(2,4,0),(1,7,1),(2,7,1)],

                  columns = ['x1', 'x2', 'y'])

X = df[['x1', 'x2']]

y = df['y']


dtree = DecisionTreeClassifier(criterion = 'entropy')

dtree.fit(X, y)


from six import StringIO

from sklearn.tree import export_graphviz

import pydotplus

from IPython.display import Image


dot_data = StringIO()

export_graphviz(dtree, out_file = dot_data,

                filled = True, rounded = True,

                special_characters = True)


graph = pydotplus.graph_from_dot_data(dot_data.getvalue())

Image(graph.create_png())
```

```
Requirement already satisfied: pydot in /Users/parthamajumdar/opt/
anaconda3/lib/python3.9/site-packages (1.4.2)

Requirement already satisfied: pyparsing>=2.1.4 in /Users/parthamajumdar/
opt/anaconda3/lib/python3.9/site-packages (from pydot) (3.0.4)
```

```
Requirement already satisfied: pydotplus in /Users/parthamajumdar/opt/anaconda3/lib/python3.9/site-packages (2.0.2)

Requirement already satisfied: pyparsing>=2.0.1 in /Users/parthamajumdar/opt/anaconda3/lib/python3.9/site-packages (from pydotplus) (3.0.4)

Requirement already satisfied: graphviz in /Users/parthamajumdar/opt/anaconda3/lib/python3.9/site-packages (0.20.1)

Collecting package metadata (current_repodata.json): done

Solving environment: done


# All requested packages already installed.
```

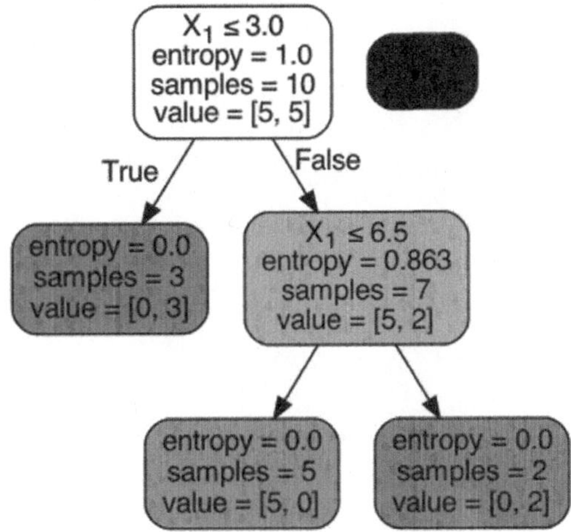

Figure Annexure 8.8: *Decision Tree formed using Scikit-Learn*

Conclusion

Both Entropy and Gini index can be used for forming Decision Trees. There is no preference for one over the other. The CART algorithm uses the Gini index to create decision trees, while the ID3 and C4 algorithms use Entropy to form decision trees. The only significant difference is that the Gini index for maximum impurity is 0.5, and the Entropy for maximum impurity is 1. The maximum purity for both Gini index and Entropy is 0.

Points to remember

- Entropy is a measure of the randomness in a dataset.
- Entropy has a value between 0 and 1.
- When the Entropy of a dataset is 0, the dataset is pure.
- When the Entropy of a dataset is 1, the dataset is entirely random.
- Information Gain at a Child node is the difference between the Entropy of the Parent Node and the Entropy of the Child Node.
- Decision Trees are split at the Child nodes where the Information Gain is maximum.

Index

A

B

C

D

E

L

M

N

O

P